Voices OF Resistance

MUSLIM WOMEN ON WAR, FAITH & SEXUALITY

EDITED BY SARAH HUSAIN

SEAL PRESS

D0354060

Voices of Resistance
Muslim Women on War, Faith & Sexuality

Published by
Seal Press
An Imprint of Avalon Publishing Group, Incorporated

AVALON
publishing group incorporated

1400 65th Street, Suite 250
Emeryville, CA 94608

ISBN-13: 978-1-58005-181-1
ISBN-10: 1-58005-181-2

9 8 7 6 5 4 3 2 1

Library of Congress Cataloging-in-Publication Data

Voices of resistance : Muslim women on war, faith, and sexuality / Sarah Husain.
p. cm.
ISBN-13: 978-1-58005-181-1
ISBN-10: 1-58005-181-2
1. Muslim women. 2. Muslim women—United States. 3. War on
Terrorism, 2001—Women. 4. Women and war. 5. Muslim women—Attitudes.
6. Muslim women—Social conditions. I. Husain, Sarah.

HQ1170.V63 2006
305.48'697090511—dc22

2006005459

Cover design by Gerilyn Attebery
Interior design by Megan Cooney
Printed in the United States by Malloy
Distributed by Publishers Group West

To all my mothers, here and past:

Ummie Sajou, Bajji Appa, Bari Ummie,
Zaida Aunty, Chewappa,

Mom . . .

To all my sisters, our present:

Ayesha, Cheenu, Muni,

Shaista . . .

To my daughter, the future:

A'asia-Thara

"You see. You are made to see.
You see and you know. For yourself.
The eyes have not been condemned.
You see inspite of. Your sight.
Let that be a lesson to you."

—Theresa Hak Kyung Cha

Presented To
Cedar Mill Community Library

By

Sushi Town

CONTENTS

INTRODUCTION

Iqra!: a poetics of resistance

"Change don't come easy. For anyone. But this state of war we live in,
this world on fire provides us with no other choice."
—from Cherrie Moraga's foreword to the second edition
of *This Bridge Called My Back*

This anthology *re*defines the stereotypical definitions of "Muslim" women that overflow Western discourse on the "Islamic" Other. The veil, seemingly the age-old symbol of our repression and the archetypical rationale for our rescuing by the West, has become a transparent symbol of "Islamic barbarity." This anthology moves beyond such sterile representations and narrow debates and engages the complexities that make up the contemporary realities of "Muslim" women and our affective lives. We construct here a multiple-voiced text and many-sided vision of our lives as "Muslim" women by forging ourselves into new creative collectivities. In this process, the category "Muslim" is rendered anew through our own politics and cultural practices across gender, sexuality, race, and nation. Such a rendering reflects the many valences of our multiple histories and selves as we come from and form heterogeneous parts of a "Muslim" world—from Yemen, Iran, Palestine, Afghanistan, Kashmir, Pakistan, India, and Bangladesh, to Malaysia, Thailand, China, Canada, and the United States, straight, bisexual, veiled, transgendered, married, *kafirs*. Part Hindu apart from being "Muslim," mothers, queers, activists, writers, outsiders, painters, poets. . . .

We are against wars—all wars the United States (and its allies) have been waging against people of color and the poor all over the globe. This collection culminated over the past year and a half amid Tsunamis, Hurricanes, Earthquakes, earth's anger over the continuous spilling of blood over lies; indictments, trials turning professors into "terrorists." The winds of Western Democracy continue to blow swiftly across the globe; it constructs its own theaters wherever and whenever it chooses, strengthening the ever-quivering *takht—of power*. Setting up its own satellites, cameras, backgrounds filled with its own imaged geographies. Buildings haven't stopped falling, nor being blown apart, since before or after September the 11th, five years ago. The legal and militarized looting of Iraqi oil by corporate America continues as Exxon, Shell, and Chevron have made record-breaking profits, and at the same time, poor and Black "citizens" of New Orleans were left to drown, often at gunpoint, in the name of a catastrophe labeled "natural." Amid the suffocating inertia of a corporate consumerist culture that would rather siege and ignore than face the fear of self-criticism, self-reflection, perhaps even self-destruction, some resisting voices come together and make their way through these pages.

This collection is a departure from some of the anthologies that have been published recently about "Muslim" women in America in several ways. It is not involved in a politics of representation but is instead concerned with creating a dialogue, first, among "Muslim" women around issues concerning our bodies and our communities, struggles that have existed long before the 11th of September. As such, this project is involved in creating a community whose *priori* frame of reference is neither the U.S. war machine nor the stereotypically termed "Islamic" patriarchy—it is a mode of intervention in both. We do not represent all of "Muslim" women, we do not think our collective representation will be secured by better, more authentic representations of "us." Second, among the project's many aims is to connect with the broader community of women of color and those people resisting and organizing against the war today generally.

This anthology does not suppose any real "truths," nor does it claim to construct a "reality" or one homogeneous vision of our struggles and resistances. Although throughout the introduction there is an overarching "we" that is used, it does not mean that everyone in this anthology agrees with one another. We certainly do not, but what we are more concerned with is forming a collective resistance. At the core of this is our poetics, which engages and puts to the forefront our varied differences and multiplicities. It is precisely being armed with those differences—in a radical poetics in which difference becomes an actual force—that enables us to critically engage the public through our work.

As our lives become targets of manufactured "truths," and the real questions are hidden behind corporate media sound bites, "Islam" becomes the new demon to be exorcized. The reason why "Muslim" is in quotes throughout this introduction is *not* to just move away from those tendencies that seek to reduce us to monological stereotypes and to define us in one homogeneous way. Our work subverts stereotypes, claims them, often with humor, moves beyond them, or simply ignores them, but, in doing so, troubles the dominant generalizations. Writing our selves into quotes does not mean that we are not a legitimate or a "real" force in our communities. What it means is that we are not one fixed homogeneous body that is always ready to be written by, and in, someone else's language. We seek to move sometimes as whole and sometimes unholy, perhaps as shadows, but like water, always fluid, constructing our myriad selves.

For us as "Muslim" women, the struggles we face today are not just limited to those against colonial legacies and its inherited regimes of control, or against today's imperial war, but what are also central to this anthology are the struggles we face within our own "Muslim" communities, our families, our homes—indeed, the struggles within ourselves. In this anthology we see the necessity of connecting all aspects of violence, from the struggle against domestic violence, women's bodies, and their health, to state-sponsored brutalities and wars. We construct here the effects of violence on our psyches, our spirituality, our bodies, on every sense of ourselves, and our art. One of the main concerns of this anthology is to question the privilege we occupy as women living in the West. This further necessitates *how* we use those various positions, a task that we collectively must begin to interrogate knowing we might lose respect, with the potential of being excommunicated from our families and/or communities, even lose citizenship, and arguably face indefinite sessions of questioning by authorities, if not full detention.

The title of this introduction, *Iqra!*, in Arabic means "Read!" This was the first command revealed to Prophet Mohammad as he sat in a cave of Mount Hira. Traditionally it has been told that the angel Gabriel came to him and said, "Read!" and the prophet replied he couldn't because he was an illiterate. Gabriel commanded him three times, to which he conceded and repeated after him. It was in this exchange that the first words of the Quran were revealed and became the beginning of the ninety-sixth sura ("verse"), al-Alaq, Iqra, or al-Qalam, meaning The Clot, Read, or The Pen (all simultaneous titles of one sura):

1. Read: In the name of thy Lord Who createth,
2. Createth man from a clot.
3. Read: And thy Lord is the Most Bounteous,
4. Who teacheth by the pen,
5. Teacheth man that which he knew not.[1]

The significance of this verse is tremendous, and the most simple reading suggests that the *ahlay kitab* (one who is of the book, a "Muslim") must seek knowledge wherever and however it is necessary. Even if it means going to China—meaning if need be, one must go to the other side of the world to obtain it. Thus, this sura instructs that obtaining knowledge is integral to one's spiritual/religious practices. To invoke *iqra!* here means that we insist on a politics and a spirituality that command knowledge, not some pure knowledge existing in a fixed past either, but one that is fluid, engaged with the changes taking place in our lifetime historically, politically, socially, and economically. It's a twofold message: First, that as "Muslims," we must generally understand and arm ourselves with the knowledge of all the complexities of transnational lives, today, living under global capitalism. We are a chiasma, those X-shaped configurations, that can no longer be measured in separate luxuries; our lives connect and at times disconnect each other, and as "Muslim" women living inflected lives, we will not stop seeking knowledge and answers, ever. Second, this invocation is also meant for the general non-Muslim readers, that they should begin to read! and seek knowledge outside of what is generally offered them. In order to understand and come out of the current crisis, they, we, must learn to re-read between the lines and unlearn histories, their/our own privileges, racism, and violence.

This anthology is not engaged in a fight with "Islam" so as to create another "Islam." In fact almost all the work collected here has deep roots in a faith of "Islam." What we are constructing here is a space of faith both politically/critically and spiritually/self-reflexively of a feminine divine engaged in resistance. The reason why this project seeks to anthologize "Muslim" women is so that we are agents of writing our own histories, struggles, and resistances against wars the United States is waging across the globe. We're aware of the fact that the market is very hungry for such "voices," but there is no lack of "Muslim" women's writings and views; one just has to do some research! We are involved here in an identity politics only as far as it concerns our own naming, because we are constantly being defined and framed by the state, its military, and its policies. We hope that this collection will be a catalyst for "Muslim" women in North America to collectively organize ourselves in order to put forth the issues we face both locally and globally.

While corporate radars drain our economic and natural resources, and warlord militias backed by the United States confiscate our lands, our cultures are "Occidentalized." It becomes even more urgent to open ourselves to the multiple forms of struggles—to the many becomings that our survival demands. "Muslim" women are at the forefront of struggles and war all over the globe. We are targets of hate crimes in the United States. We are suicide bombers in Palestine. "Muslim" women are taking up arms and throwing their bodies against military machines while sacrificing their mothers, daughters, sisters, sons, brothers, husbands, fathers, and friends to . . . war.

The works collected here speak of "war" broadly but of struggles specifically, redefining war and warring, from our bodies to the so-called war against terrorism, from the war against heteronormativity in our homes to the construction of the nation, from the war for control over our sexuality to the war against cancer and its attendant biopolitics. We begin to break through and create fissures in the artificial peace maintained today under Western eyes by signaling a color not part of the spectrum of safety selected by Homeland Security's "threat advisory." Fervently refiguring the banality of war being experienced today, the writings collected here begin to redraw the "official" maps of our multiple War Zones in order to begin forging peace.

Most of the contributors in this collection live in the United States—some are second-generation daughters of immigrants, while some have come here for higher education and have stayed in exile both forced and voluntary. But all of us come from "homes" being either bombarded by U.S. warplanes or blown apart by (right-wing) regimes of control, and almost all of us have been targets of hate crimes post–September 11. We begin here to document and give voice to the many forces stirring in our communities, histories, bodies—in us; we write, we create, we struggle in the tradition and legacies of Black, Latina, Indigenous, and Asian women who have come before us and have helped shape the contemporary contexts of resistances.[2] Stripping America's own veil of convenience and comfort by laying naked the "terror" circulating through every corner of its culture, we come together to bear witness, to refuse silence, and to imagine and work toward constructing other futures. As Audre Lorde wrote, "It is learning how to stand alone, unpopular and sometimes reviled, and how to make common cause with those others identified as outside the structures, in order to define and seek a world in which we can all flourish. It is learning how to take our differences and make them strengths. *For the master's tools will never dismantle the master's house.*"[3] And so we begin to (re)construct our lives in order to survive and create tools necessary to shatter that "master's house."

This anthology is divided into four parts: I. (Un)Naming Wars, II. Witnessing Acts, III. (Un)Naming Faiths/Unclaiming Nations, and IV. Re-Claiming Our Bodies/Re-Claiming Our Sexualities. In the first section, (Un)Naming Wars, our writings address current issues facing "Muslim American" communities, from hate crimes and indefinite detentions, to the wars taking place "abroad," such as in Iraq, Palestine, Afghanistan, and Kashmir. In order to begin to voice the contemporary struggles, it becomes necessary that in this section we, first, begin de-mythifying the current hysteria that uneasily erects September 11 as the beginning of all evils by re-membering and situating current experiences with, for example, our stories of the Gulf War. It's important to point to two facts here: first, that the current war on Iraq is a continuation of the Gulf War; the bombing of Iraq didn't stop with Clinton but continued for more than a decade. Second, the U.S.A. Patriot Act is a solidification of the antiterrorism laws written and passed under the Clinton administration. The aim of this section is to historicize contemporary struggles with those of the anticolonial struggles generally.

In the second section, "Witnessing Acts," our writings deal with struggles that we are not engaged in directly but are affected and informed by. The primary focus of this section is on issues concerning the thin lines between violence, resistance, and the suicide bomber, from Palestine to Kashmir to Pakistan. Our writings en-gender the image and affect of this figure within a politics of (dis)location; as "Muslim" women, we are privileged and far removed but nonetheless stand affected. Our writings are acts of witnessing! But they also, equally, bear witness to the poverty that the highly sensational U.S. media spreads about war and death generally.

The third section, "(Un)Naming Faiths/Unclaiming Nations," struggles through the encounter between a recolonized public and the policing of families in our homes, specifically and in the broader "Muslim" communities. Here the concept of "faith" engages not only a religious faith but also the political, cultural, sexual, and national. For example, within this section there is an effort to name the violence that borders Pakistan, Kashmir, India, and Bangladesh. Here our writings are not just simply (un)naming histories and struggles, but actively constructing new visions.

The last section—"Re-Claiming Our Bodies/Re-Claiming Our Sexualities"—centers on the politics of the body and primarily sexuality, the effects of these struggles on our bodies, and the question of struggles over our sexuality and gender, linking it to politics, war and spirituality.

This anthology produces a heteroglossia of "Muslim" women struggles in which "every utterance contains within it the trace of other utterances, both in the past and in the future."[4] Although the work is generally organized under the four categories, each piece spills beyond the frame, speaking in and to multiple histories and issues. Weaving together the multiplicities of struggles that are generally understood to be separate is essential to the politics of this collection. In order for us to construct genuine democratic futures, we must face the differences that seek to divide us. Our bodies become mapped images, sites, and constructs of multiple wars. It is a body on whose back the nation reproduces its laws, its armies, and its decisions, as it is simultaneously a body of the outsider, the Other, the foreigner. However, we find ourselves further complicated and divided within our "own" communities, such as between those who veil and those who don't as portrayed in S.N.'s poem "Woman." Through mapping that woman's body, this anthology not only names the differences but also claims them as our own, as insiders/outsiders—a part of and apart from the United States, the "Muslim," and even the ("white") "feminist" community.

Our writings begin to articulate the experiences of growing up in the post–Gulf War United States as "Islamic" outsiders, living in racist war zones where our bodies, our cultures, our desires are spectralized in "zones of exception." The writings begin connecting histories of migration, memories of "home," and stories learned growing up in the harems[5] of "Muslim" households to present-day experiences, the everyday lived in the United States inside its own Camp X-Rays called "rights," "citizenship," "patriotism," "security," and "feminism." Here harems should not be only understood as gendered spaces of domestic surveillance but also as constitutive of a certain politics of masculinity in the public sphere; similarily, the legitimating strategies of Western counterterrorism need to be understood in terms of these memories of "home." Connecting the wars "back" home—the ones stored in our memory and in/on our bodies—to the wars being carried out today under the dictates of democracy and security, our work seeks to create the *disturbances necessary to build peaceful futures*.

In her three poems, Zohra Saed re-members her family's forced multiple migrations from Afghanistan to Saudi Arabia to Brooklyn in the late 1980s, sketching a history of Afghanistan when it became the battlefield of an imperial war between the ex–Soviet Republic and the United States. Her calligraphy of memories, "lit with the names of martyrs,"[6] is a rewriting of a palimpsest (hi)story in an effort to trace the "topography of loss" through self, community, and memory caught in decades of violence. Saed's poems drive "home" to Brooklyn, a history of displacement of an Afghan community whose refugee status is denied today.

Her poems historicize a crisis that, although termed by all human rights organizations as a "humanitarian" crisis, is left ignored when U.S. military planes invade and carpet bomb Afghanistan.[7] Her poems allow us to interrogate the ways in which wars and struggles affect us and inscribe us as we walk into and through (our) neighborhoods in cities across the United States. As we unearth those sites of struggles rendered invisible by the dominant war machine and start to paint these white pages, we begin to refigure struggles over our faiths, our bodies, our languages, and our histories.

Soniah Naheed Kamal also seeks answers from histories hidden between nervous acts and carefully chosen words our parents conjure in order to "save" us but also to minimize their own remembering, the often painful and violent histories they've lived. "The Fall" begins by asking Kamal's father about Bangladesh and what's called the war of 1971, but has been more aptly named one of the largest genocides of the twentieth century—with no accountability. Despite history's silences, Kamal's piece illustrates that we cannot remain silent about our own struggles. Her piece goes on to document her experience when her father, a Pakistani government employee, was detained by the current military dictatorship of General Pervez Musharraf, who took power through a coup d'état in 1999.

What comes to occupy a central concern of the contributors to this anthology is in fact the struggle over the very aesthetics of our politics. Indeed, we understand the political and ethical relations of resisting the multiple violences that cathect our desires, our memories, and our communities. This has the potential to present a fundamental problem, but it also provides an opportunity to practice a new political aesthetic. Our different arts and voices begin to redefine war, not as the unrepresentable lack supposedly at the center of our ravaged psyches, but rather as the sometimes violent, sometimes spiritual, sometimes humorous, and sometimes bodily demand for justice. Renaming our struggles to take on new forms of resistance, developing collective resources as the means of survival, we confront the terror that lives around us, within us—the terror that is us. . . .

As images of "Muslim" women's dismembered bodies air across the seas, as bits and pieces of flesh fixate the pornographic gaze of Western eyes, as pieces of her still mark the site of a suicide bombing or a demolition by Caterpillar bulldozers[8]—as these images, memories, and acts make their way into our lives, they leave their traces in our blood and in the hunger on our tongues, and our imaginations begin to paint. Even as warlords—we call them politicians in the West—continue to create bases on our bodies and continue their democratic rape of whole peoples, we begin to interrogate our faiths and dig out those narratives of women that silently linger on in the background of *khutbas* (decrees, sermons, declarations) pronounced by politicians, imams, chaplains, and ultimately history. We begin to seek possibilities outside the realm of patriarchal households, outside of the "under One God, under One Nation" discourses. Our imaginations re-trace possibilities between, for instance, Safa and Marwa, those two mountains where Hagar sought desperate possibilities. Bushra Rehman's poem "God Gave Me Two Children" is involved in this complex negotiation and witnessing by refiguring the connections between narratives, the body, and the historical meaning of a "*mujahidat.*" Engaging the story of Abraham's second wife, Hagar, who is largely a forgotten character in "Islamic" history, enables a radically different image of "Muslim" histories to emerge, indeed presents us with another kind of political aesthetics of "Islam" that is gendered. Rehman reminds us of Hagar's banishment and her struggle, by disconnecting her from "Islamic" history, of the dispossessions of "Muslim" women throughout the world, particularly of Palestinians under occupation. Through such re-imaginings we begin to refigure our histories, religions, and myths, and re-construct, re-image, and re-imagine contemporary wars, violence, and our spirituality in the face of dominant religious and political doctrines.

This refiguring allows us to engage with and go beyond the dominant moral parameters in which the suicide bomber, for example, is constructed in the West. Such an intervention is particularly crucial here in the United States, as the United States is the largest funder of the Israeli State and has hegemonically defined what constitutes a "moral" or "legitimate" war and death. These definitions help maintain the conditions that lead to suicide bombings in the first place.

We dare to move forward and challenge these ethical dogmas and interrogate the conditions, realities, and the very myths of the suicide bomber in order to forge new possibilities of political and spiritual resistance. The question isn't about whether we condone suicide bombings or romanticize them as a form of resistance. It is, however, to recognize them as such and to name, unapologetically, all the sites of violence that the blood stains and to question their ability to be a form of struggle, "to fight violence with violence."

This critique is forcefully expressed by Muna in "The Letter" by Shadi Eskandani. As the Western media would like to de-legitimize the Palestinian struggle for self-determination and further dehumanize them by veiling the conditions they live in under Israeli military occupation, while the International Monetary Fund bankrolls Israeli checkpoints, we never hear the other story behind the resistances. In at attempt to give voice to that story, the story of a suicide bomber, Eskandi also gives voice to the families and communities that are part of that dismembered body. At the end of "The Letter," it isn't enough to just "hear" the story either, indeed one can very much question whether the protagonist really "hears" it, but what is more urgent and necessary is the haunting question of "what can *we do* from here" about the conditions that the Palestinian people live under. What are we going to do about those conditions that lead to such acts of resistances? The myths the Western media constructs around this issue evade such a questioning. Indeed, if such acts are so horrific, what about the millions of U.S. tax dollars that fund the Israeli apartheid state? What are we going to do about the United States funding and creating right-wing dictatorships throughout the world, from Indonesia to the Congo, Haiti, and South America?

Chaumtoli Huq's essay "Violence, Revolution, and Terrorism: A Legal and Historical Perspective" urges us to question the neoliberal's demand that all "moderate" Muslims immediately denounce "violence" and "terrorism," excluding, of course, the terror that the U.S. state spreads. Her essay points to many different histories in which violence has been used, from the American Revolution, the abolition of slavery, to the struggle against British colonialism in India. As history is rampant with such uses of violence as heroic examples to end injustice, Haq points out that today we cannot denounce violence without examining how violence is connected to, and a means of, continuation of the nation-state, and its legal systems and regimes of control. Thus, the demand on

"Muslims" to denounce violence is not only a means by which they automatically become guilty and must blame themselves, but by which they simultaneously become victims without a right to resist. When violence is the rule of the day, it becomes necessary to find other ways of resisting; but for people who do not have the military capabilities to fight on "equal" terms their oppressors, such questions still remain drumming in our ears. It's important, here, to paraphrase an important question raised by the-soon-to-be suicide bomber in *Paradise Now*—how do we build a resistance based on morality when the occupiers have no morals?

The events of September 11 have dramatically redrawn the cartography of war zones, traditionally understood as war carried out in a particular space and place, fought by state-backed armies and through an official language. The West's military and political response has maintained, or better, re-energized the colonial legacies of "democracy" (that is, capitalist, racist, and sexist violence), even as new regimes of "security" and (counter)terrorism develop and deploy more effective technologies of death. However, there is nothing terribly new about the policies that the U.S. state is instituting in its so-called war against terrorism, either at Camp X-Ray in Guantanamo, Cuba; Abu Gharib in Iraq; or through legislation such as the Patriot Act and its ongoing rewriting of the U.S. constitution. We need only remember in this regard that the mechanisms of torture that seem to most revolt the supposedly humanitarian mind in Pontecorvo's *Battle of Algiers* are precisely what is being taught at the Pentagon today—with all the blessings of the State Department.[9] Despite the liberal faith that these torture chambers are exceptions to the rule of law in the United States and in its satellites abroad, or that they are something new, horrific, and thus correctable, a careful reading of the work of these contributors point us to the abject histories of dispossession that will always haunt our "civil liberties." With one eye on the West's (neo)colonial histories and another on today's prison industrial complex (the fastest growing industry in the country), this anthology urges us to contextualize "Muslim" communities in North America in terms of the struggles for empowerment and civil rights in the 1960s and 1970s. Indeed, the FBI's Counter Intelligence Program that materially aided the assassinations of key Black Panthers has today transformed into a pedagogy of citizenship called "Total Information Awareness."

We have been torn between two empires: one that claimed our freedom in rapacious capitalism and another that claimed to break these bonds by normalizing and commodifying our cultures—corporate multiculturalism. Both were caught in a shadow dance of proliferating arms. Now with the end of the so-called Cold War, the nuclear race is considered over, yet dirty bombs hide under every pillow; we find ourselves on the precipice of another divide. Today, the United States and its military are seeking to impose a (new) world (dis)order by creating new dictionaries of control and by defining and normalizing which person and which population, which nation and which culture, can enter the theater of "civilization." We are living in a period in which violence is the rule of the day, in which states sponsor and legitimize violence, seeking to control populations, to define a "just" death, and to monopolize the right to kill. Given the radical indistinctness between the Democrats and the Republicans eager to go "hunt them down and kill them," either in the caves of Afghanistan or the slaughterhouses of Baghdad, we begin to see a certain regularity between the racist policing in communities of color in the West and the privatization of prison technologies. If we could come to terms with those faces that occupy life behind prison in this country, we would not be so shocked at the speed with which civil rights have been overturned and thousands of immigrants detained or deported. The fear that exists today in the United States is merely the symptom of the violence of a too-long-repressed haunting. The cases of political prisoners in this country who have been wrongfully accused, mistried, and denied justice— such as Mumia Abu-Jamal, on death row for more than two decades, and Abner Louima and Amadou Diallo, in which racist, violent, state-backed practices were deployed—point to the imprisonment, sexual assault, quarantining, and murder of working-class, poor communities of color. Such histories only ricochet forty-one times (as did the bullets shot into Amadou Dialllo) with the bombs being dropped on Afghanistan, Iraq, and Palestine by the U.S. military.

This collection continues a long and complex tradition of resistance—with, first, a war cry, a ululation for survival. By beginning to articulate our resistances to the very Rationale, Politics, Languages, Traditions, and Walls built to police our bodies and homes, we can only then begin to wage peace. When a whole people is labeled as "terrorists" and arbitrarily rounded up and kept in indefinite lockups, carpet bombed, left floating in a sea of land mines, and sodomized, it is clear that the current political climate necessitates that we not just re-think or re-write, but name, launch new untimely becomings, and re-connect histories, struggles, and strategies. It is to respond creatively to this necessity for struggle that brings together this collection of poetry, prose, and other creative, personal, political writings. These voices allow us to enter the multiple worlds that we as "Muslim" women occupy under conditions of incredible violence. Articulating a collective vision allows us to come to terms with the possibilities of imagining peace as we learn to use, negotiate, and explode the fires within ourselves, our homes, and our communities.

Tina Zaman, in her poem, links the struggles of being "Muslim," a bisexual, and a brown woman living in a racist and a heterosexist society that seeks to reduce her to an exotic other. Central to naming her sexuality are the struggles of her working-class Bengali background. She refuses the guilt that works to police the boundaries of "authenticity"—how can we re-create ourselves, our communities, even as we become "Americanized" or "Westernized," in other words "*haram*"[10] in the eyes of our immigrant communities, parents, and families. By re-claiming herself and her sexuality, she also refuses the Western feminist construction of what constitutes liberation for women of the global south. Hers is a refusal to take part in a "free market feminism"—what Chandra Talpade Mohanty and M. Jacqui Alexander call a "... feminism [that] has been quantified for consumption within the global marketplace of ideas. ..." As transnational feminists, we struggle to redefine the core of our histories, our selves, and our communities, and articulate the new relational conditions of our autonomy.[11] We simply cannot walk out and turn our backs on our families, histories, or communities in some multicultural sound bite of a "better" life out here in the United States. Her series of poems ends with a call to (white) feminists to "wake up," because the struggles that we must fight together can only be addressed when we confront our differences. Struggles cannot be won in silence or under the totalizing banner of a universal sisterhood/womanhood.

Although originally one of the intentions of this anthology was to stay away from addressing the issue of why "Muslim" women wear the veil, Z. Gabriel Arkles's piece called "The Scarf" was deliberately placed for several reasons. As his is the only voice of a white transgendered person who is now a male, it was crucial to include, because he is able to address his own (white) community and its studied ignorance. His piece not only serves as an alliance between our two communities, but it also complicates issues around gender, sexuality, politics, culture, and religion. What his work does practically is make the construction of gender difference radically fluid—between bodies and matter, between culture and nature, and between our lives and another future. One can argue that in any transformation, one doesn't excavate what one has lived before; there isn't a simple cutoff or erasure/amnesia and a clean/pure beginning. For many "Muslims" and non-"Muslims," these identity categories (themselves seemingly fixed for all eternity, *qayamat tak*), such as transgendered and queer, are forever incompatible with "Islam." Arkles's piece testifies to the continued salience of such struggles around our fluid identities. In asserting an alliance here, we also affirm a spiritual practice in which we can explore, become, and celebrate our sexualities, politics, and religion.

Jawahara K. Saidullah's essay "War Stories" is not a "traditional" story about wars, but one voice that seeks to articulate the violence some "Muslims" grow up with in India, home to the world's largest Muslim population. Bush's war on terror has re-energized right-wing regimes throughout the world, namely the Bharatiya Janata Party (BJP) and Shiv Sena in India, which fueled the 2002 massacre in Gujarat that claimed more than two thousand lives. Human Rights Watch released a seventy-five-page report in April of 2002 titled "We Have No Orders to Save You: State Complicity and Participation in Communal Violence in Gujarat." This report concludes that the violence against Muslims in Gujarat was premeditated and planned before the Godhra massacre and at length supported by the local state apparatuses. When officials of a state are directly involved in such carnage, these violences can no longer be termed or understood as "communal violence." Such a label assumes that violence is an inherent part of a community and its makeup. Saidullah's war story is a testimony of the effects of this continuous tension, but it's also a testimony to the fact that Hindus and Muslims in India have been living together for centuries—marrying, negotiating, celebrating—but nonetheless, struggling together. It's about the complex negotiations of the ways some of us continue to re-form families, beyond religious doctrines and nationalist boundaries.

Organizing and fighting against domestic violence within the "Muslim" American community is complicated by the racist Western assumption that domestic violence is an inherent part of "Islam." This policing of the "Muslim" family makes it all the more difficult to articulate, as the ("white") "feminist" method of battling and surviving such violence in America requires "Muslim" women to reject their religious practice *tout court*. In Sarwat Rumi's poem "ramadan mubarak for 's,'" the experience of domestic violence and the struggle over the practice of faith is subverted, as violence is battled through a new articulation and a re-practicing of faiths (spirituality and identity) that enable strength and healing to take place collectively. Rumi's poem bodies forth a hunger for a new religious practice that will no longer be contained by the gendered disciplines of a sexual service to the masculine demands of a husband or a religion. In this specific way, faiths find a new entry into the struggles to re-define resistant spiritual practices collectively.

Aisha Sattar calls attention to the "McDonaldization" of Mecca and the thoroughgoing commodification of Hajj by the "Muslim" *umma* and by the Saudi government in "The Politics of Hajj." Her critique focuses on the "Muslim" woman's body in the organization of the five-day pilgrimage and asks how the corporatization of Hajj sanitizes the political and spiritual risks of the journey. By evoking a tradition of Hajj as a long-forgotten Mecca of global exchange, where ideas, politics, spirituality, and goods circulated, Sattar re-imagines the pilgrimage to Mecca as a journey that the "Muslim" *umma* could use today to cleanse and purge itself (but not through an ethics of purity) and that it could be a space of organizing dissent against war.

In this collaboration we begin to realize peace and its impossibilities. That without first laying naked the "truths" that continue to rape us, our lands, our cultures, our languages, and our very existence, and beginning to re-define and name our struggles, we cannot survive. That is, if we are not detained. As the war against "terrorism" unfolds, we seek to address everyday "Muslim" women's lives and reconnect our resistances, spirituality, and religion to our memory, loss, violence, sexuality, and love. This anthology is a vital intervention in today's discourse on war, peace, gender, sexuality, religion, politics, civil rights, humanitarianism, activism, and art. This anthology moves the current debate around "Muslim" women in significantly new directions. There is an argument here for a new aesthetics rooted in heterogeneous practices of the body, sexuality, religion, and creativity: an embodied poetics.

We hope to utilize this collectivity of "Muslim" women beyond the pages of a book and extend the discussion started here to communities, universities, galleries, and various public spaces. We hope to organize community discussions, academic conferences, and cultural and visual art exhibits around the themes of this anthology. We hope to further this dialogue and bring together other communities, both in North America and the West more generally, but also in the "Muslim" community all over the world, by linking women's struggles together and creating new methodologies in the battle to resolve the current crisis that has us all in its clutches.

—Sarah Husain

NOTE FROM THE EDITOR ON TRANSLITERATION

The transliteration of words in Arabic, Urdu, Farsi, etc., have been kept as the contributors wrote them. The reader will find variations of the same word, such as *hejab*, *hijab*, *chador*, and *chadar*. The words have been kept in their original form to respect the different pronunciations, spellings, and indeed differences that exist within the "Muslim" diaspora. We come from heterogeneous regions, and our choices are symbolic of the ways we inhabit and wear our words through difference. It has been important since the conception of this project to present the multitude of experiences that exist, not only in life, but in the spelling, pronunciation, and very meaning of words. As readers of difference, it is valuable to feel alienated. Not everything can be translated, nor is it necessary that it should be all the time. As "Americans"—as consumers—we expect everything to be presented perfectly packaged and in a proper line/order in each and every aisle of choice. Because we contributors consider the worldview that reduces everything to commodities to be destructive, it was imperative and therefore intentional to let language and difference in this anthology be little rocks in the reader's throat—so they are not easily digestible, and thereby encourage thoughtful reading and discourse about the value of our differences.

one:

(UN)NAMING WARS

Woman

S.N.

most certainly your body
is for us to mark our territory
and to conduct our wars

and it is nation that marks your back
like a map
roads twisting down the bones
and in your womb
waits the government
wishing to decide
on its fate
the sterilizations
the control of decisions
the abuse of space
prison shackles in labor
and secret bruising.

body always public
for the slashing of face if it is uncovered
and kicking of belly when it is covered
the not getting the job
the getting kicked out of school
the threat of violence daily
covered or uncovered
it is the same here
this body.

For Afghanistan, 2001

Salimah Valiani

This
is a clock
whose time tells horror
whose alarm rings oblivion.
We can't undo time.
We can stop the ringing.

Circumstantial evidence
upon circumstantial evidence
does not make Intelligence.
Military might without Intelligence
flies smart bombs without direction.

A 1000-pound bomb
explodes the heaviness of shame.
The heaviness of land mines lost over 20 years of time.
The heaviness of herds of livestock—once an economy—
pasting the hills with bones.
The heaviness of plastic tents
bursting
when the -20C air blows.

A mother or a father
did not lose four children
because of the war today.
The world is losing its families,
We are losing ourselves.

Heights of wacky, civilized war-calls.
Rocky caves of wacky, holy war-calls.

Pits of cut-off hands, blasted limbs, our muted minds.
We can't kill a beast which is already dead.
We can bring back to life collective responsibility—
the heartbeat of human dignity.

The Day After:
A Cento Based on Hate Crimes Filed Shortly after 9/11

Anida Yoeu Esguerra

1942: Executive Order 9066 authorized the U.S. military to incarcerate 112,000 Japanese Americans in ten internment camps, many of whom were second- and third-generation American citizens.

1967: "Those of us who struggle against racial injustice must come to see that the basic tension is not between races . . . The tension is at bottom between justice and injustices . . . We are out to defeat injustice and not white persons who may happen to be unjust."
—*Dr. Martin Luther King, Jr.*

Awoke to signs,
TERRORISTS sprayed in red paint across their family's driveway,
TERRORIST ON BOARD written on their white car.

Awoke to find,
freeway sign says, KILL ALL ARABS
elevator sign says, KILL ALL TOWEL HEADS.

A Pakistani Muslim living in L.A.
awoke to find his car scratched across
the right side with the words NUKE 'EM!

Awoke to find
300 march on a mosque in Bridgeview, IL.
300 American flags shout "USA! USA!"
Mosque awoke to find a 19-year-old shouting
"I'm proud to be American, I hate Arabs and I always have."

Firebomb tossed,
Taxi driver pulled out and beaten,
Vandals in Collingswood, NJ, attacked two Indian-owned businesses.
Vandals spray-painted LEAVE TOWN.

Awoke to find
a South Asian American,
Sikh, chased by a group of four men yelling "terrorist."
Sikh mistaken as a Muslim American.

Back up.
Sikh man, 69, shot.
Body found in a canal
He had a turban on.
Turban mistaken as a Muslim American.

A vehicle of white males,
followed and harassed a 21-year-old female.
Attackers yelled, "Go back to your own country!"
The attackers' car pinned her against another vehicle.
Then they backed up and ran over her again.
Kimberly—a 21-year-old
Back up. A 21-year-old full-blood Creek
Back up. Full-blood Creek Native American
Mistaken as a Muslim American.

Awoke to find,
a Pakistani native beaten by three men.

Back up. Egyptian American, 48, killed point-blank.
Back up. Sikh man, 49, shot.
Shooter shouted, "I stand for America all the way."

Back up.
A man pushing a baby stroller walked by a mosque.

He stopped and started yelling,
"You Islamic mosquitoes should be killed."
Mosquitoes mistaken as Muslim Americans.

Awoke to find two women speaking Spanish in a doctor's office.
A Caucasian woman yells, "You foreigners caused all this trouble,"
and begins to beat one of the women.
Spanish mistaken as Muslim.

Back up.
She asks the woman if she is Arab,
and then punches her in the eye.

Awoke to be mistaken.
A woman wearing Muslim clothing was shopping.
A Caucasian woman began attacking her and yelled,
"America is only for white people."

Back up. America mistaken for white people.

Armed man sets fire to a Seattle mosque.
300 march on mosque in Bridgeview, IL.
Mosques in Carrollton, Denton and Irving, TX, attacked.
Muslim student at Arizona State University attacked.
Afghan restaurant in Fremont attacked with bottles and rocks.
Two suspects wrote DIE on a Persian Club booth.

A gasoline bomb is thrown
through the window of a Sikh family's home,
hitting a 3-year-old on the head.

Two women at a bagel store.
Woman attacked for wearing a Quranic charm around her neck.
Attacker lunges,
yells, "Look what you people have done to my people."

No one in the store tried to help.
The owner apologized to the attackers for any inconvenience.

300 march on two women
No one tried to help.

Two women awoke to find
an explosion from a cherry bomb
outside the Islamic Center of San Diego.
San Diego mistaken for Muslim Americans
"Look what you people have done to my people."
300 march on mosque in Bridgeview, IL
No one tried to help.
Sign says, KILL ALL ARABS.
Sign says, KILL ALL TOWEL HEADS.
Towels mistaken for Muslim Americans
No one tried to help.
Vandals attack.
No one tried to help.
He had a turban on.
No one tried to help.
Sign says, LOOK WHAT YOU PEOPLE HAVE DONE
Flags wave in an Afghan restaurant.
300 march against Spanish spoken at a doctor's office
Spanish mistaken for Muslim Americans
300 march on two women at a bagel store
Bagels mistaken for Muslim Americans
300 wave cherry bombs.
Bombs march on 300 Sikhs,
hitting a 3-year-old on the head.

Look what you people have done.

Human Services

Leila Montour

"Where's the WIC office?"
This building twists;
her knees hurt;
the appointment is at three.
The guide eyeballs her headscarf, hands out
a map and questions:
"Diocese volunteer?"
and she blurs
into the blue-white
stripes of Theresa.

In knotted hallways
with fluorescent blares,
and in hours of butt-numb
waiting, the secretary
s-l-o-w-l-y-s-p-e-a-k-s
English.
She must be
the prisoner of dusky men
who spew explosives,
who tent-creep.

Food vouchers in hand,
she unravels toward
an exit. The security guard
circles tighter
to sniff her aura, to listen

for the sound of ticking
underneath her clothes.
Omniscient,
it is three years before the Twin Towers.

Shadow Nation

Leila Montour

On Occupation and Resistance:
Two Iraqi Women Speak Out[1]

Azza Basarudin and Khanum Shaikh

PREFACE

The fall and capture of Saddam Hussein, the appointment of the provisional government, the January elections, the transitional government, etc. have not provided a glimpse of the "democracy" that the American establishment had desired for Iraq. Instead, destruction, violence, revenge, and death reign free in the land where civilization began. The opposition, or, as they are labeled, "insurgency," are still faceless and nameless (despite claims that they are mostly connected to Al-Qaeda, or that they are individuals who come from all over the Arab and Muslim worlds to fight in the name of Islam); the exact number of civilians who have been killed in Iraq is not known; and the number of American military personnel dead has reached more than two thousand. Amid world outcry against the violence, abuse (i.e., Abu Gharib), and dehumanization that are taking place in Iraq, it has been recently reported that the U.S. military has been "planting favourable stories in the Iraqi press . . . *The Los Angeles Times* reported . . . that articles trumpeting the work of U.S. and Iraqi troops were written by U.S. soldiers, and translated into Arabic by a defence contractor, who then helped place them in Baghdad papers."[2] How is this conduct different from that of Saddam Hussein when he was in power?

Violence against women, or, as we label it, "sexual terrorism," in Iraq is on the rise. Women Living Under Muslim Law (WLUML) reported that the U.S. occupation has fueled violence against women and rising religious extremism. This report cited evidence obtained by Amnesty International and Human Rights Watch that "jailed Iraqi women have suffered abuse and torture at the hands of the U.S. military."[3] According to the Ministry of Public Works and Social Affairs, there has been a marked increase in violence against Iraqi women since the U.S.-led invasion of Iraq, especially in the capital, Baghdad. While specific statistics are lacking, since April 2004, nearly four hundred women and thirty-five men have reported cases of rape to local nongovernmental organizations (NGOs). One NGO, Women for Peace, estimates that the numbers could be more than twice as high.[4] In addition, the lack of security and the threat of rape, kidnapping, and prostitution of girls and women have led to parents encouraging their daughters to abandon their schooling. Women and girls are being sexually terrorized every day of their lives to the extent that they are no longer safe in their own houses. WLUML reports that "threats of sexual violence and murder have also led professional women to quit their jobs . . . violence also affects women's political participation: Following the 2003 murder of Akila al-Hashimi (one of only three female members of the Governing Council), many activists were forced to retreat from the public sphere."[5] Religious extremists are policing women's bodies and sexuality, and women who are deemed to be "Westernized" (i.e., who refuse to cover their hair and/or wear the *abaya*, a full-length veil) are threatened with various forms of violence, from acid attack, to rape, to murder. Women who "cross" the preset borders of religious extremism are seen as subjecting themselves to violence, and the act of transgressing these borders allows for violence against women to be normalized, produced, and reinforced.

Rubina Saigol points to the resemblance between the treatment of women and nation/land. She connects how the nation/land is perceived as feminine in construction and the desire for the land is masculine: "the desire to possess it, see it, admire it, love it, protect it, and die fighting for it."[6] The aggressiveness with which men protect their country is similar to how they control and treat their women. In Iraq, women's bodies have become a site for contestation of the U.S. military occupation, nationalist sentiments, and affirmation of masculinity where violence such as rape, torture, and murder are inscribed onto women's bodies the same way a land/nation is fought for. Therefore, the female body has become a brutal tool not only in reproducing opposition to occupation and patriarchal control, but also nationalist ideologies.

What does the rhetoric of democracy mean within a context of occupation? How do militarized spaces and ideologies impact the lives of women in contemporary Iraq? What is the connection between sexual terrorism and occupation? How is patriarchy reproduced? Even though the following interview with Amal Al-Khedairy and Nermin Al-Mufti was conducted in 2003, the issues raised continue to be relevant today as we see an escalation in violence against women in Iraq.

THE INTERVIEW

On November 17, 2003, Amal Al-Khedairy and Nermin Al-Mufti, two visitors from Iraq, gave a talk at University of California, Los Angeles on the im-pact of the United States' military occupation on Iraqi men and women. Khedairy's opening comment to the audience was, "I see your beautiful universities here, and I ask why did your government have to destroy our universities?"

They were enraged by injustices committed on Iraqi civilians and were determined to speak out against the United States' occupation of Iraq. Insistent that the occupation of Iraq must end, they believe that the international community must be a part of the reconstruction of their country. "This is not a war, it is an aggression, a vicious destruction of our country and its people," said Al-Mufti.

Amal Al-Khedairy is the founder and director of Al-Beit Al-Iraqi, or Iraqi House, an arts and cultural center in Baghdad. Ms. Al-Khedairy opened the center in 1988, and it is located in her family's Ottoman-style home. She is a widely traveled expert in Iraqi history, regional culture, arts, archaeology, and music. She is fluent in French and English, in addition to Arabic. Nermin Al-Mufti is an internationally recognized Iraqi journalist. Through scholarships and invitations, Ms. Al-Mufti has received fellowships in international journalism from Hungary and the U.K. For more than twenty years, she has served as a consultant and writer for many international media agencies. Until this year, Ms. Al-Mufti produced weekly columns on corruption, environmental issues, gender issues, contemporary literature, human rights, education, nutrition, and disease for a well-known Iraqi weekly. With her extraordinary grasp of the social, economic, and political history of Iraq, Ms. Al-Mufti writes articles on sanctions, war, and history that appear on a regular basis in *Al-Ahram*, a weekly paper in Cairo. Ms. Al-Mufti is also an expert in the archaeology and art of her country.

The following is our interview with them:

BASARUDIN AND SHAIKH: Can you explain why you have embarked on such a tour in the United States? What is your purpose and what do you hope to gain by doing this?

AL-KHEDAIRY: We don't represent Iraqi women; we are women from Iraq who have witnessed the occupation, and we are here to tell our side of the story.

We want people to know how the Iraqi people have not only suffered from the severe sanctions but are now suffering again from this unjust war. Our basic infrastructures such as schools, bridges, hospitals, sewage, and water systems have been destroyed. Everything was destroyed completely, and only the Ministry of Oil was saved. In the search for Saddam Hussein, our children, women, and men are constantly under bombardment. We ask ourselves, how and why did this happen? Iraq is even smaller than the state of California. All this destruction was done under the guise of searching for weapons of mass destruction and toppling Saddam Hussein. Instead, the U.S. administration toppled the whole of Iraq, destroyed houses and the lives of people.

AL-MUFTI: We are here to raise awareness on what is going on in Iraq. We were in opposition to this occupation from the beginning. The U.S. administration launched this occupation on my country based on false documents given to the U.S. administration by Iraqi opposition groups who are in Iraq and in exile. Iraqis are being killed every day, in every city—not just in Baghdad—by so-called "friendly fires" of the American army, who are "trigger happy," ready to kill any Iraqi while at the same time they [American soldiers] are also being killed.

We are here to say, end this occupation and pull out all the American troops as soon as possible, not only to protect the Iraqi people, but also to protect the young Americans who are being killed. . . . We are here because for thirteen years, twenty-six million Iraqis have been demonized in the Western media in a very ugly way, as if we are not human beings, as if we are not the same Iraqis who have a rich history, as if we are not the same Iraqis living where civilization began, the same Iraqis who introduced the very basis of mathematics. So we are here in a very simple way to shake hands, to see our American friends and let them know what is really happening.

BASARUDIN AND SHAIKH: We know that Iraq is a very culturally rich country. Can you share with us a little about Iraqi culture and people, and what the impacts of the war have been on Iraqi culture and the people of Iraq?

AL-MUFTI: [In tears] I spent three days crying when our museums were looted. It was not just Iraqi history but it is the history of the world. You cannot find those old Iraqi statues anymore, the ones that were stolen from the museums. The statues were always of a man and a woman, and between them a child or children, and most of these statues were twenty thousand years old. This proves that Iraqi civilization was filled with love; we have a very old civilization passed down from generation to generation. Do you know that when Allah expelled Adam from paradise after the first sin, he [Adam] sat crying for years and years, looking for another place that resembled paradise . . . and that place was in southern Iraq, in Basra, a place called Al-Qurnah, which is where Adam and Eve met for the first time on Earth, and for the first time on the Earth, a love act took place between Adam and Eve. So the first time in the world a love act took place it was in Iraq, an act that gave birth to all humankind.

So I say, how can such a history be lost? You can find from East to far West, from North to South—we had 140,000 historical sites. These sites now are being dug up and we are realizing that all the genuine artifacts that were thousands of years old were stolen, but the duplicated ones were left behind—all under the protection of U.S. military. Important documents of all sorts for the last one hundred years—real estate, birth certificates, etc.—have disappeared. The looters burned the university library and the general library of Iraq, so two and a half million books from libraries were lost. They burned and ransacked Bait-ul-Hiqmat [the House of Wisdom], which was an institution created in the Abbasid period. With my own eyes I saw people selling the most valuable historical books from Bait-ul-Hiqmat on the streets, ten books for $1.

I must say that this is not an accidental erasure of history. It is a very deliberate and calculated act. It was very well planned out in advance. And don't forget that one thousand Free Iraqi Forces were very well trained by the Americans in Hungary before they even entered Iraq. Many things point to the fact that this was all a calculated destruction of the very foundations of Iraqi history, Iraqi dignity, the erasure of Iraqi history and pride.

BASARUDIN AND SHAIKH: It was widely reported that the cultural center, the Iraqi House, was looted and ransacked during the chaos that followed after U.S. military occupied Iraq; why do you think this happened and could it have been prevented by U.S. troops?

AL-KHEDAIRY: It is a systematic way of destroying culture and all aspects of life. This was not only my house, you see, it was a cultural house as well as an arts and crafts center. There used to be many women who worked in that house, earning a living and supporting their families by selling their crafts. So many of them at the moment are feeling very bad about the destruction of the Iraqi House.

But the destruction was everywhere in Iraq. The second day after the occupation started, I went to a bridge to get a view of Baghdad, and it was the most tragic thing that could happen to any city, especially a city like Baghdad, which was once the seat of the Abbasid empire, which ruled for six hundred years from China to Spain. Iraq was also the first independent country in the Arab world and the Middle East. To see everything burning around you, week after week after week, was very painful. I really believe that this was part of a systematic elimination of the culture of our society and country.

Just before coming on this trip, we [Al-Mufti and Al-Khedairy] were searching through the rubble left behind from the destruction of the Iraqi House, and we found looms that were used by craftswomen and men—they even destroyed the looms. Why did they have to destroy the looms? Had they stolen the looms, I could understand that people wanted them. They just destroyed everything that was there. Another example is the museum; it is a clear example of the international and systematic nature of this operation. Why else would the looters leave the fake pieces in the museums and take the original ones? How do the looters know which is original and which are the fake artifacts? Why did the U.S. military just stand by and let the looters run wild? This could have been prevented. One warning shot into the air would have scared the looters away, but this was not done.

BASARUDIN AND SHAIKH: Can you describe the life of Iraqis in general and women in particular over a decade of war [Iran-Iraq War], Gulf War, international sanctions, and now under U.S. military and economic occupation?

AL-MUFTI: As an Iraqi woman, let me tell you what the impacts have been on my life. I was just twenty years old when the Iran-Iraq War began. In my twenties I gave birth to my son, so he was a baby in the war. He became a child in the 1991 war, a teenager under very severe sanctions, and a young man under U.S. military occupation. Thank goodness I have a very good mother who assisted me financially, helped me raise my son, and gave me a choice to be a journalist. But other women do not have the same options. You know, in 1979 Iraq won the

United Nations Education, Scientific and Cultural Organization prize because the literacy rates among both men and women were extremely high. After years of wars and sanctions, 45 percent of our younger generation below the age of fifteen is illiterate. . . . Iraq had the finest education system, free healthcare system, and excellent social services. Now we have nothing.

However, the most important thing we lost is our value scale. Our values are now upside down. During the sanctions many people got involved with smuggling and other illegal and immoral activities in order to make money, and through such activities have accumulated some measure of wealth. Such illegal activities are so commonplace now that they are affecting the dominant moral values of our society. Within twenty years, Iraq has gone down from being number 14 in the United Nations Development Programme list of most developed countries to number 156. Seven million Iraqis are now under the poverty line. We have three million single women who have lost husbands and sons through sanctions and wars.

One of the impacts of wars and sanctions has been a rapid increase in prostitution in Iraq. Prior to 1991, levels of prostitution were relatively low. However, over the last decade, prostitution rates have skyrocketed. Many men have died in the wars and sanctions, which has left women in financial difficulty. More and more women, as well as children now, are involved in prostitution in order to make a living. I recently completed a project working with children who are ten, eleven, twelve years old—not even teenagers—who are working in this industry.

BASARUDIN AND SHAIKH: The Human Rights Watch has published a report on how the failure of Iraqi and U.S.-led occupation authorities to provide public security in Iraq's capital has increased incidences of rape and abduction of girls and women. Can you comment on this report?

AL-MUFTI: I have seen many cases of violence against women recently. One specific case that stands out is that of a nine-year-old girl who was brutally raped and continued to bleed for ten days, and her body was bruised in ways that are hard to even imagine. When I asked her what had happened, she could not even explain to me what she had experienced.

BASARUDIN AND SHAIKH: Noeleen Heyzer, executive director of the United

Nations Development Fund for Women, said the poor security situation is also preventing women from taking more responsibility in rebuilding Iraq. What are your opinions on this and what roles do you envision women taking on in this postwar society?

AL-KHEDAIRY: Yes, this is a serious problem. Because of rampant abductions, rape, and other crimes against women and also men, many women are afraid to come out of their houses. Iraq is a lawless country now. Some people are out of control, and women become victims; so when they can't even leave the house without fear of rape, how are they going to take part in rebuilding the country?

I see women taking up active roles, just as they once had, in postwar Iraq. Before the Gulf War, sanctions, and now occupation, women had active roles in society.

BASARUDIN AND SHAIKH: There have been numerous reports lately that the U.S.-led occupation in Iraq is fueling extremist groups, whereby women are being intimidated to take on the veil. Any comment on this?

AL-MUFTI: Before the war, some religious extremists spoke out against women who didn't wear *hijab* in the streets. However, the highest Sharia court issued a wonderful fatwa in favor of women, saying that no one has the right to force women to wear the *hijab*. This was a great fatwa, and women in Iraq rarely veiled, although this practice varies according to region. Now, however, violence, sexual coercion, and rape are on the rise due to the chaos in the country. More women are seen wearing the *hijab* on the streets now, and fewer women are seen walking in the streets due to the fear of violence. I can't say if this is directly linked to U.S. occupation or not, but perhaps foreign presence, coupled with incidences of abductions and rape in the country, has increased the need for protection of our women.

BASARUDIN AND SHAIKH: What roles do you see Iraqis in exile having to play in rebuilding Iraq?

AL-MUFTI: Everybody must have a role in rebuilding Iraq—not just Iraqis—because everybody is responsible for what happened. International organizations as well as political leaders like Nelson Mandela who have dealt with serious challenges in their own countries could serve as an important voice. And what happened to the United Nations? Where were the international organizations like the United Nations in the destruction of Iraq?

BASARUDIN AND SHAIKH: Is there anything you would like to say to the American public?

AL-KHEDAIRY: People should not be deceived by the media. The American public needs to think of us [Iraqis] not as things but as human beings who also have a right to live and have our children educated just like children here. Why were our universities destroyed when they look after your universities so well? Our museums, all the historical and cultural aspects of our lives, have been destroyed as well. Why did the occupiers do that?

They [Americans] should ask themselves why they waged this war—it is not just one man—it is the whole nation. One man cannot wage war just because he wants to. I know there were demonstrations in opposition to the war, but if you are a democratic country, there should be more than one voice making decisions and declaring war on another country. This was not war; it was aggression, and it was violation of human rights against people of one country and against all of humanity. In front of the eyes of the whole world, we saw houses being violated, windows being broken, just under the pretense of finding Saddam Hussein. Can you imagine us coming here and doing the same to this country?

American Flag as *Pardah*

Saba Razvi

Baghdad, of its magic carpets, lost
one thread and another—like a crumpling row
of soldiers—in turn the rectangles folded
back over themselves and the tasseled fringes
of sky and soil met, across the horizon.

A hem was pulled from the vertical center—
one row of stitching, square knots
of windows and curtains—and another
above, higher, above, unraveled
into the collapsing spine of the building,
sides falling into the center, into a plume
like an ash flower, an asphodel—
the ghost of bodied breath swelling
under a snapping sky.

In TX, I folded my *jaan-e-maaz*, fringe to fringe,
to place my peace on an American shelf
beside the TV screen
on which the whistles of bursting rocket lulled
my brothers' screams—
until I stopped folding
my scarf into smaller angles in my frozen hands—
my scarf on my hands, under my eyes opening,
fell open unfolding—openmouthed, unsilenced.

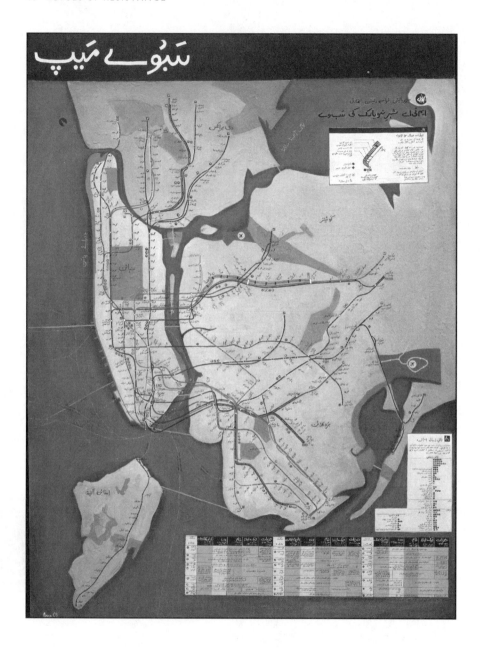

Vanwyck Details

Asma Shikoh

Homeland Security: Crossing the Border

Leila Montour

The van rumbles
as we sit, waiting for our turn.
Tense eyes, and the handover
of passports. How long will we stay
and for what?
Welcome to Canada;
a smile spreads to the eyes
of the woman in the booth.

A long line, a long warning.
The terror alert—a canary
in the mines, awaiting suffocation.
Beefy men multiply by three.
They say our passports
haven't been signed;
they ask every question twice
with un-subtle variations.
Our heads reflect
in their accusing sunglasses
as we cross back home.

Dear Honorable Gentlemen:
Re: Religiously Motivated Discriminatory Conduct at Peter C. Rodino Federal Building in Newark, New Jersey

Engy Abdelkader

Thousands of ordinary Muslims or "Muslim-looking" people continue to be profiled, indefinitely detained, and harassed, sometimes for hours, throughout North America, either at airports or in public places by local, state, or federal authorities who often deny that racial and/or religious profiling is a tool used in securing our safety. As this debate continues within the formalities of political correctness, politicians' dogma, and biased media reporting, the real issues concerning the Patriot Act and the insidious attacks on our civil rights are going largely unaddressed and are often obscured. Reprinted below is a letter written by Engy Abdelkader, a prominent lawyer from New York/New Jersey, addressed to major politicians, varied officials, and national civil liberties groups, highlighting the discriminatory practices and attitudes American Muslim women confront routinely amid the challenges inherent in security personnel jobs.

The letter is reprinted in this anthology for several reasons: namely, to bring the ways in which "Homeland Security" secures America to our nation's collective attention but also to draw attention to how American Muslim women donning the hijab *in accordance with their religious beliefs are targeted in all facets of their lives, and the numerous ways we are organizing and challenging such biased conduct, stereotypes, and misunderstandings. While many remain cynical of letter-writing campaigns as an effective form of protest or an adequate means of effecting a necessary change, in Engy Abdelkader's refusal to tolerate such mistreatment, and in her utilization of her own position of power as a prominent attorney, her protest has in fact effected change for both herself and others: When she returned two months after the discriminatory incident to the same courthouse, she was "greeted" by the same officer and immediately asked whether she would like to be checked by a female officer on the premises; she has also witnessed other Muslim women being treated more humanely at the same facility. Currently, this case is being investigated by U.S. Federal Protective Services in Washington, D.C., and*

the Honorable Congressman Christopher Smith's office. As a result of New Jersey
Attorney General Peter C. Harvey's pushing, cultural-sensitivity trainings are
now mandatory for all New Jersey State law enforcement, and Engy Abdelkader
conducts such trainings on American Muslims and Islam for both New Jersey and
New York local and state law enforcement and for U.S. Department of Justice
officials in order to prevent similar incidents from occurring for other Americans.

July 4, 2005
Re: Religiously Motivated Discriminatory Conduct at Peter C. Rodino Federal
Building in Newark, New Jersey

Dear Honorable Gentlemen:

My name is Engy Abdelkader, and I am a United States–born citizen, practicing attorney, and registered voter. While visiting a federal building in a professional capacity recently, I was harassed, humiliated, and denied access to the building as a result of religiously and racially motivated bigotry.

I am a staff attorney with Legal Services of New Jersey (LSNJ), which, as you may know, is a preeminent organization providing legal services to low-income New Jersey residents who cannot afford private counsel. At approximately 8:00 AM on Thursday, June 30, 2005, I was en route to a court hearing before Judge Franklin at the Peter C. Rodino Federal Building, located at 970 Broad Street in Newark, New Jersey, when I passed through an entrance metal detector and it beeped. In response, privately contracted Security Officer Smith* instructed me to remove my outer blazer jacket, and I calmly explained that the tenets of my Muslim religion prohibit me from doing so in the presence of a male officer. I requested for a female officer to conduct this more intimate search in a private area.

Unfortunately, Security Officer Smith answered abrasively, "Thank you and have a nice day" while directing me to the exit. Surprised, I reiterated that I was Muslim, advised him that I was an attorney required to appear in Judge Franklin's courtroom, and articulated my complete willingness to comply with the prescribed security protocols but explained that I could only remove my outer blazer jacket in the presence of a female officer, in accordance with the

---

*Note: Names of all individuals referenced herein have been altered.

religious beliefs underlying my modest dress. Officer Smith bellowed that he did not care who I was and that I was not entering the building unless I removed my blazer jacket. He falsely informed me, "We don't have female security officers," while directing me once again to the building exit.

I immediately demanded to speak to a supervisor. Officer Smith stated that he would call a supervisor, and as I stepped to the side, he forced me to exit the building. Several minutes later I met Officer Doe, who was dressed in a dark, seemingly Department of Homeland Security officer uniform. He had been misinformed that I had refused to pass through the entrance metal detector in the first instance. I explained that I had in fact set off the detector after passing through it and had simply requested a female officer when I was instructed to remove my blazer jacket, in accordance to the tenets of my religious faith. I further informed Officer Doe that I was willing to comply fully with all security procedures and protocols and would even remove my headscarf if deemed necessary, but only in the presence of a female officer. Further, I reminded him of the federal government's policy of cultural sensitivity accommodating Muslim women's religiously motivated requests for private secondary searches and that same be performed by female officers—this is specifically true of the Transportation and Security Agency, whose customers routinely undergo similar initial and secondary security searches at our nation's airports.

Officer Doe called for a female security officer, who performed a private external body search that yielded nothing. I expressed my desire to file a formal and official complaint against Officer Smith. As she escorted me to the building's lobby, after informing her colleagues who had congregated in the area of her search results, Security Officer Smith yelled in front of security officers, attorneys, customers, and government personnel, "And you have to go through the same process before you leave, too!" I chose not to respond, but I had visited the building on prior occasions without incident and always left through the lobby doors without being subjected to any such search before departing.

As I waited to file my complaint with Captain Jack, two men dressed in dark Department of Homeland Security uniforms stood near me as one said to the other, "If you don't want to go through the metal detector, then you shouldn't come into the building"; aside from being factually misinformed, it appeared as if these men were attempting to intimidate me. Accordingly, I turned directly to the unidentified officer and advised him that I was an attorney and fully aware of my rights. I apprised him of the facts at hand, advised him of our government's policy of cultural sensitivity in such situations, and reminded him that all human beings deserve to be treated with respect regardless of race, religion, or gender. Neither officer said anything in return, and quite honestly, both looked somewhat shocked; I am not certain if this was the effect of the substance of my statements, my ability to speak English flawlessly without an accent (despite my headscarf), or that I responded to the officer's remark in the first place. Finally, I spoke with Captain Jack, who appeared sympathetic and apologetic while providing me with an incident report form to complete. Note: I arrived at 970 Broad Street that morning at 8:00 AM; however, I did not in fact appear before Judge Franklin until approximately 9:01 AM.

I was harassed, humiliated, and denied access to a United States federal building because of my observance of modest dress in accordance with the tenets of my Muslim faith, Islam. This is unacceptable. Not only am I an American-born and -bred citizen, but I have always been a law-abiding and upstanding member of the community: I was the secretary of my public high school's National Honor Society and Russian Language Club and a photographer for our school yearbook; I graduated Phi Beta Kappa from the Rutgers College General Honors Program, where I served as a dorm resident advisor and tutored English as a second language on behalf of Rutgers University; at the Rutgers School of Law–Newark, I was on law review, participated in the Public Interest Law Foundation, and wrote articles for the Law Students Guild's publication; as an attorney I have dedicated myself to serving and protecting the more vulnerable among us in society—hence, my current post with LSNJ.

Since September 11, I have repeatedly and consistently condemned the terrorist attacks carried out by so-called Muslims and worked earnestly at establishing a dialogue among the government and the Arab, South Asian, and Muslim American communities by serving on the Arab and Muslim Advisory Committee to Attorney General Peter C. Harvey and attending a Ramadan *iftar* hosted by former New Jersey Governor Jim McGreevy at the State House as a representative of the Muslim New Jersey community. Yet, last week, I was reduced to an "other," an "enemy," a "terrorist" by fellow Americans and my government's employees. Do I fit the terrorist profile simply because I am a Muslim woman covering my hair and practicing modest dress in the same vein as the Virgin Mother Mary or Orthodox Jewish women?

The vile, un-American conduct of Security Officer Smith et al is wholly unacceptable, warranting appropriate disciplinary action and corrective measures to prevent such incidents from recurring in the future to me or others. Indeed, how will someone without the benefit of a law degree or specific experience in civil rights advocacy fare with Security Officer Smith et al? How have they fared? In fact, all state and federal employees required to interact with members of the general public, and particularly those doing so while functioning in a security capacity, should be required to attend cultural sensitivity training to help ensure the highest quality of customer service and professionalism. Cultural sensitivity trainings, such as those provided by the Department of Justice's Community Relations Service, will enhance security by enabling officers to easily identify sincerely held religious beliefs along with related requests while ensuring the proper allocation of officer time and resources to legitimate security threats. Indeed, we must "secure our homeland," but with respect and sensitivity for all Americans, regardless of race, religion, or gender.

To my knowledge, such cultural sensitivity training sessions are largely voluntary at this time. Security Officer Smith's conduct highlights the necessity of making such sessions mandatory for all those who wear the face of our state or federal government when interacting with the public. No one should have to suffer harassment, humiliation, or discrimination in any building, and particularly not a state or federal building, in America. Amid abuse of Muslims in Iraq, Afghanistan, and Guantanamo Bay; "extraordinary renditions" by the CIA of Muslims to Third World countries to be subjected to torture; and the 70 percent increase in discrimination against American Muslims in 2004, per a recent civil rights report issued by the Council on American-Islamic Relations, it is imperative that each of you send a strong message to the offending officers, to potential future perpetrators, and to Muslims that such behavior will not be tolerated here at home. This country was founded upon principles of religious freedom by men who left their native lands because of religious persecution— what is becoming of our great nation?

By way of this letter, I am filing a complaint with the American Civil Liberties

Union, Department of Justice, Department of Homeland Security, American-Arab Anti-Discrimination Committee, and the Council on American-Islamic Relations.

Thank you for your time and consideration, and I look forward to hearing from you in the near future.

Sincerely,
Engy Abdelkader

Subway Negotiations

Sherien Sultan

"IF YOU SEE SOMETHING, SAY SOMETHING. If you see a suspicious package or activity on the platform or train, don't keep it to yourself . . . call the Terrorism Hotline at 1-888-NYC-Safe." The words stare at me as I sit on the R train making my way home to Queens from the Financial District. I turn my gaze only to feel their weight bear heavily on me, and I start to fidget in my seat. There should be no reason for me to be so uncomfortable. But as I sit there, the only emotion I do feel is absolute terror.

I am an Arab American Muslim woman residing in New York City, and I spend approximately twenty hours a week riding the subway. For the past couple of months, I have been negotiating my existence on a daily basis. It has become almost mandatory for me to do this. If not, I take the risk of becoming absorbed in the current climate of public hysteria, where people applaud the American government for its use of violence and clandestine behavior. My "war zone" does not consist of tanks or stealth bombers. There are no soldiers breaking down my door, no land mines threatening to blow me up. My war zone instead consists of symbols that bring comfort to so many others around me. The American flag, which once represented freedom and liberty to me, now stands for tyranny and repression. No one knows about the battles I fight, and no one will welcome my victories. Regardless, my war zone is quite real, and I am in battle every day.

Shortly after Bush declared his intention that "Saddam must go," New York City straphangers who never really read newspapers that often during their commute all of a sudden were in possession of either the *New York Post* or the *Daily News.* I had never seen so many newspapers, so many eager readers. I was bombarded daily with outrageous headlines that provoked hostilities toward Arabs and Muslims, and I gradually found myself feeling out of place. Physically I began to occupy less space by crossing my arms or legs. I did not want to share a space with the burgeoning readership of the *New York Post.* I grew more and more frustrated as each day passed and as each headline became more blatantly racist.

I remember the day I took out the Quran from my bag in order to read it on the way to work. It was, I am ashamed to admit, my first and last day. It took only a couple of stops for someone to make a comment. "You're making people uncomfortable." I turned to find a man scowling and a couple of people staring blankly at me. I asked the owner of the voice what exactly I was doing that was making people uncomfortable, and he told me straight out that it was the Arabic "shit" I was reading and that I should put it away. Anything written in Arabic has to be threat, of course. I did not quite know how to respond to him. I looked around and saw the clutter of newspapers declaring war on innocent Iraqis (is there even such a thing?). I saw women reading their bibles in English, Spanish, Cantonese, Polish. Were the other commuters going to put away their newspapers that make me, as an Arab, uncomfortable? Were the women around going to put away their bibles, symbols of the Christian fundamentalist thought that only a holy crusade would save America from the evil of the Arabs?

I was told by friends and family not to read the Quran anymore in public. "No sense in provoking people," they said. And as I mentioned before, I am very ashamed to admit that I have not read it on the subway since that day. I have developed a certain kind of self-censorship that I am not proud of and try to fight daily. My war zone scares me because I do not know what I am fighting against. I do not have anything tangible to battle and do not even have allies. How can I protect myself against something I cannot grasp? How can I reclaim my space?

I am scared. I will not deny it. A couple of weeks after the incident I had with my Quran, I found myself on the subway again with another book. This time it was in English, and I hesitated to make it public because the title, *Classical Islam*, was guaranteed to draw attention. I managed to find the strength to start reading it, however, only to have a fellow commuter ask what I was reading. I froze. I showed him the title, and he asked if I were reading it for school. I froze again. Do I legitimize it? Do I give him a valid reason for my reading this book instead of simply claiming that I am interested in learning more about my culture? I cannot quite remember the answer I gave him, but I do know that I tried to give the book some kind of academic credibility by rambling on about how the author was one of the foremost scholars on religious texts. The gentleman left at his stop, and I was left feeling shame once again.

What one considers a simple subway ride, I have begun to consider a daily struggle. I struggle to maintain my identity, struggle to find the strength to stop hiding. I do not want to live in a war zone. I do not want to feel terror. Every moment I spend on the subway, I spend *fighting* for my existence. I have not taken my Quran out again; maybe I have not been able to be quite that defiant yet. Not too long ago, when Iraqi casualties were being announced on CNN, Torie Clarke impatiently directed this statement to journalists: "This is a war zone; what do you expect to happen in a war zone?" I cannot expect not to feel fear in this time of turbulent historical change, where diplomacy gives way to war, and killing is tolerable if it means getting your way (except of course if this killing happens to Westerners). Although I do feel shame in monitoring my actions, I understand that it will take time for me to build up my determination and defiance. I will continue doing this every day as I ride the subway. And one day I will no longer look at the NYC terror hotline ad and feel fear because, if I have my way, one day it will no longer need to be there.

The Tragedy

Salma Arastu

Grandpa was a terrorist

Leila Montour

My grandpa was a terrorist.
He was a Navy man
an engineer, a pragmatist
and farmer with a plan.

He used to grow hot chili pods
for government report
and dared some guy to eat one for
a weapons-grade man's sport.

I tell you he was dangerous!
He'd tickle kittens' feet
to watch their spastic kicking
as they took off toward the street.

And once inside an airport's line
the people went berserk.
They asked him what was in his crate
he giggled with a smirk:

and even though inside there were
some avocados from
his family's farm, he told the men,
"They're guacamole bombs!"

For Farouk Abdel-Muhti[1]

Aisha Sattar

i needed the eloquence
of a river
to tell you my story
but this poem
will have to do

my home became
imaginary
mythical
lost like Atlantis

visible only to those
who write history
with their bodies
and remember it too
with their bodies

i needed the power
of a river
to tell you my history
but this poem
will have to do

bulldozers razed through—
as if plowing land
empty of houses and life

and to the settlers
for whom history
began with persecution

and ended
with their migration/settlement
the land was empty

i needed the urgency
of a river
to tell you my story
but this poem
will have to do

mine is the story
of occupation
deepening over time—
of my land
within (palestine)
of my body
without (america)

having no land
i plowed the airwaves instead
planting palestinian voices
in american heads

these olive trees did not grow.

oil kings
pawn my freedom
for a prison bed
and an 8 x 10 cell
and i'm supposed to forget
to forgo my rights
to forfeit my body, too

i needed the perseverance
of a river

to tell you my story
but this poem
will have to do

apartheid seems
a forced birthright
barbed wire & checkpoints (palestine)
plexiglas & solitary confinement (america)

my bones are a matrix of resistance
making visible
to the naked public eye
my stateless state

as i starve
i sustain
the intifada

may this olive tree live and grow.

Dhikr—

Nuzhat Abbas

Muharram 14, 1427/February 13, 2006

Four years have passed since I first wrote these words over the course of a single sleepless, grief-stricken night. Four days ago, it was Ashura, once again. I sat in a rented hall, listening to *marsiyas* about the ancient massacre at Kerbala, remembering the 32,000 Iraqi bodies silenced by this war. On the same day, February 9, 2006, thirty-two people were killed in Pakistan in the name of faith and identity. Today, people are gathering on the streets, filling pages with words, trying to control what can, and cannot, be spoken.

Calendars collide. Our days and nights are riddled with history's echoes. I wish I could tell you that these words, today, bear no repetition.

Ramadhan 21, 1422/December 8, 2001

> At a certain point I lost track of you.
> They make a desolation and call it peace.
> When you left, even the stones were buried:
> The defenceless would have no weapons.
> —*Agha Shahid Ali*, "Farewell"[1]

Tonight is a night of anniversaries:

Tonight is said to be one of the possible nights of Laylatul Qadr, that night of glory, fifteen centuries ago, when the Holy Qur'an was revealed to the Prophet Muhammad. Forty years later, on this same night, his nephew Ali died from wounds inflicted by a Kharijite assassin.

Two nights ago, over a decade ago, fourteen women lay dead, murdered by the misogynist rage of a desperate young man called Marc Lepine.[2]

One night ago, fifty-six years ago, the Japanese bombed a naval base called Pearl Harbor in the United States. On a night like tonight, all those years ago, a few powerful Americans began to imagine the obscene beauty of a mushroom cloud rising over Hiroshima and Nagasaki to avenge the deaths of two thousand U.S. soldiers.

Tonight, eighty-eight nights have passed since some airplanes crashed into the World Trade towers, damaged the Pentagon, and killed, by some estimates, four thousand people.

And tonight, sixty-two nights have blazed with the flares of bombs falling over Afghanistan in the name of those deaths.

Tonight, I have received no names and no numbers to record the ones who receive such terrifying gifts from the sky amid the grieving valleys of Kabul and Kandahar.

Tonight is the night to remember the gestures that open a conversation. An angel comes to a man in a cave and recites: *Iqra!* ("Read!") And the man repeats after him: *Read in the name of your Lord who created humans from a clot of blood....* The Qur'an enters his tongue, and he descends from the cave and repeats. Over the years, some men transcribe these recitations. Later, Umar, one of his followers, will codify and canonize the text. Some will contest this fixing of holy words, but soon, it will become the standard, and those who follow it will forget its fluid origins, its passing from tongue to tongue, and the time it took for these words to become a Book.

Centuries later, barely literate Pashto-speaking boys will stumble over the Arabic of the text in the Saudi-funded *madrasahs* of Pakistan. They will descend as soldiers into the valleys of Afghanistan to found a culture in the name of this book. Tonight is the night words fell from the sky into the ears of a yearning man. Let us remember the yearning, the gift of words.

Tonight is a night to remember gestures that open a conversation. And to figure the response. Fourteen dead bodies in Montreal testify to a young man's inchoate rage at what he believes has been stolen from him. Refused entry into the school of his choice, he roams the city furious, drifting into unemployment and misery. Modernity and the privilege of being in Canada should, he believes, have entitled him to more. He blames women. He believes they have trespassed into territories that do not belong to them. He does not know the women he kills; they are simply symbols, substitutes for the powers he dare not attack.

Across the ocean, there are more unhappy men like him. In countries like Egypt, Pakistan, and Algeria, young men prowl the city streets in discontent, beneficiaries of improved educational opportunities but barred from jobs by massive unemployment and entrenched class prejudices. The decolonizing nationalisms of the 1960s and 1970s have failed them. The engines of globalizing capitalism have left them stranded in their yearning, and their fragile masculinities begin to fracture in such spaces. Thousands of them drift into the welcoming brotherhood of political Islamic groups. Their sisters, new to the cities, studying in schools and universities, put on the modern veil to negotiate the strange spaces of cities while reassuring their families and villages of their unspoiled chastity. Political Islam, in all its reassuring garments, its promise of unbroken history, becomes shelter, provides a seemingly authentic voice with which to chastise the new brown colonialists who have made no room for more at the table.

Whatever might take away this fragile dream of resurgent Islam will be greeted with obsessive hysteria. In Egypt, scarcely legitimate fatwas farcically declare divorces for the noted feminist Nawal El Saadawi and other "apostates." More frighteningly, the Egyptian state continues its contradictory policy of imprisoning and torturing Islamist radicals while placating popular Islamism by echoing its demands. Thus, dozens of men accused of homosexuality are exhibited in courtroom cages while local human rights groups fall silent out of fear of similar accusations of immorality.

Writers, in particular, become the Islamists' favored targets. Iran's fatwa on Salman Rushdie is soon followed by the persecution of Taslima Nasreen in Bangladesh. Even "U.S.-liberated" Kuwait has no qualms about enforcing such laws, charging feminist authors Alia Shuaib and Laila El-Othmani with blasphemy and obscenity. Meanwhile, hundreds of writers and journalists continue to be killed in places as disparate as Algeria and Iran.

This is just the surface. Pakistan, with its long history of militarization, gratefully receives millions of U.S. dollars in the early 1980s to fight the threat of Soviet communism with the carefully harnessed zeal of Islamic fundamentalism. The leaders of both nations shake hands to seal the deal and look away as laws are enacted to suppress women, and starving refugee boys are forced into Saudi-funded *madrasahs* to produce the Taliban.

Everywhere, anxiety is gnawing for what modernity has failed to deliver. Across the table, the rich grow easy with each other, imagine borders collapsing, find commonality with English, Coca-Cola, and MTV. But outside the lights of their cosmopolitan parties, the discontented gather in the ruins of destroyed homes, congregate in mosques, churches, and temples. Some find answers in the lost certainties of indigenous religions and the invention of new traditions. Others take to the hills in places like Chiapas and refuse the temptations of simple victories.

In Canada, the beginning of the new millennium arrives with the multiplying murders of women within the privacy of their homes and families. There is news of escalating suicides in native communities and the uncomprehending faces of young, glue-sniffing teenagers stare back at the nation that destroyed them in order to flourish. In a small Ontario town, contaminated water kills fragile children. On the streets of the world, young people greet the millennium with a refusal to let the promise of a borderless world erase the existence of such impermeable borders, persistently rewritten with secret and visible violences.

This is a night of remembrance. The bodies gather. It becomes difficult to write.

The bodies of the dead accumulate, become statistics. What are their names? Who will remember their faces? Who will mourn them for forty days and forty nights?

In the United States, the talk shows still feature survivors and the families of the dead. In the days following the attacks, newspapers carried a running strip of faces and names to personalize the uncountable dead. All over New York City, posters stared from walls with the faces of the missing and the dead. But in Afghanistan, the dead have no names and no faces. Instead, one face, the strangely gentle face of a Yemeni man from Saudi Arabia, has become America's strategic sign for an entire country. In pursuit of this face, wanted dead or alive, bombs have fallen from the sky for sixty-two nights and murdered thousands who bear no resemblance to the desired one. Today, pamphlets fall from the sky offering $25 million for a body to match that face. A whole country has been bombed to annihilate the terror written over that face.

The dead in Afghanistan are not even allowed to become statistics. They are invisible, given over to their rulers by the obscenity of words like "collateral damage." Worse, the dead are made to disappear. Given over to the unmarked mass graves of those the world can choose not to mourn. On the horizon, a number given by UN aid agencies hovers as a terrible warning. By winter, seven million may die for lack of food and shelter.

There are many ways to kill a people. Since 1945, the world has been obsessed with the Nazi's technology of murder. But there are other, simpler ways to "purify" the world for those who would like to rule over it. Tonight, eighteen days lead us to Christmas and the orgy of consumption that it entails for wealthy Christians in the world. Tonight is the twenty-first night of the Ramadhan fasts that teach Muslims to empathize with the hungry and the poor. But each day's fast is punctuated with the feasting of the night. Real starvation, like real yearning, is of a different kind. Unfed, it leads to myriad forms of death.

There are many ways to kill a people. In Iraq, bombs have rained since 1990. Eleven years of terror falling from a sky now grown foreign to its people. The trade embargo has killed millions of children by the simple gesture of denying the sick medicines that might heal them. Collateral damage? Madeline Albright has shrugged her shoulders. All the dead children are made to wear the mask of their putative father, Saddam.

This is how an entire country is given over to its leader. This is how the patriarchal family of the nation is reinscribed by the West. These sons of America, Reza Shah, Saddam, Noriega, even Bin Laden, were paid to be proper sons, and like all aging patriarchs, the United States was dismayed when they wanted to reproduce themselves in their father's image. Like frightened Cronos of the ancient myth, the United States has become obliged to devour its offspring. Unfortunately, in this scenario, there are more bodies involved, and in a strange chain of substitutions, the United States sends its citizens to murder its opponents' citizens. The fathers sit and watch such slaughter and count the victims. Each side calls it collateral damage.

There are many ways to kill a people. The old battlefields of war are shrinking. Now cities are targeted from the air and the bodies of citizens evaporated in the phallic rush of hitting an on-screen target. On *Oprah,* a woman serving on

USS *Carl Vinson* smiles at the camera and says, "September 11 solidified the desire to serve my country and go kick some butt." She navigates the planes that drop the bombs. But flying above a place, staring at a computerized screen, can leave you unscathed, utterly ignorant of the devastation you have wreaked. No blood on your hands. No terrifying glance into the faces of the dying.

It is simple, this gesture of lowering your eyes to focus on a screen. Every day, hundreds of poor U.S. citizens, undocumented workers, and those without proper addresses are turned away from U.S. hospitals to die in silence and obscurity. Every day, we, in democratic North America, walk over the sleeping figures of the homeless on our way to earn our paychecks. Every day, we gratefully purchase goods at cheap prices produced in places that treat factories like labor camps. Every day, we murmur pious platitudes about the suffering of native communities, the rash of young suicides, the suffering swallowed in alcohol. President Bush informs us that he is out to protect "our way of life." This is what it means to live our way of life. It is impossible to live it unless you conscientiously practice a peculiar form of myopia and blur your vision at the borders.

In Palestine today, one needs to go through checkpoints to go from one Palestinian town to another. The Israeli border guards have become masters of the techniques of delay and intimidation. Hundreds of stories circulate about women forced to give birth in the taxis taking them to hospitals, of the sick dying as they wait in the long lineups at checkpoints. These are the simple deaths that do not bring out international cameras and outraged reporters. Strangely, not so long ago, the prophets of globalization were speaking of open borders and dissolving states. Today, guns patrol Canada's border with the United States, and thousands of people are being arrested for lack of proper papers.

A curious effect of September 11 has been the clarity with which the unspoken assumptions of the powerful are now manifest. Meanwhile, the bodies of the dispossessed drift over oceans in the fetid containers of ships, suffocate in the trunks of cars, get caged in the detention camps of Australia and the secret jails of the United States and Canada. These bodies flee, escaping terror, poverty, the kinds of fears unimaginable to the scornful officials of the border gates. *Prove your identity*, they ask. *Give me a reason for your arrival here.*

At the same time, over there, men and women in expensive suits are signing multimillion-dollar deals, pipelines are being planned, resources are being extracted while factories churn out goods labeled for the West. These men and women travel differently. For them, borders are porous, mobility swift; the world grows more and more into a habitat for their tastes and their desires. Some would say, there is a terrible hubris involved in making the world over in your image. In wanting the world to become a mirror for your longing. The refugee whose motion is arrested at the border is allowed no mirror. The border guard stares down at a piece of paper and continually repeats: *Who are you? I do not believe you. Prove to me the truthfulness of your name.*

Reaching the border is in itself an achievement, despite the humiliations imposed by the guardians of frontiers. As millions of Afghans disperse into the valleys to escape the U.S. bombing and the Taliban's retaliations, stories come to be told of how entire villages contribute to the safe passage of one sick man, and how highway bandits steal this money, leaving the sick man and his friends destitute and indebted as they arrive to face the obstacles of the border. In Toronto, young Asian girls tell of similar debts incurred to the men who smuggled them into Canada; they now must use their bodies to earn their freedom. In Afghanistan, twenty years of war has meant unspeakable stories of parents selling their young daughters to the men who would smuggle their families across borders for a price. Such families need to forget their daughters to survive their escape. *Who will remember these daughters?*

In the name of the daughters, Mulla Omar took power. The story goes that two young girls were kidnapped and raped by members of the Northern Alliance then in power. Mulla Omar and his men rescued the girls and massacred their rapists. It was to keep women safe, it is said, that the Taliban, on gaining power, enforced the burqa and the enclosure of women within the family house. The borders of inside and outside had to be zealously patrolled in the name of security, in the name of property. Women who transgressed this boundary, not surprisingly, threatened the security of the state and struck terror in the hearts of the fundamentalists. They needed to be punished, detained, controlled before they contaminated the hard-won purity of the emirate.

In Canada, Bill C36 works in much the same way. Except this time, the subjects of such obsessive surveillance are those who look Arab, who bear Muslim names, those whose citizenship might be suspect. Like women under patriarchy who need to uphold the values of male supremacy because of their dependence on men, Arab and Muslims in Canada have had to vow the purity of their faith in Canada and pledge loudly to become fundamentalist Canadians in order to escape being branded treasonous. The ones who have spoken out, Sunera Thobani being among them, have immediately been marked as "poisonous," ungrateful, the not-quite-Canadians they have always been suspected of being.

These are strange times to be among those who are accused of being not-quite-Canadian and not-quite-Muslim. These are strange times to want to weep for the daughters but not speak in their name.

In the United States, images of women in Kabul pulling up the burqa to show their faces and men shaving their beards are used to symbolize the "civilizing" force of the United States' "liberating" war on the Afghan people. Here, the burnings of mosques and temples and ongoing attacks on people perceived to be Muslim have driven the Muslim community to organize a united front and to participate politically to protect their rights. It is strange, in this climate, to want to criticize one's own people. It feels unseemly. The way antiwar voices may seem unseemly to Canadian patriots. It opens me to accusations of betrayal, of being among those who are too "Westernized."

If I speak of the Iranian government's intention to execute a noted filmmaker, I am asked to keep quiet. *This is not the time.* If I talk about the injustice of Shari'a laws on evidence and inheritance, I am reminded of the separate spheres of men and women. Worse, if I argue for the rights of women to the erotic powers of their bodies, I am accused of obscenity and depravity and declared an apostate to be denounced within the community of Muslims.

Not long ago, I wrote an article critical of the drive in Muslim communities to build private Islamic schools in Ontario. Ingrained sexism and rising homophobia are at the root of such separatist desires, I argued. But the Canadian education system's ingrained racism and Eurocentric curriculum are equally at fault in creating such alienation and fear among Muslim immigrants. The Canadian state continues to fail its minorities.

The West's desire to see the world in its own image found its first expression in the colonial enterprise. People in Canada and the rest of the world have borne witness to these violent experiments in territorial expansion, nation building, and the containment, if not annihilation, of other cultures. If Islamism, in the Middle East and elsewhere, can be read as a response to such disregard for other peoples and cultures, it is not surprising that it has found ground here in Canada to counter the racist discourses of the state. Like other nationalisms, including Chicano, Black, Quebecois, and Native, Islamism wants to claim women as the sign of its realized identity. Errant women, women who cross borders, contaminated women remain troublesome.

At each border point, we are asked to produce proof of our identities, marks of our allegiances, evidence of our purity.

In the refugee camps that populate the borders of Afghanistan and Pakistan, women weave rugs to make a living. After the Soviet invasion, the patterns changed. One rug shows helicopters invading the sky over an inverted map of Afghanistan. A bomb with a hammer and sickle falls over it while tanks and jet planes hover to the side. On the rug's border is the repeated imagery of *aqrab*—the scorpion, symbol of darkness; and the broken rays of the sun rising, promising life.

These days I read reports that tell me how infected wool is making these weavers sick. As in many parts of the world, children in Afghanistan are forced to weave on account of their small and nimble fingers. The rug continues to tell its story despite the suffering of its maker. Who knows what images will emerge now as the United States turns another page on Afghanistan and prepares to wage war on Iraq.

Winter is still coming over the mountains. People are starting to flee their new masters, and the refugee camps can barely hold all those in need of food or shelter.

The poet Rumi, born in what is now Afghanistan, wrote:

"Silence, for the mirror is rusting over: When I blew upon it, it protested against me."[3]

Answering . . .[1]

Zohra Saed

Henna or black ink
a woman with calligraphed knuckles

madar   *zan*

the use of Farsi script to name

mother   *woman*

"I'm very aware of my limitations"

a birthmark
a star mole over
dark eyebrows
a woman in a floral veil
"guns and bullets to suggest terrorism
. . . fear of Muslim identity in the West"
the smudge of black eyeliner
a white wall
a shifting ground
lit with the names of martyrs.

April 1978

Zohra Saed

April. The aroma of cloves and saffron wafts from my plate of rice. 1978, Riyadh.
I blow into my spoon so it is just right. I am three and trying to impress them by
mastering the spoon. But they are mesmerized by the television.

There has been a coup d'état in Afghanistan. Another one. Saudi news flashes a
picture of Daoud Khan. Five years ago, he had toppled a monarch, a cousin.

A bloodless coup in 1973 meant to bring a new republic,
instead became an unhealed wound and began drawing parasites.

Our neighbors, migrant workers and overnight exiles like us, share what the
news keeps from us, gossip.

They say that Daoud Khan's head was impaled on a stick in the center of Kabul.
When it decomposed and fell off the pole, they kicked his head amongs them like
a moist soccer ball.

While we children played in our large air-conditioned rooms, the women tearfully
whispered to themselves the story of Daoud-e-Diwana[1], who went mad, killing
his entire family before committing suicide.

A Communist fabrication, others say, his family was massacred and their
undergarments were put out for sale in the bazaars of Kabul, so the masses could
feel, at a basic level, equal to royalty.

We children hear through the cracks in the wall of our play. When we sleep, we
dream a topography of loss in the inner coils of our hearts.

The Things That Still Reach Us in Brooklyn

Zohra Saed

My brother, named gentleness in the midst of fire and blood, is born. 1979, Soviets invade Afghanistan. I am a few months from turning five years old. A leather businessman from Parsippany smuggles us into New York.

1980. I start kindergarten in Brooklyn. Mother and Father rely on the television and on other refugee stories for news of homeland.

We hear no news of our own family until 1983. Then grandparents and aunts arrive at a refugee camp in Pakistan.

My eighteen-year-old uncle was arrested, tortured for days then executed for attempting to flee.

People tell Grandfather that they have seen my uncle, that he is being held at a prison on the border. Grandfather reaches the prison only to find another eighteen-year-old boy held for ransom by members of the Pakistani border guard. He has the same name as my uncle, Mir Wais.

Grandfather claims him, pays, and frees him. He returns home, sweat-soaked from the heat and dies gently on his prayer mat, face first in eternal humbleness. Grandmother tells us this five months too late.

Only daughters and children survive his death. The second Mir Wais appears in time to bury his new father in Karachi.

Death reaches us in the form of photographs and damp, pale blue letters.

My brother, named humanity in the midst of cruelty, dreams of uncle's torture at the hands of Soviet soldiers. At age four, he struggles with nightmares of a war that missed us.

Why enter our dreams when we are safe in the red-brick neighborhoods of Brooklyn?

Until the news of death, bomb drills at school were a curious break from class work. But when I overcome shyness and ask whose bombs we are practicing to hide from, my bones shake and I crawl under my desk.

Coiled up like a small pretzel, I am too frightened to come out. Mother has to be called in. Still wearing her black mourning veil, she gently convinces me that Soviets are not invading Brooklyn.

She carries me home that afternoon and does not complain that I am too big. We drift by the bagel shop, the Laundromat, and the Waldbaum's supermarket with bright red lettering. Her long dark skirt with white flower-stitching grazes the sidewalk. My breath dampens her shoulder as we wait on the corner for the traffic light.

Home, in front of the television, exhausted, Mother and I fall asleep on the couch and slip into the constellation of each other's dreams where tears bloom into stars.

Narration: The Tragedy of the 15th Shaban Movement

Leila Montour

In Basra's streets, and Najaf's hawzah doors
it trickled down to Karbala: a plan.
The monster's weakened; let the felling blow
and rise; a distant country lends its hand!
Wa ant? And you?

In honor for the last Imam, the men
and women chose his birthday, on the Ides,
not knowing modern Rome lies over seas
with double-tongued face. Expanding sides
may switch at whim, inconstant slips at night
of lunar phase or guile.
Wa ant? And you?

And on that day, this rabid Ides of March,
was flipped on head, another knife was sunk
in dusty grit, and helicopters spun
their blades of death, in nineteen ninety-one.

The revolution ran to shrines' thick walls
and knew their guns would fire shots alone.
No foreign troops emerged from promised lips,
they didn't come, and far-off eyes were closed.
A federation loosed the monster's wrath,
by choosing, then, to squeeze it in a cage
called neutral zones, and set along a path
that only brought about starvation. Blights
came slinking, cancers rose, a pox was spread
in bodies dumped in trenches, plagues of pain
in empty bellies wept while infants passed.

"A weakened monster's easy slaying now
that nearly thirteen years have come to pass,
and what's another hajji's death in light
of middle earth's control, our business class?
There's weapons, terrorists, they say Allah is greater!"
And such it runs, the white man's burden, too little
and much later.

Wa Ant?
And you?
Et Tu?

The epilogue: And now the land is stretched
like carded wool, the bodies hang like light-
bulbs strung across the street. They hang from bridge,
and drag along the ground to chap in shades
of red; their photos blare from both sides, brown
or white, my sons, your sons, two thousand four.
I hear the shriek rise up from continents,
as cracks erupt despite tectonic plates:
a growling heat in Babylon, it wafts
as hate, unending, gnaws the heads that watch
the cancer-dance: Amrika and Iraq.

Whirling Darvesh

Salma Arastu

The Fall

Soniah Naheed Kamal

The history I was tucked in with at bedtime always left me cozy. Tales of family vacations, weddings, and birthday parties. The seamy underbelly, the unpleasant anecdotes, why one relative wouldn't look in another one's face, these never qualified as bedtime tales, or as I grew older, anytime tales. But I'm a nuisance, and the older I get the less I allow what's past to rest.

"I need to know the bad and the ugly, too," I tell my father, "in order to know you, yes, but also in order to know *me*."

I've just asked my Pakistani father, an immigrant from India, about his leaving Bangladesh, where he happened to be working during the 1971 war. He sits back in his armchair right in front of the TV, which some unspoken law has decreed his. His long fingers drum on the glass ashtray always by his side. He lights a Dunhill and takes a small puff. His jaw automatically adjusts his dentures. Then he mumbles about terrible times, very bad, everyone gone quite mad and, picking up the *Daily Jang,* seeks refuge behind sheets of black-and-white ink.

I sigh an umpteenth sigh. So he doesn't want to talk; he's taciturn by nature, a reserved accountant in his early sixties who in photos stands at the back, though he's looking straight into the lens; no fear, I'll try again later.

My mother, however, can't be quieted, a regular chatterbox even when you don't want to know, so I ask her, instead, about the time in Kashmir, was it, when my uncle, then a child, was arrested for his father's involvement in politics. She says she wasn't even born then. Fine. But what has she heard about that time? Was he tortured? And when he returned home, how long did he cry? Did he cry? And were they the sort of cries that a promise of candy and toys can end? My mother said she didn't know, she'd never asked what she wasn't told.

Forty-odd years later, my uncle is a doctor in England, nice, big brick house with jade creeper, gravel driveway, and, at the back, a sprawling lawn with a red seesaw set under a weeping willow and barbecue grill cemented in stone pavement. He's flipping a hot dog when I ask him.

"I don't really recall," he says, scratching his graying temples, the tightness in his voice belying his claim.

So what do you do when history won't talk to you? In my case you eat your hot dog, scratch your head, and go on to read books. That's what I was doing one morning in 1999, when my mother telephones from Pakistan to the United States, where I now reside. She starts crying at hello.

From the apartment building window, I can see it's a really nice Virginia day. Winter sunshine trickles down from an ice blue sky. Tree trunks rise from anklets of unblemished snow, their bare branches alert in the December air. A black crow sits on the baby blue bonnet of the Honda Accord owned by the Afghan couple who live a floor up. The woman is the fashionable type, moss green woolen scarf with matching gloves, coiffed, bleached hair, suede boots with just the right length heels, and she clip-clops toward the car at precisely that moment. Crow goes.

"What, Mummy?" I say, resting my book on my thigh. "Has the cook been rude to you again?"

My father has been taken away. For questioning, they say. By the new government of Pakistan, which has toppled the old through a bloodless coup and now wants to hold the old fiscally accountable and therefore has arrested the top accountants that worked, mind you, in the overthrown prime minister's mills and factories. She's telling me details I suddenly don't want to know: The police knocked on the gate with batons even though the doorbell worked perfectly fine; my dad put in his dentures in a hurry; they were kind enough to allow him to wear his shoes.

I think of the father who hugs me close during thunderstorms because he knows I'm scared the sky might break. The father who kisses my forehead when my novel isn't going right, imprinting me with forbearance, honesty, and belief in hard work. The father who lights up because I light up when he calls me Soniah Rani, Princess Soniah, those uneven dentures of his flashing between his ruddy, bee-stung lips. The silver day before me has gone decidedly gray.

"I'm coming home," I say.

Absolutely not. It would jam my green card process. Your future is a priority, Mummy says, and then she tells me to pray. And I do, of course, but in my own way. I'm a spiritual person—humanist and all that—but not big into rituals. The only time I actually pray is when someone close to me passes away, and my dad is alive, will stay alive, through it all, okay, okay!

I begin calling home every day. I call when I wake up. I call before I sleep, if I sleep. Sometimes I call right after I've already called. Lame phone calls—are you okay, are you okay—because the phone might be tapped. And I learn that it is I sitting far away who am needy for consolation. It makes me feel guilty. I am not like my mother, who is waking up to an empty other side of the bed. Or like my brother, who returns to Pakistan for the summer from college in D.C., decides his task is to make my mother laugh though he's finding it very hard to laugh himself. Or like my sister, who accompanies my mother on visits to the detention center/jail where my father is growing thinner and thinner and quieter and quieter—how much quieter can my quiet father get—and covering the bruise on his cheek with his palm only to betray the one on the back of his hand.

Days turn into weeks turn into months. I wonder is it easier to have seen a bruise and know its shape than conjecture sometimes a mere ochre dot, sometimes a plum blot, over and over and over again.

I learn I'd rather be the one to call. A Marlboro already lit in case of bad news. When they call, I scramble to find the pack. A ringing phone portends dread and only dread, although my husband reminds me that good news travels over the phone lines too.

One afternoon I return home to a blinking red eye on the answering machine.

"Call me back please."

It's all the message my uncle from England leaves. He's never called before. Not on a birthday, a graduation, an anniversary, not even when the pressure cooker went off in my face.

My father is dead. What else?

An impossibly hard *whoosh* of air punches me in the solar plexus. I'm going to throw up. No, I'm going to fall down, instead. Bile rises; I taste terror on my tongue, stale, metallic. I black out.

When I come to, it's a false alarm. Uncle just wanted to know how I'm holding up. My dad is okay; in fact, soon eight long months will come to an end. It'll be confirmed that my father was never party to any hanky-panky, and he'll be home, forever a quieter and increasingly godly man, but back home and back in front of the TV in his armchair, the one no one sat in while he was gone.

When I talk to Daddy, his voice seems unsure of how to speak, baby steps, it's taking baby steps. He says, "As long as you children are safe . . ."

And I look out of the window, at the cloudy August sky, and think, like a traitor, I live in America, thank god.

I'm a default immigrant. I entered college in the United States, already eager to return home and begin life, only to meet the man I was going to marry. I remember walking across a campus quad one evening complaining to a friend that I'm going to miss home so much. She nods sympathetically. She can't quite grasp "overseas," for she's never left Maryland's shores. Stars nest in the fluffy night sky like sparkling eggs.

"Well," I say bravely, "at least it's safe here. No threat of civil war or coups or sectarian strife or interfaith shoot-outs, bombs, the sky falling on top of us, etc. . . ."

It's been a year or so since my father came home. A blinking answering machine is slowly reverting to being just that, phone calls have reverted to once a week, and sometimes not even that. I've been busy. We've moved to Colorado, new place, new people, new shopping, and a new baby. So, when the phone rings early Tuesday morning and my husband says hello, I merely pull the pillow over my head. It's probably one of those damned sales calls, but no, he's not hanging up, and his voice is getting louder. I hear him say my brother's name, then he says, Aunty don't worry—Aunty for him is my mom—Don't worry, Aunty, he says, We'll try calling him, then we'll call you back.

I sit up. What's that fun-loving twit of a brother of mine done now—run off with a girl of his choice? For all of my bravado, though, I'm not brave anymore. A siege of days, weeks, months spent on the phone has left a mark.

I hoist my infant up and lumber out of bed to find my husband in front of the TV. He's rubbing the back of his head, flipping from BBC, CNN, MSNBC, NBC, ABC, CBS, and back again. I yawn. A shawl of early-morning sunshine spills in from the bay windows onto our electric blue Microsuede love seat.

"What did Mummy want?"

"Apparently," looking at our babe, he bites the bullet, "there are planes falling out of the sky."

And that's how Pakistan informs us of what's happening in America on

9/11. The role reversal is unnerving, because this is America and phone calls should not be flooding in to ask if we're all right, but America is, it seems, part of the world after all.

We finally get through to my brother in D.C. He can see, he says, a smoky cloud over the Pentagon. We get through to a cousin. She's in New York. Safe, though the smell of smoke, the fuzzy black of it in the air and on faces, contradicts her assurance, almost. I call the same friend I'd walked across the campus quad with five years ago. She lives in Pennsylvania now, though far from Shanksville, where the only plane that did not reach its destination made the most difference.

Are you okay? I say.

Are you okay? she says.

We're as okay as anyone can be while thinking about people in planes and people in towers and people in places where they can get in trouble for the misdeeds of others and people who will talk nonstop about this day and others who will try to forget it by going mum. A safety net seems to have fallen, and we're all tangled up.

Take care, she says.

Take care, I say.

red clay women

Sarwat Rumi

taught   to be a father's daughter.
a brother's sister.   a husband's wife.
taught   the roles that defined honor
in peacetime.

fathers, brothers, husbands
should have known better than to shape us this way
to carry safety   sanctity   ancestral red clay
in the earthtone of our skins   the timbre of our bones.
they should have remembered
nine generations of colonization destruction healing
and colonization again;
should have remembered
that there is no such thing   as peacetime
that rebuilding is as melancholy
as the catalysts of grief are traumatic.
how much they lost, our men
when we lost it all
again.

child-size saris twisted
to strangling a shower
of shimmering bangle-glass shards
bridal gold ripped   from fingers
ears necks nose wrists
widow's white
was not meant to be spattered   with the red
of blood   weeping   from wrenched wide
open legs.

we returned to the earth
who birthed us
    burying our safety, our sanctity
        our honor in red clay
to be cradled in the stillness
of our longest peacetime
and our men could not even stay.

taught   to be a father's daughter
a brother's sister   a husband's wife
we learned that in this man-wrought world
there is no such thing   as peacetime
or rescue   or victory   except
within a wise witch
a fiercely loving woman
      a warrior girl
for we are of moonrise red clay   stillness
we are of the earth
of the earth.
inna lillahi wa inna elayhi rajiun.[1]

If This Were My Family: Relearning Important Lessons of Organizing after the Earthquake

Bushra Rehman

On October 8, a 7.6 earthquake radiated through Kashmir and the North-West Frontier province. A total of three and a half million people lost their homes, and more than eighty-seven thousand people lost their lives. Among the many places that were devastated was Oghi, a remote village in the mountains, the home of my mother's family. It had been a few years since I had been there, and a whole year of natural disasters. With each one, I felt the panic, the powerlessness that comes when nature stamps its feet. I had grieved and helped raise funds. But the headlines on October 8 hit me in the gut, an invisible umbilical cord that connected me to those mountains had just given a harsh tug.

Three years ago, when my grandmother was ill, I went to Oghi. While there, I had climbed up and down the thick pine valleys visiting family. I have backpacked in national parks in the United States, even climbed to Cloud's Rest in Yosemite, but nothing had prepared me for such a natural beauty. Nothing had prepared me for the warmth of the villagers. Everywhere neighbors came out of their homes, asking, "Is this Fatima's daughter?"

They invited us in, not taking no for an answer, brought out food, chicken, potatoes; they gave me gifts, sheets, clothing. They laughed at me when I said I loved the wild, the mountains. "Yes, this is Fatima's daughter."

Like all children, I had a limited view of my mother. She was the one who fought against roaches and mice in her Queens home, and now guarded her suburban home in New Jersey fiercely while trying to grow tomatoes in the back yard. I found out she had been a wild child, unafraid of landowners as she broke into their fields, stole their fruit, and ran off.

I also learned that when the twin towers fell, my mother's sister, my *khala*, had organized the village to pray for weeks, doing Quran *khanis* for our safety. I thought of those horrible days, with the city reeling from death and hate crimes. All that time, when we had felt so lost, this village had been praying for us.

Now, of these people, there was no way to know who was alive and who was dead. There were no phones in Oghi.

When I called my family, my sister, Aisha, answered. She said my mother was busy, and no one knew what was going on.

"Please, Allah," I prayed while packing my bags, "let them be safe."

When I got to my parents' house in New Jersey, I steeled myself for the scene. There had been other times of loss when I had come home, walked in, taken off my shoes; my nieces and nephews had come to the door happy to see me, fighting to hug me. And then I would hear the tears; my mother would be in the living room crying. The children would look at me. Their faces would be tight, and I would wonder how much they understood.

When I got to my parents' house, my nieces and nephews ran to the door to greet me as they always did, but my mother wasn't crying when I walked in. She was on the phone, squinting over her bifocals. Before the earthquake, she would have given the phone to me when she needed to make a call, saying, "Here dial this." But now she had somehow become adept at working not one, but two phones—the cell and the kitchen phone. She hugged me quickly and then went back to her conversation. I raised my eyebrows, and Aisha said, "She's been like that since it happened."

The doorbell rang. It was an aunty asking, "Is your mother here?"

I pointed upstairs, but she pressed an envelope into my hands. "If your mother is busy, don't worry, tell her this is for your village."

This is how my parents' community works. They don't have endless meetings and minutes. When there is a birth, the aunties know immediately. When someone dies, it doesn't take long for the food rotation to be set up. It is from my parents that I learned my first lesson of community organizing: *You must first have a community, one that you share joy with as well as suffering.* My parents had a certain amount of respect and trust among their friends. It hit me that being trustworthy was essential to being involved in community work, and being worthy of this trust took a lifetime. My parents knew they could call on people because they knew the community could call on them.

For the next two days, my parents were on the phone nonstop to friends in the United States and relatives in Pakistan. There was still no news, so they arranged for cousins from my father's side to go to the mountains. My cousins reported back that Oghi and the neighboring villages had been destroyed; the survivors were living under makeshift tents in the fields, where a freezing cold rain was falling.

This was in direct contrast to what PTV (Pakistani Television) was reporting. In those first weeks, PTV was on continuously in our home. Bodies under ruined homes, children lost—we felt that we could not turn it off. It became our portal to the other side of the world. Over the footage, PTV said the government was sending food and clothing, but my cousins reported that supplies and tents had not reached Oghi yet. This is the second lesson my parents taught me: *Trust your eyes and ears, never the government-controlled media.*

My parents knew Oghi was a remote village with very few monetary resources. They knew they couldn't wait for the government. My parents got on their phones all over again, to store owners they knew and more cousins in Pakistan. They got in touch with one, who got in touch with another, who got in touch with more store owners. Food was bought and packaged. The packets contained rice, dal, sugar, chai, and ghee. Another cousin rented a truck, which they filled with packets of food and supplies; it reached Oghi two days before the government officials arrived. This was my third lesson: *urgency.* How many times have I and other activists wasted time getting involved with red tape, with personal issues? But my parents knew each wasted moment was a moment our family and their neighbors were out in the cold rain, with destroyed homes.

While watching my parents, I couldn't believe that all these years I saw them as old-fashioned and myself as the radical one. Watching them in action, I relearned the most important lessons of activism: The strongest, most effective form of community activism is not complicated. It comes from a sense of family, love, urgency. It's not something that can be taught in a college classroom or learned from a book. It comes from a sincere belief that we are in this world together and must take care of each other, as well as ourselves. How different my own activism would be if every time something happened, I asked myself, "What would I do if this were my family?"

As I write this, my parents are in Oghi, sleeping in those makeshift tents with my mother's family. They could not rest until they went themselves. I spoke to my mother the other day. She said, "You cannot imagine. Nothing can prepare you for this. There is still so much need." The tremors were still happening. I wanted to tell her to come home, but I knew she wouldn't, because I know myself. I am her daughter. I knew I had to raise funds. When I got off the phone, I started calling all my friends, all those in my own community.

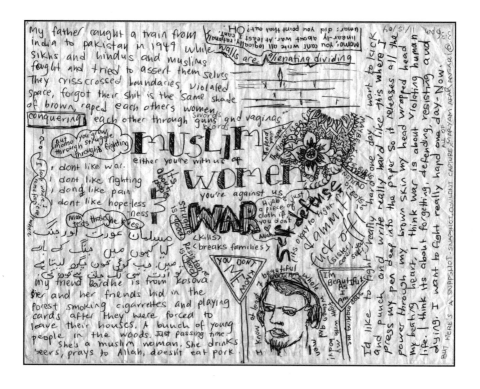

Sketches of My Palm

Maryam Ansari

Yimberzal[1]

sarah abid husain

glassy waters reflect infinitely
black eyes. leaning
over the edge of the *shikara*[2]

i look carefully

they tell me
peace in the valley is imagined
by the dal[3]

deep waters preserve my reflection:
    mountains smoke and sky

my grandmother looks back at me
and a tear drips from my eyes . . .

    allah

sending ripples through my dream.

black widow

sarah abid husain

Major "Rehman"[1]
stands guard at
Hazratbal[2]

sacred hair to be kept hidden
but i submitted
now my belly is marked
by a diminishing time that germinates hate

Bismilah-ir-Rahman-ir-Raheem

my black burqua conceals
our fate

remember
it was me that you raped,

and isn't it true

Black Widows Kill Their Mates . . .

Tongue Tied with Cancer Wars

Sarah Husain

In memory of my brother Hassan

Congratulations on becoming a mother
during this September war.

Aye shaam,[1] this morning I closed my brother's eyes shut.
Tied his feet in a ritual of sum   un-ending sleep. Knelt
before shadows of chewed up bones and kissed wrinkles
of dried skin condemned to no future—a body drained
of all its waters.

Aye shaam, this morning displaced night
and lingered on as a specter, tracing shadows
with his chewed up bones. How will we know
to tell our children of the beginnings of these wars?
Of dreams of homes now built on graveyards
and this love buried too soon
unaccounted for?

How should I congratulate you
when my tongue is a hostage
a requiem of dirty words tied
to the dead weight of this civilization
my vocabulary possessed needing a language
to map its destruction of love and its splendor
ghost?

Aye shaam, how will we grow
out of this tongue tied war and
re-member our mothers who tore

every dirge song out of folklore
and stripped every ceremony
ten times of its meaning
before beginning
another poem.

"Line your eyes with soorma²
and look through its well.
At the bottom of that darkness
you'll find my spell."

Her spoons weren't made of silver
she didn't teach me to expect
with every bite she held out
she taught me how to chew
each bone   and dream
with no expectation.

We were never children
in open fields of hope
we would run around polishing shields
and cleaning guns for dirty wars
we didn't choose nor control.

How should I congratulate you
amid this ending, *shaam,* of love
unaccounted for and strip this poem ten times
of its meaning before beginning
another war.

two:

WITNESSING ACTS

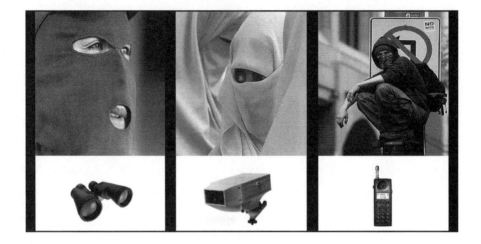

Surveillance

Farheen Haq

revisionist history

S.N.

we sit in silence
thinking of her.
so many others
women not read
about but have
gone missing
found dead.

what will they say years from now?
will they know
the countless stories
that soak into earth quickly
seep and go missing into
smoke and chaos?
the stories of war
not in the headlines
but caked in the fingernails
of those passed
burrowed in wounds
and glazed eyes closed?

will they remember
moments not caught on camera?
immediate
urgent moments
laced with fear
her will to live
pulsating rapidly

in out of breath
sweaty heart beats
gone cold?

will they remember this history?

ya sin

sarah abid husain

ya sin[1]
your final testament
whispers to me

allah
is our lord
prophet is our commander
qu'ran is our constitiution
jihad is our path
shahadat is our

desire

like a silent offering

my love
falling from infinite pathways
into a single moment
and we recognized
the possibility

maybe it was the universe
meeting in our eyes—
and understanding
you needed
before
you
died

now my heart
is left alone
and this pain is
dropping me to my knees

pressing my head into the floor

oh allah
please forgive me
an*other* woman

left behind.
somehow it's me
who must reclaim

the piece of you
transgressed.

for
our fathers
who remember
the horror of your body
hardly recognizable
except for
blackened lips
and a solitary tooth.

an evocative smile

for
our mothers
left to wonder
if their breast milk
spilled in vain

what is left to nurture,
blood mingled with ripe earth?

in the chill of our kashmiri winter
that raises goose bumps upon our skin

my martyr
i'll remember you

burnt tissue and charred bone

shuddering
i hold my *kangri*² close to me

warmed by the stirred embers
praying i feel
complete.

God Gave Me Two Children[1]

Bushra Rehman

> "God gave me two children and I loved them so much.
> Only God knew how much I loved them . . ."
> —*Reem Salih al-Rayasha, Palestinian martyr/suicide bomber*

When I first started wandering this land long ago
there was nothing but desert for miles.
Water, no, just sand in my mouth
hot rock, the bottom of my feet
the fussing baby,
and my Lord's betrayal
that tasted like blood on my tongue.

Back then,
there was nothing but sky, flat
land, no footprints but my own. Now
there are children with broken

skulls denting the side of the road.

I used to come
to this desert for solace
for solitude, a thousand years ago.
When I was looking for Allah,
I knew where to find Him. Now
Allah is nowhere to be found.

There are children
with broken skulls denting
the side of the road.
And I tell you,

I don't want to be
an old woman cutting up stones.

There was a time
when Allah listened. When
I wandered between Safa and Marwa
from mountain to mountain, abandoned
by lover, father, friend,
searching for water,
but there was no water to be found.

I thought Allah had abandoned us as well.
I hid Ishmael where I couldn't see him die of thirst
and I prayed one last time to my Lord.

Just then I saw Gibreel
with his heavy wings come down.

He knelt and struck the earth.
With his heavy wings,
he scratched the dirt, until
a spring of water burst forth.

But now, I can't wait anymore.
I'm going to see my Lord.
I wrap my heavy wings around my body.
Taped to my skin, they itch.
I am no angel and won't be until the fuse is lit.

When I close my eyes, I see my children.
There is one in each eye like an explosion of stars.
When I open them, I see Gibreel descending,
his wings glinting light off the bombs.

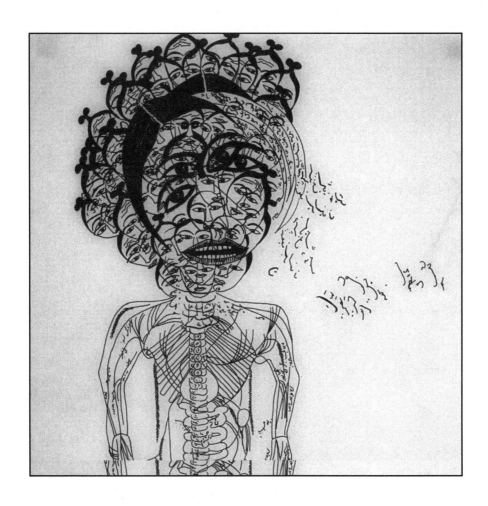

When Alone

Samira Abbassy

rhung[1]

sarah abid husain

rhung
for the One who dyes
can reflect so many shades.

deep cuts smear me across reality,

but truth
like 5x prayer,
   fajr-zuhr-asr-maghrib-isha[2]

seams of a single cyclical journey.

where breath and death
stain in your name . . .

bismillah-ir-rahman-ir-raheem[3]

The Letter

Shadi Eskandani

Let Sharon the coward know that every Palestinian woman will give
birth to an army of martyrs, and her role will not only be confined
to weeping over a son, brother, or husband; instead, she will
become a martyr herself.
—*Dareen Abu Aysheh*

It happened like this. She walked into a store and blew herself, and everyone in
her vicinity, into pieces.

*No. That is not how the story went. That is what you read in the paper the
next day.*

So what is the story?

That depends. Which story do you want to hear?

I want to hear the real story, the one that lies outside the realm of propaganda,
hypocrisy, and hysteria. I want to hear the story from the heart. What did she say?
Let me hear it from her. I want to hear it from her.

So listen . . .

*My name is Wafa Idriss. I died on January 27, 2002. I was twenty-eight years
old. I was the first woman freedom fighter to take her life in the mission for her
people. . . .*

*My name is Dareen Abu Aysheh. I was a twenty-one-year-old student at Al-
Najah National University in Nablus. I was the second woman to give her life for
the cause. I died on February 27, 2002. . . .*

*My name is Reem Salih al-Rayasha. I was a twenty-one-year-old mother of
two. . . .*

My name is Zeinab Abu Salem. I was eighteen years old . . .

My name is Ayat Akhras . . .

My name is Andaleeb Takafka . . .

My name is Hiba Daraghmeh . . .

My name is Hanadi Tayseer Jaradat . . .

I awoke from a nightmare. I dreamed I was floating in the sky, and then I fell. I fell with great intensity, hit the ground, and saw myself die. There were broken bones and blood everywhere, so much blood.

I looked over at the alarm clock, and it was only 5:50 AM; I had another hour and ten minutes left to sleep. But how could I sleep now? I was shaken awake by a dream that made no sense to me. I recited the Surat-al-Ikhlas under my breath and prayed the bad omens away. I stayed in bed for a few minutes, trying to think of a way to fall back asleep until it was time to get ready for work. It was no use, I was wide-awake. Troubling thoughts were weaving their way in and out of my mind. *What if I didn't get the report to the manager in time? How come I hadn't heard back from the doctor about my pap results? Why did I dream about dying? The damned nightmare! What did it mean? Jaddah would know, she deciphers everybody's dreams. Maybe I should call her. But Grandmother is probably taking her afternoon nap; it is well past noon in Palestine right now.*

My thoughts were interrupted by the ringing of the phone.

"Hello?"

"*Habibti,* I'm sorry to wake you, but there is some upsetting news I must tell you," said my mother in a quivering tone.

"Ma, what is it? Is everything okay?"

"Your cousin Muna is missing. She never returned home after her classes. Uncle Abbas just called to tell me. He said Jaddah collapsed when she heard the news. She's at Um Ahmad's house where they're taking care of her. You know they couldn't take her to the hospital because of the delay at the checkpoint. This time of day is very bad. They keep everyone waiting in that horrible lineup, and Jaddah would have been sicker under the sun, in that heat. They are worried sick over there, Leila. Where could a nineteen-year-old girl disappear to? Have they taken her?"

"Ma. Are *you* okay? You don't sound good at all."

"I will be okay *habibti,* don't worry about me. Your father is at the store, but I stayed home in case there was more news."

"Should I call? I mean, what should I do? What can I do from here? What *can* we do from here? Except worry . . ."

"Leila, you just go to work and call me from there."

"Okay. I love you, Ma. Things will be okay."

"*Inshallah,*" she said in a pleading voice.

"I'll call you later."

What was going on? Was it the Israeli authorities? What would they want from a nineteen-year-old girl? It must be a mistake. There had to be some way to clear this mess up. There had to be. Poor Jaddah, she had worried herself ill.

Muna, who had just turned nineteen in August, was the youngest of my sixteen cousins. Despite our nine-year age difference, we got along really well. Having grown up with two brothers, Muna had always looked to me as an older sister. She even called me *ukhti* ("sister"). Her father and my mother were siblings and very close to one another. My mother, being the eldest of five, took on a motherly role to help out Jaddah. Khali Abbas, Muna's father, was the youngest child and the favorite of his eldest sister. Inevitably, my mother and Abbas formed a special bond, and as a result, we cousins became close. That is what made our move to Canada most difficult. Being apart from Uncle Abbas and my cousins, especially Muna, was the hardest part of leaving Palestine. Since my parents' emigration to Canada in 1986, we had never returned home. My relationship with Muna had been based on countless letters and occasional phone conversations. Over the years, through words, I watched her grow up and shape into a different person than the little girl I remember playing with years ago.

I got out of bed and decided to call in sick. How could I go to work? I felt a migraine coming on. I made a call to the office and went into the kitchen to make some chamomile tea in the hope of releasing some of the tension in my body. I took two aspirin and went back to the bedroom. I turned on the computer and decided to check my emails in case Muna had sent me a message. She sometimes emailed me when she had the opportunity, either from an Internet café or from Uncle Tariq's office. She would send brief messages in broken English or an Arabic that was phonetically typed in English letters. I opened my email, but amid all the junk mail, there was no sign of Muna.

She had not written in two months. I had sensed some changes in her tone over the last year; in fact, ever since the second intifada began. This was the winter of 2000, which also coincided with the death of Muna's mother. Auntie Souad and Muna were close, closer than any mother-daughter relationship I had known. Souad's sudden heart attack came as a shock to everyone, but especially Muna. I remember feeling her pain through the letters she sent me. There wasn't a letter that I finished without crying for hours after. She had suffered the loss of her mother, and now with the second intifada, and Israel's aggression, Muna's letters had taken a particularly dark tone. After a few letters of this kind, she stopped writing all together. I didn't hear from her for almost three months, although I received news of her from my mother.

When I did hear from her again, I sensed a different Muna, a more mature Muna, a politically conscious Muna. She was writing to me about the strife of the Palestinian people and the atrocities of living under a brutal occupation, an illegal occupation, by a state that was obliterating our people, our culture, our history. She told me it was genocide. She would mention the youth and how they needed to educate themselves to resist. She spoke of the Algerian revolution; she spoke of the South African apartheid; she spoke of Che Guevara, Fanon, and intellectuals I had never heard of. She told me that it was up to women to take on their role, not only as mothers to a new generation of fighters, but as liberators of Palestine. Like Leila Khaled, she told me, Palestinian women played an important role in the struggle: Freedom of the nation was in the hands of our Palestinian sisters.

I was thinking about my role as a Palestinian woman who had spent a large part of her life outside of Palestine, and those Palestinian women who had never seen Palestine, and the refugees in the camps of Lebanon, and all those who had been exiled to different parts of the world, expelled from their homeland: homeless, stateless, lost, forgotten. Then the phone rang. I nearly fell, tripping over the chair as I plunged toward the bed to grab the receiver.

"*Allo?* Ma, is that you?"

"It's over. It's all over. What can we do now? What are *they* going to do now?" My mother said this and began sobbing uncontrollably.

"Ma, what is it?"

No response. Just the sound of my mother's weeping.

"Ma, please, what happened? What happened to Muna? What *happened?*"

"She is dead."

"What? What are you talking about? What do you mean, 'dead'?"

Again, my mother's crying, which now had turned into loud wailing.

"Ma, I'm coming over. I'm calling a taxi right now. Okay?"

I called the cab immediately and put on whatever clothes were in my reach. I couldn't think straight; my head felt fuzzy. No, it felt full. My migraine had turned into an unbearable pain that I could feel in every inch of my body. Was

I still dreaming? Was this all part of that nightmare? I felt like I was floating. Maybe I was the one who was dead?

I looked out the window and saw the taxi pulling up. As I reached to open the front door, I noticed a letter stuck in the mail slot. I could see the stamps on the envelope; they were from Palestine. I put the letter in my purse and got inside the cab. Knowing it would be a long ride to Markham, I settled into my seat and took out the letter. I could feel my heart beating in my throat as I looked at the envelope and recognized Muna's handwriting. I wanted to rip open the envelope and read my cousin's words, my dead cousin's words. How could she be dead? She was dead, and I was holding her letter? But she was here; she was in my hands. My head was spinning. I felt faint. I remembered the dreadful images of broken bones and blood. But this time, there were pieces of human flesh strewn on the ground.

"Lovely day, isn't it?" The cab driver said.

I did not respond right away. I could not speak; my throat was dry. I managed to say, "Yes."

"Where are you from, miss? I have a feeling we are neighbors."

"I was born in Palestine. I'm Palestinian."

"Ah, Felestini! I sympathize with your people's suffering. I am an Iranian, and I have seen plenty of suffering. But you see, we are surviving, because our people are survivors. And so are your people, my friend. Don't forget that."

"Yes . . . I won't. . . . Thank you."

I did not know where the words were coming from. I did not know how I was managing to hold an everyday conversation with this man, when I could not feel the limbs of my body. I excused myself from the conversation and looked down at the letter in my hand. I began to rip the edges; my hands shaking, I pulled out a sheet of paper. There they were, Muna's words, in front of me. And I could almost hear her voice. . . .

Dearest Leila,

I'm sorry if I haven't written you in a while. Things have been very hectic for me. I miss you with all my heart. I wish I could see you to say these words to you in person. Life has been unbearable over the last few months. As you know, Israel is coming down on us harder than ever, especially since September 11. They are continuing stronger with their genocide mission of our people. The second intifada, *ukhti*, is the time for us to become liberated. But what is happening? We are dying. That is what their occupation is doing to us. Barely surviving, we are floating bodies.

Our people are tired of just barely getting by. Our people are tired of this illegal occupation, of having their homeland run by a murderous army. Our people are tired of curfews, tired of having their homes demolished, tired of having their olive trees uprooted, tired of endless checkpoints. Our people are tired of home raids, tired of being poor, tired of being shot at, arrested, interrogated, tortured, raped. We are too tired.

The other day, Umm Ahmad's youngest son was shot in the back of the head because he had peeked out of the window during curfew. This happened the same week that Abu Salih's house was bulldozed because of his son's supposed involvement with Hamas. Remember Akbar? Jaddah's neighbor's son, the eldest? He was teaching mathematics at Birzeit University, but now he has been thrown in jail because of the discussions he allowed the students to have in class. They spoke of 1948 and the expulsion of our people from their homeland; they spoke of 1967, and Israel's illegal occupation of Palestinian land; they spoke of massacres like Sabra and Shatila; they spoke of Israel's violations of UN resolutions that condemn the occupation, they spoke of these things and much more. But someone snitched on him, and they took Akbar away in the middle of the night from his parent's home. I heard it was an awful scene with his mother screaming and wailing, and the soldiers beating his father. They hit him so hard that he broke a rib. A sixty-five-year-old man with a broken rib and a bruised-up body. I heard there was blood, a lot of it.

Blood is all I see around me, *ukhti*. Red like the color of the rage burning inside me. Red like the blood they spill. Red like the blood our people are shedding for their freedom. All I see is red.

My studies were going well until they closed the university down for a few days as punishment for last week's suicide attacks. I have been attending extra classes though, which I haven't told you about. They are not really classes, more like group meetings. Some of us feel strongly about this second intifada; this is the time. My role as a woman in the struggle has become clear to me. I have thought about different ways to resist, like writing or teaching or working for some aid organizations. But I know now the only way to resist a state of violence is through violence only. Armed struggle is what this intifada is about. We fight their state terrorism by resisting with our blood. By resisting with our bodies. Flesh and blood is resistance.

Ukhti, there are countless voices and unheard sorrows. There is endless sorrow and unheard suffering. There are too many voices of suffering. But is anyone listening?

I tell you this, though, and I'm smiling. I am happy because I see a future that is as bright as the sun, where another generation of Palestinian people will know a life without occupation. A life of freedom, justice, and peace. That is what we are fighting for.

It's all in god's hands, but I will make sure that I do my part, my duty for my people. Inshallah, I will see you, *ukhti,* maybe not any time soon, but we shall meet in another time and another place.

All my love,

Muna

I folded the letter and looked out the window. The brightness of the outside world made my eyes water. I watched the people on the street, walking, talking, waiting, breathing . . .

I closed my eyes and began counting to a hundred in Arabic.

wahid, ithnan, thalatha . . .

Images of blood, bones, and flesh were floating in my mind as I counted. The more I counted, the more vivid the images became.

arba'a, khamsa . . .

I saw Muna, lying on the ground and looking at me, with open flesh, drenched in blood. She was speaking to me, but I could not hear her voice. I tried listening, but I just could not hear her. I just couldn't.

sitta, sab'a, thamaniya . . .

Collateral Damage

Sarah Husain

My cousin, Qudsia, emailed two weeks ago telling us of a bombing she thought was directed at an empty lot. We were scared; it was much too close to home. . . . I imagined Sialkot, the city, and how it was sustaining its wound, even to an empty lot. Mostly afraid for my young cousins who could've been there, I began to picture our neighborhood, just over the little bridge where the Coca-Cola factory lies, right across the street from the graveyard where my grandmother is buried, by the movie theater where more dust collects than films. . . . Closing my eyes, down the street on Allama Iqbal Chowk, near that hospital where last year my cousin had appendicitis. . . . Trying to imagine the hole.

On October 1, 2004, thirty-one people had been killed in a suicide bombing while praying in a Zainabia[1] Masjid in Sialkot.

Today, two weeks later, I receive another message:

> Asad died
> Bomb Blast

She had been misinformed. That empty lot was a mosque where Shia Muslims prayed.

> Sarah, Asad died!

Asad had gone there for Jumma[2] prayers and decided to stay for As'r.[3]

Zainab's house burned this is not the battle at Karbala, Iraq   tell yourself   Imam Hussein is already dead   but binti Zainab   where are you tonight?

I need to close my eyes shut because she stands directly in front of me, Mrs. Jaffri, my third-grade teacher. Her long black eyes outlined with *soorma*[4]—bright. Can I conjure her voice, instead? Her voice so far from where I am right now? That voice, which sang in my childhood ear every Moharram, calming my nerves after the neighborhood's daylong *matam*.[5] How do I remember her voice that enchanted all those moonlit nights, intoxicating the city to help heal its wounds?

But today is the first day of Ramadan and endurance has failed you   left you to your imagining   her soorma   thick blackness   staining your face   and every city   its future   every calm   every silence   every shriek   her eyes bloodied   her twenty-five--year-old son burnt to death   no, not at the battle of Karbala, Iraq   but in Zainab's own house

burned   sitting here so far I can imagine you wearing black   all black   without a song   sweeping the ashes of all the dead   at your *masjid*   your only child   burnt has left you screaming   "No, not Shaheed,[6] how when I've been looted can you imagine?"

Where are you Hazrat Zainab tonight?   Bear witness!   These deaths are no longer at the battle of Karbala, Iraq   no   not of your brother Imam Hassan or Hussein not of your two sons but her child the only son Asad   Can you offer your strength you the grand daughter of the prophet? What shall her lesson be, this twenty-first century's teacher?

It had rained the day of the mass funeral in Sialkot. Newspaper reported that people of all faiths joined for the *namaz-e-janaza*.[7] Asad's body was buried last. His mother, from one hospital to another, carried him, but there was no treatment for the type of degree burns he had sustained. The hospitals were unequipped in Sialkot, the largest exporting city in Pakistan of pharmaceutical, leather, and sports goods.

Untitled

Samia Saleem

Oil Field. Mine, Field. Afghanistan.

Saba Razvi

Workers below do not work to throw rocks or other missiles.
Workers below are pelted with rocks and other missiles.
Workers before sometimes bulldozed, preventing future missiles,
and un-misled voices, standing guard against the door to home,
scraped away the bones of the unloving and unloved.

No man that is not man needs a guard, no-man
is man that is bluffed by missile. Noman is man that has
become nomad, in tents and graveyards, where a plastered poster's
picture depicts how to tie a tourniquet when no-man nomad
has stepped through not a missile's arc but a mine-field.

Once, here, were pomegranate trees, once whooping birds and
Jasmines big as a fist, until a fist took,
shook fistfuls into sand and caves and sand replaced the places
where missiles later sought and demanded misled bones,
bones like those fleshed bones standing in front of bulldozers.

On Loan to the Public

Shahrzad Naficy

Inspired by a glimpse of two orphans in Afghanistan on CNN.
(October 2001)

I must be fertile. I can tell because they can't stop poking their fingers inside me as I go back and forth to the well to draw water for my sister. They push me down in the dirt, weight splitting my ribs, flesh crowding my breath, they spit in my face, call me a whore, and suck skin with mouths croaking with black teeth. I can only see purple flapping beyond my eyes. They shot my mother two days ago in the same dirt. She pleaded for them to leave, falling to her knees, "I only have my daughters; we only have this, please, please, please—" Their laughter synonymous with desert coyotes, choking babes.

Somewhere, thousands of miles away, someone is chewing on a popcorn kernel; another is swinging in the park, chasing pigeons into scattered rivers bobbing gray. Someone is singing unconsciously as he waits for the light at the corner of the street.

My sister is nine years old. I use my mother's scarf to wash the dried blood from the creases of where her legs meet her small body. "Soraya," I say, "you have mother's skin. You are my mother. I am your mother." She holds my hands firm. I know the water is muddy. I know the orange cloth is soiled with the salt from my palms. I know how it stings. She holds my hands firm, so that I don't need to look up at her face. Her slow, fawn eyes are laced with black, as if drawn permanently with ink; the tears fall like shadows, as patient as breathing, as undeniable as the sun rising. She doesn't make a sound.

They point their pistols in the dirt and draw maps, or routes, or characters. They take turns, between my sister and me and their pistols in the dirt. There are three of them. When night falls they close the doors and leave us with the stars. I fold Soraya's hair gently beneath her scarf, framing her round face with turquoise. We watch the darkness move into the sand like waves. When it is dark enough, Soraya pulls herself up. Limping, she wanders toward the ditch where our mother is planted. I follow her.

When I awake, I am holding my belly. Soraya is at my feet. Half her face buried in the dirt, her mouth slightly open; she is wrapped in her own soil. I turn her on her back, and some vomit slides from beneath her lobe down her neck. The corner of her mouth and cheek are crusted with saffron-muted flakes. "Soraya, wake up now. Did you forget? You are my mother. Wake up, now, dearest mine." I take the corners of my purple scarf to my mouth and lie beside her, bending far enough to wipe the dry silt from her face without revealing my dark hair. She opens her eyes wide and still. I kiss her face again and again, holding her against my lungs.

I know somewhere a dog fetches a ball. Bread is baking; storefronts are being swept. Someone is balancing her weight on her toes, and another is collecting shells. I know a child is fleeing his mother to escape the boredom of shoes, and an elephant is stepping on a land mine.

When we reach the house, the men have gone. Traces of their beards are found in bowls and cups. The door is still swinging from the winds of their breath. Tables have marked dents in the wall. Landscapes, still remnant in the dirt. I draw some water from the well and throw it upon the scratched earth.

Zaynabe's Militia (*from* Re-Aiming the Canon)

Amitis Motevalli

The Immortality of
"Tribute in Light"[1]

Sarah Husain

No need for rules
We know no boundaries.

March 11, 2002. NYC

Don't speak to me of rules, my
love, knows no boundaries
today's ritual in light beams
erected a new morality,
over savagery,
a limitlessness of power
in a space odyssey.
Immemorial two white lights
beaming sky high,
once again
Victoriously

beyond the eyes
God!
Hallucinating
15-year-old girls leave suicide notes
with *not* plastic knives
but shattered homes and run
straight at armed soldier's

staccatos of bullets
unsettling your imaginable dreams
so, Victory
take your boundary
past these lights
and look
we too are a people
in need of no rules, my
love, knows no boundaries.

Violence, Revolution, and Terrorism:
A Legal and Historical Perspective

Chaumtoli Huq

> The task of a critique of violence can be summarized as that of
> expounding its relation to law and justice.
> —*Walter Benjamin*[1]

After the London bombings, media commentators have publicly called upon "moderate Muslims" to denounce violence. One such article, "Where Is the Gandhi in Islam" (*Telegraph*, July 9, 2005), queries why Muslims have not advocated for the use of nonviolence as a means to champion the causes of concern for Muslims globally. While the media calls to denounce violence have provoked religious debate among the "moderate" Muslims here in the United States (who exactly these "moderate" Muslims are, and whether such a religious identity label exists, is another important question that needs to be addressed), there is, however, no debate as to why the dominant media believes that such public declarations from Muslims are so critical. Or as to why the use of violence by groups self-identified as Muslim resisting what they perceive as U.S. aggression on Iraqi sovereignty in the current political context has been made synonymous with terrorism; yet, the United States' use of violence in the invasions of Afghanistan and Iraq has not been identified as terrorism. Why do Muslims in particular need a Gandhi or a nonviolent advocate for their cause when India did not have Gandhi as its sole advocate for independence? The civil rights movement in the United States did not have Martin Luther King Jr. as its sole voice. Among the key voices were those of Malcolm X and the Black Panther Party, who believed that armed revolution might be necessary in the face of persistent and pervasive injustice. History is replete with examples of individuals or groups who see the use of violence, informed by a sense of injustice and confronted by legal systems that are deficient in redressing that injustice, as the only means by which to address the pressing social issues of their day. What, then, is the purpose for the dominant media and society to denounce violence, especially when such a denouncement fails to examine the underlying roots of violence? Further, such a denouncement of violence fails to recognize that violence is a part of the state and the legal system. Even Gandhi recognized the violence of the state when he said, "The individual has a soul, but as the state is a soulless machine, it can never be weaned from violence, to which it owes its very existence."

American jurisprudence also does not absolutely denounce violence. Our criminal laws recognize justification defenses, where illegal and criminal acts are not punishable because the crime committed was justified based on the specific facts of the case. A popular example of a justification defense is self-defense. If an aggressor lunges forward with a weapon, and you fear for your life, you are justified in responding to the aggressive act by protecting yourself. Individual states are limiting how much force an individual can use; but, nonetheless, the criminal law allows for limited use of violence. While the act is criminal, society has determined to excuse the criminality for some extralegal notion of justice. Finally, while beyond the scope of this essay, the existence of the Second Amendment right to bear arms makes the question of violence a part of state formation and our jurisprudence, even if we may differ on the scope of that right. Thus, American jurisprudence recognizes and sanctions violence in limited circumstances.

Given that both history and our laws reveal examples of society permitting the use of violence in very specific contexts, why is violence viewed as anathema to the rule of law, and the public asked to denounce violence? It is, in my view, because the state's legitimacy and stability rests on a characterization of violence as not being an inherent part of the rule of law but an aberration, to prevent lawlessness. Paradoxically, the legitimacy of the rule of law must also allow for violence in limited circumstances to achieve just results, to ensure the public's confidence in the legal system. It is in this conflation and contradiction of law and justice that we must, as philosopher Walter Benjamin advises, locate any critique of violence. Our critique cannot be in absolute or static terms. It cannot be an outright denouncement of violence. The existence of violence must be understood in relation to law and justice. Only then can we differentiate violence, terrorism, and revolution.

Separating violence from terrorism is not a purely theoretical exercise, but also has concrete implications in the ability of oppressed communities to express themselves in the context of a system that deprives them of this ability.

In absence of an opportunity to meaningfully participate in civil society, such communities resort to violence in response to an oppressive system. If the use of violence as a political ideology and tactic to resist an unjust state is equated with terrorism—which has as its goals to instill fear and maintain the status quo— then all revolutionary movements that may use violence may be suppressed under the guise of labeling it terrorism. Therefore, it is important for us to better understand these terms theoretically, because they have concrete implications for social justice movements.

Because history serves as my compass to current questions of the day, I look for analogies that could shed some light on what are becoming blurred lines between violence, terrorism, and revolution. In the 1770s, the Sons of Liberty were a loose coalition of American revolutionaries who used violence and intimidation to force the repeal of a stamp tax imposed by British colonialists. While not all members of the Sons of Liberty believed in violence, many of the members did intimidate British officials from collecting the tax. "No taxation without representation" became the revolutionary cry of American "patriots" and the foundations of the American Revolution. Confronting an unjust law, and being denied any meaningful participation in the system dominated by the British, American revolutionaries used violence to challenge unjust laws.

In the mid 1800s, white abolitionist John Brown murdered pro-slavery men and justified the killings as being the will of God. Born into a deeply religious family, he was open about his view that there was a need for armed insurrection to dismantle slavery in the South. Despite his religious underpinnings and his use of violence, he is viewed as an ardent abolitionist and martyr for human freedom. Would we see John Brown as a terrorist today? Would we call upon antislavery activists to denounce his actions because his actions led to the deliberate murder of people who were pro-slavery? Would we denounce his role in abolishing slavery because he believed that slavery could only be abolished through armed intervention? Is he a terrorist or the revolutionary that history seems to regard him as?

In India, around the same time, we find martyred freedom fighter Bhagat Singh, who believed in armed revolution to fight British colonialism. In 1928, Singh expanded on the distinction between terrorism and violence. He stated that when an oppressed person takes arms to eliminate exploitation, they use violence, but they do not spread terror. Here, Singh made a strident distinction between violence and terrorism. Should Sikhs and Indians denounce Singh as a terrorist? Mainstream Indian nationalists at the time, while opposing Singh's ideology and use of violence, did not denounce Singh. Even Gandhi, the symbol of nonviolence, publicly opposed his tactics but praised Singh's heroism in the face of British oppression. When we read how these historical figures and struggles are characterized as revolutionaries fighting against oppressive laws and states, we cannot ignore that they did use violence to redress their grievances. In fact, historically and in our legal system, we as a society have accepted the use of violence when social, political, and economic conditions have systematically denied people an opportunity to enjoy basic human rights.

In the current form of globalization, in which capitalism continues to expand through the consolidation of financial organizations such as the International Monetary Fund and World Trade Organization, which dictate social policy through trade agreements such as NAFTA, usurping the traditional functions of the state, the lines between violence, terrorism, and revolution become ever more blurred. Once, violence that was directed at the state and its laws was easier to understand because the state was viewed as the oppressor, and those impacted by the policies of the state, as the oppressed. Now, when states do not necessarily act in tandem with the directives of global capitalism (e.g., economic demand for cheap foreign labor, and restrictive immigration law) as it once did under colonialism, and financial organizations are not accountable to democratic processes, poverty and exploitation caused by global capitalism become difficult for people to fight against, because the nonviolent modes of redressing grievances—i.e., electoral process and courts—do not work. Without a clear institutional target for people to channel their activism through peaceful means, and with the absence of any real process, people feel disempowered and marginalized. Violence then becomes the only remaining means to end exploitation.

Thus, if we were to categorically denounce violence, we would eliminate a mode of expression for people whose only resort to self-actualization, defense, or independence is through violence. As Bhagat Singh tells us, violence can be utilized not to spread terror but to end exploitation. In denouncing violence, we are consequently also denouncing revolutionary expressions against exploitation that take form in violent acts. American revolutionaries who took up arms to fight the British would be American terrorists. In this context, we can then understand why the dominant media and states are so insistent that we denounce violence. The reasons advanced for the use of violence are to end the occupation of Iraq, to reclaim the right of Palestinians to their own nation and land, and to redress countless other grievances from the Muslim world. Yet, the targets of the violence are vehicles of capitalist expansion—trade and transportation. Stateless multinational corporate entities that operate with a similar profit motive to that of the British colonialists, profit-mongering slave economies, and de jure segregration are the new targets of violence, because these institutions reflect the unjust laws of our contemporary society.

If we are truly interested in combating the violence to which we all find ourselves victims, we have to make efforts toward a just society. We cannot limit ourselves to the independence of one nation-state but must work together for a just global society—politically and economically. Otherwise, we are doomed to continued violence and lawlessness. Violence is not an aberration of rule of law, but is in fact a product of an unjust system, a product of law. It is in the interest of an unjust system to denounce violence to create an illusion of violence being outside the system, when it is the violence of the state and the international economy that people are reacting to. It is not surprising that all revolutionary historical struggles, including the ones described above, have used violence. So, when we are asked to denounce violence in absolute terms, and stifle any discussion on the roots of such violence, we should hesitate, because unwittingly, we may just give up our opportunity to forge a more just society.

three:

(UN)NAMING FAITHS/
UNCLAIMING NATIONS

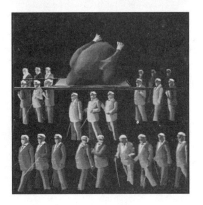

The Procession

Asma Shikoh

Abida

Saba Razvi

She sits in the dawn silence—
house pulsing with dreams
& *muezzin* echoes of a faith
deeper than sleep—
fingers holding prayer beads,

counting each worry
& pushing it away
with a small *tick*
to clash into the others
on the strand of her *tasbeeh.*

Her prayer rug secure beneath her—
threadbare reds & blues
where knees & forehead have
ground faith deep
into terra firma.

A flame to burn down heaven,
& a sea to quench hell
& like Rabia
she sits before God,
offers her love for itself alone.

Later, there will be coffee, tea,
to be made,
sugar spoons & aspartame,
too many kinds of cracked
& cooking eggs, a rush of hands.

The sound of crumpling paper
sacks, screen doors slamming
against *Thanks*,
echoed in the scattered, unrinsed
mugs & shells.

And every 4am,
her threadbare rectangle like solid stone
waits, the beads ticking
a loop of steady gratitude.
Everywhere—peace.

ramadan mubarak *for* "s"

Sarwat Rumi

well enough into ramadan
just days before the solar anniversary
of your death, rebirth
and first steps toward freedom.

you broke my heart back then:
two months of house arrest
two months of answering to calls of
fucking bitch slut whore fucking
bitch
with a smile and sweets
in your open palms.

his hands   smacked   strangled   shoved
and worse.

what broke you   was the daylight
molestation by a marital rapist on the first
friday of the month of fasting.   hours of begging him to
please wait until the sun goes down
please stop.

by sunset the next day
you'd come to the shelter unwinding
the history of a five-year love
spanning three continents.   years of waiting
to finally share a life with your *praan*   your soulmate
the one who made you laugh   feel protected
who asked honorably for your hand   more than once
convincing your brothers, your father

trading the name   kevin mcgill   for thick flowing arabic
to seal a love based on faith.

no wonder disbelief   made your voice
catch: who wouldn't be perfectly deceived?

days later   a week
then two   three   four
speaking of   nightmares   the snakes that crawled
all over your violated skin   while waking.

i couldn't   didn't tell you
that there at least   i had been
and still was
now and again
and again
and again.
didn't tell you
about the rapes which had
shattered my faith in divinity   years before
so that ramadan had meant nothing
until your story
made even more melancholy
this bengali heart.

didn't tell you either
about the craft which returned me
to the religion of my raising
the doors which swung open
to allow room within
for one faith with two different faces.
no need: i am the only one
who must understand it.

so in a year, woman
you've come so far   standing solid at the edge
of your new dreams realized:
resident status   self-sustenance
a return to the healing you'd given
so selflessly in the decade before you were
lured here and eaten alive.
this time they won't slip through your fingers
like water.

here i am a year later
fasting for the first time
since i was seventeen
still integrating the religion of my raising
with one which has cradled eve
to her divine breast since before eve
ever had a name:
different faces   one heartbeat.

this morning, still dark out
forty minutes until one could distinguish a
white thread from a black
i woke with someone next to me
woken with me:
forty minutes . . .   do i eat
not quite wanting to so early
or do i feed other hungers
curl deeper between the sheets?

considering my decision
over peanut butter and jelly
a cigarette and tea:
the claim to *choice discipline empowerment power*
living the right of respect for these
has brought you up from memory

and the nightmares we banished ourselves.
thank you s------
for reminding me to notice
how bright, soft and strong
a cold predawn can be.

ramadan mubarak
and happy anniversary.

Our Memories of Islam:
Pakistani, Malaysian, and Palestinian Women
(Re)imagine "Muslim" and (Re)define Faith

Azza Basarudin, Maddy Mohammed, and Khanum Shaikh

Dear Azza and Khanum,

I have been thinking about that intimate evening in which we started testifying about what it was like to grow up and be raised a Muslim child/girl-daughter/sister/woman/"wife" and the expectations and negotiations we have made (continue to make) as adult women. I cannot help but think about how harmonious it was to talk/share with you both on that night in November of 2003 at Azza's place. I hold the idea that people from multiple cultural backgrounds, geographies, and languages, *yak'ni,* have human condition commonalities, and it is especially galactic when they actually reveals themselves, as they did in our dialogue. It serves as a reminder that we can indeed move, shift, and find spaces and places to locate ourselves safely among others. At times it seems impossible, though.

I can record only a few times in my life when it was relatively painless and actually fruitful to dig up my own "Islamic memories." *My very own.* It was almost as if that space we created positioned me in such a way that I felt comfortable, familiar, and safe to explore, share, pose questions, witness, and listen. I did not have to waste a lot of time explaining or deal with the added burden of choosing my words so as to carefully communicate what I meant in someone else's language. I did not feel the *gaze or contempt* for saying something like, "*I was not allowed to date boys, growing up on the southwest side of Chicago.*" And how I shared my pain and silence over how my dear family ceased "normal" relations with me (thus cutting me off from my existing Muslim/Arab communities) for over seven painful years because my chosen partner was not a Muslim[1] (man)—"*Without paper or pen into your heart I reach Listen is more poignant than any speech.*"[2] I felt relatively "free" from the (North, Middle, South) stereotypical dichotomized limitations, locked ideas/everyday practices, and even from American, Palestinian, Arab, Muslim, feminist diatribe—all sides of my (dis)connected living world(s). I was able to express my narrative and what it means to me in my living life to be born a Palestinian American Muslim woman (I dislike labels because they are most always limiting and constantly evolving and sometimes deceitful, but feel it is necessary to point this out even at the risk of essentializing).

Perhaps the seed that spirited that blooming evening was planted earlier in the day. Remember? It was Edward Said's "After the Last Sky Symposium" at UCLA. *Even in death he gives us something back.* I can still recall the paper that spoke to part of the indescribable loss(es) I was feeling, "Edward Said—Accidental Feminist: Orientalism and Middle East Women's Studies" delivered so tenderly by Sondra Hale. In addition to this, perhaps, it was the temper of Azza's place—the warmness and hospitality, Khanum's sweet smile, the *shisha* (I would say *argilah*), which I tried for the first time, the *shay na'na* and French florentine cookies that I brought from Chicago. Reflecting, it was one of those evenings when time stands still—the self-recognizing a critical (collective) time and how to safely use it and pass through. Lately though, friends, my safety (public-private-real-imagined) has been evaporating around me (once again). I'm reminded through daily life experiences that I am living in a geo-socio-economic-political place and time where human relations and understandings are at a all-time low, and the everyday, silent, bloodless wars are high with casualties, as are the larger, louder, bloody ones.[3] I feel that I do not even have words/language to name the ongoing and simultaneous "little" and "big" wars that attack my person, my body, my space, my mind, my spirituality, my love, my communities, my work, my wages—even with the time that I spend thinking and working to understand, to find solutions. In the meantime I have poetry:

I am the history of the rejection of who I am
I am the history of the terrorized incarceration of my self
I am the history of battery assault and limitless armies against whatever I want to
do with my mind
and my body and my soul and whether it's about walking out at night
or whether it's about the love that I feel or
whether it's about the sanctity of my vagina or
the sanctity of my national boundaries
or the sanctity of my leaders or the sanctity
of each and every desire

that I know from my personal and idiosyncratic
and indisputable single and singular heart [4]

While that shared evening in L.A. has passed, what has not is the need for creating a safe space to explore what Islam means to me and how it has shaped and formed the very person I am today. Honestly, I do not talk about it in such ways (especially publicly), and indeed for the longest time I did not think myself Muslim for various simple and complex reasons that I hope to expose in our exchange. I suppose that's one reason that night was lasting for me: I was able to cross into and speak from my living born Muslim location(s) with you two and not feel judged, stigmatized, afraid, shamed, preconceived, or used, nor have the heavy feeling one gets from battling others who question their identities, authority to narrate, authenticities, and loyalties (inside-outside-real-imagined). How did you all feel that night? Any lingering thoughts, feelings, and ideas? What was it about that night that allowed us to willingly split open and testify to each other?[5] What brings us to this (white) page where we will turn oral talk into (black) written word, to be documented, processed, consumed, judged, and concluded? It is difficult for a private person such as myself to write such personal things, and I am asking myself, "What is my hope in writing this?"

Maddy—Chicago
July 10, 2004, 6:20 PM

Dearest Maddy and Khanum,
I write to you both from Cairo, Egypt. . . . Being in a Muslim country, living once again among a majority of Muslims, forces me to acknowledge, understand, question, and (de)construct my identities (e.g., Muslim, woman, Malay, feminist). Therefore, this dialogue comes precisely at a time when I am at crossroads of (re)defining what it means to be not just a Muslim but also a woman who is a firm believer in the ideas espoused by feminisms.[6] I, too, have hungered for the candor, companionship, understanding, and intimacy we shared that night in November. Maddy, you asked, "What was it about that night that allowed us to willingly split open and testify to each other?" Perhaps it was our state of mind at that moment, the location, the social and political climate, and the symposium to celebrate the life of Edward Said. Perhaps it was

our struggles/resistances that can no longer suffer in silence. Perhaps we were all simply weary of constantly being told how to *be* Muslim. Perhaps it was our way of creating organic solidarity—of remembering, resisting, (re)building, and (re)connecting. I am still truly amazed at how attuned we all were about what it means to be born and raised "Muslim" and live the "Muslim" experience on many different levels, cultures, and contexts. Perhaps we could never truly understand each other's experiences because we all come from and inhabit different spaces and locations, but for once in my life, I felt like we were all talking in a similar "language." *Finally, someone understands how I feel and knows exactly what I am talking about. Finally, I can open the "gates."* After all, borrowing from bell hooks, isn't language a site of struggle?

One of the my most vivid memories growing up "Muslim" was being told by the women in my family that I should "behave like a proper Muslim girl/woman." The Malay expression *"Jangan menconteng arang di muka keluarga"* ("do not disgrace the family") was constant throughout my childhood and continues to adulthood. I was told that wearing shorts or knee-length skirts was unacceptable. Talking and laughing loudly was unacceptable. Questioning authority (e.g., elderly, religious teachers) was unacceptable. Riding bikes, climbing trees, and playing with boys postpuberty was also unacceptable. I was told that roughing it out with boys was unbecoming, and that I could lose my virginity due to all the "unfeminine" activities . . . and I was only eight years old. Stories of what happened to girls who lost their virginity before marriage used to frighten me, and in so many ways, it was a successful method of policing my mind and movements. Compared to my non-Muslim friends in Malaysia, my memory of being eight was shadowed by the realization that being Muslim meant being different. It meant regulations. It meant surveillance. It meant authority. It meant gender inequality. It meant limitations. Not restrictions set by Islam, but of culture and of the communal Malay society disguised as Islam. At eight years of age, the borders and boundaries of what it meant to be Muslim, what constituted Islam, had already been defined for me. Not necessarily new borders and boundaries, but imaginary fences that had been (re)erected for generations, and cultural traditions that had been recycled without critical thinking, reasoning, or questioning.

I also remembered Qur'an school and how the *ustaz* ("male religious teacher") would come into the room with a long, sturdy stick, which was later to be used on anyone who made a mistake in reciting the Qur'an. The *ustaz* would not even acknowledge the existence of females in the room. We were, once again, relegated to the realm of the invisible, dispensable creatures. *Why does he despise me so,* I (and my female friends) used to wonder? *What did we do wrong? Was my* tudung/hijab *so askew that it was showing my hair? Are the sleeves of my* baju kurung *not long enough to indicate modesty? Am I not sitting properly?* I used to shiver in fear and revulsion each time I laid eyes on the *ustaz*. Fear because I knew if I mispronounced my Qur'anic verses, my flesh would taste the stick, and revulsion because as young as I was, my invisibility was a result of his inability to control his sexual urges. He was a man who was hiding behind his beard, turban, and religiosity. He feared the "active female sexuality"[7] even though I was a child who was unaware of sexuality at that age. Mind you, we were not even taught to read the Qur'an; we were taught to repeat after the teacher and memorize *ayah*. This, as I later realized, was the most convenient way of discouraging us from questioning authority. After all, how could we begin to question when we could not even read Arabic? What was there to question when we were *told* the meaning of the *ayah*, or surah, and given the supposedly single correct interpretation of what these beautiful words meant?

Despite all this, Maddy and Khanum, the Qur'an is dear to my heart . . . the words, the message, the passion, and the language are so beautiful . . . reciting it soothes and comforts my soul. . . . Is it twisted that my most vivid childhood memories are my most painful? Maddy once said to me when I was at my lowest, ". . . some of my fondest moments in life are my most painful. But they don't hurt anymore. If you work them through (gently and over time) they have a way of placing themselves neatly in the chapters of one's life."[8] I believe our dialogue that night has helped me reach into parts of my suppressed memories and to better understand how Islam has been, and is continuously being, distorted by certain segments of society. *I no longer want to suffer in silence. I can no longer afford to suffer in silence. Silence is killing my soul and my passion for Islam.* In the process of remembering, dialoguing, sharing, and writing, I am mapping my journey to (re)claim Islam and (re)nourish my soul.

I feel as you do, Maddy, that my safety (public-private-real-imagined) has been evaporating around me, yet again . . . it is very disturbing to write when the public and private collide . . . putting my innermost thoughts on paper for public gaze . . . it is disconcerting, but much needed. A few days ago, I went to the famous

Al-Azhar mosque in Cairo. It was the most poignant yet alienating experience of my life: Poignant because I have always loved the serenity and tranquility of spaces within mosques (even though I was never really encouraged to attend mosque by virtue of my gender). Alienating because whenever I am in a mosque, I am "exiled" into a specific space where the partition of man-made segregation demands that women be invisible, even in the house of Allah. Are we not equal in Allah's creation?[9] I was not made from any man's rib or created as a helpmate for man. I was created as a human being, equal to man, and should be treated as nothing other than that. What would my *ustaz* say to this thought? For as long as I could remember, my elders (males and females) have always painted a picture of the mosque as hostile to women. *Orang perempuan patut sembahyang dalam rumah, tak payah pergi masjid. Orang lelaki bagus kalau boleh pergi sembahyang dalam masjid.* ("It is more advisable for women to pray at home, but it is better for men to pray in the mosque.") *The brush that strokes their canvas is tainted with their misguided aspirations of Islam and its teachings.* As a child, I was confused as to why Allah prefers girls/women to pray in their homes and not in Allah's house. At that age, I was somewhat incapable of fully understanding the power of excluding women from attending, and performing their prayers in mosques. *The point of my story is that for as long as I could remember, my Islamic memory has been blindly inherited, defined and articulated for me by others (elders in the family, religious teachers, religious community leaders, to name a few) who think that the monopoly of religious knowledge production in Islam is indispensable and divinely sanctioned for the survival of a faith and its people.* I was never in the position to ask questions, let alone (de)construct the meaning of the rules and regulations that bound me to this imaginary allegiance of what Islam should be and how it should be lived. These are the tainted Islamic memories that have denied me a space in the mosque, the ability to understand and embrace Islam as it was intended to be, the appreciation of what it means to be Muslim, and, above all, a Muslim woman.

Azza—Cairo, Egypt

July 15, 2004, 3:15 AM

Dearest Azza and Maddy,

Sorry for being out of touch, girls. My mother and little sister, Khadija, are visiting from Pakistan this summer, and not having seen them in three long years, I find myself wanting to absorb every moment spent together. As both of you know, I have been anxious about this visit. It is the very first time that my mother has acknowledged, and agreed to come into, my world, into the home I have created away from the home she created for us—her children. So many times over the years, I have imagined her moving through the spaces I have carved out for myself here in Los Angeles. Can these worlds that I so deeply love exist in one space without creating a volcanic eruption? Which ideas, habits, rhythms, words, concepts, smells, feelings, expressions, ambitions, gestures, and people associated with these different contexts translate? Sometimes I do not know what belongs where. These days I find myself contemplating the walls that have kept my worlds so conveniently compartmentalized and separated from one another.

We are learning, afresh, about each other's worlds. I am learning, for instance, how my eighteen-year-old little sister is coming into womanhood in Lahore, growing up away from her elder sisters. I am learning how she, as a young Pakistani Muslim girl, is beginning to see herself in relation to the world. This morning on our drive home, she said that men have more freedom in Islam than do women. When I inquired as to what had prompted such a statement, she shared with me a Hadith that our first cousin in Pakistan had shared with her.

"Gurya says that there is a Hadith that says that every uncovered hair on a Muslim woman's head will be burned, one by one, on the Day of Judgment. But men don't have to worry about covering their hairs—so how does that make sense?"

She went on to share more stories, stories she had heard, stories she has carried in her little body, stories about Islam and women, and sin and freedom, and the Day of Judgment. Stories about her goals and dreams, and the realities that circumscribe them, and of her plans of circumventing those realities. And as I listened, I was transported back to that magical evening at Azza's house, when snippets of our stories had so freely rolled off our tongues, stories of our relationships with our own Muslim selves in our respective cultures, stories that we had heard as young women growing up in Chicago, Palestine, Penang, and Lahore. Listening to my little sister, I began to think about how different versions of these religion-based stories travel through our respective cultures, through us, across time and space, woven into languages, transmitted across friendships and generations, and how they are transformed each time we release them into the world. Could we ever trace the routes this story traveled before its entry into

Gurya's world? How many have heard and interpreted this story? Whose ears has it touched? How many voices did it ride before hitting my ears, through my little sister's voice? Sometimes I think about how different stories stitch themselves together and wrap themselves around our bodies like chadors that we wear as we make our way through life. Do you ever think about the weight of these stories on our bodies? Or about how sometimes it is these very chadors that we pull close to our bodies for warmth, comfort, and protection as we walk through cold and unfamiliar places?

Images of women running with their scalps aflame, the smell of burning hairs conjured up and set in motion through this story. Images deposited onto the consciousnesses of those who hear it. *Does my little sister think about the beautiful, shiny, long, black hairs on her head that will burn on the Day of Judgment when she walks around uncovered every day? Will my unruly, long black hair burn, one curl at a time?* After speaking with my little sister this morning I find myself enraged once again by the insidiousness of guilt-inducing stories cloaked in Islam, dished out to little girls to monitor the contours of their bodies, behaviors, and beings.

Yes Maddy, that night in Los Angeles did open up a space for us to excavate our very own Islamic memories. In retrospect, it felt both loving and desperate, the intensity with which we each revealed our stories to one another. I remember being told that wasting food was sinful, and that on the Day of Judgment we will be required to sweep up every grain of salt spilled on the floor in this lifetime. At the age of seven, I knew that I had wasted much more than a grain of salt, and so I used to practice getting on the floor and sweeping up grains of salt with my eyelashes to gain the skills I would need in the afterlife. Isn't that crazy? Azza, as a little girl, did you used to think about the consequences of losing your virginity by virtue of playing rough games meant for boys? Visual images of raging-hot fires and sweeping up salt with eyelashes can induce fear so deep. Does it not seem sinful to inject terror into the veins of little girls to secure their allegiance to the Creator? These are the very stories that are used to discipline our unruly desires and behaviors, to sculpt us into "appropriate Muslim women" (whatever this means).

Yes, Azza, the efforts to mark the appropriate boundaries within which we must exist have been infinite. Maintaining the "purity" of our female Muslim bodies seems to preoccupy many in our communities, and hence these "imaginary fences," as you so aptly described it. Regulation comes in so many forms. Sometimes it is the watchful, piercing eyes of the aunties, fixated on our every movement, waiting patiently, in anticipation, to see if we will dare to digress. It is the tongues of the relatives, ripe with stories of *whose-daughter-did-what*, and *whose-father's-head-is-bowed-in-shame*. Growing up, my parents' favorite response to my endless stream of questions about all the restrictions imposed on us was that *"log baaten karte hain"* ("people talk"). Most of my imaginary fences were made of the *logon kee baaten* ("talk of the people"), mostly relatives and community members. It has been the stories whispered by the neighbors that have tried to dictate how I dress, study, laugh, talk, eat, dance, and love. It is *logon kee baaten*, legitimized by cultural and religion-based justifications that work to enforce oppressive notions of morality for women.

My love to you both,

Khanum—Los Angeles

July 19, 2004, 4:15 PM

Dearest Friends,

It is good to hear from you both. Oh how I wish we were all sitting together right now. Where do I begin with this exchange? *"The sleepwalkers are coming awake, and for the first time this awakening has a collective reality: It is no longer such a lonely thing to open one's eyes."*[10]

Growing up first-generation Palestinian *fellaha* and Muslim American working class in the United States has given me narratives that represent some of what you both generously mention. The word *"ayb"* ("shame") was one of the first words I learned and understood in Arabic. It would set off a hurdle of haunting emotions, and as a child it was painful to deal with, but it served its purpose and gave me female binding borders and boundaries (real and mythical). I can't tell you how or why, but I was very keen to it even though I could not name it and had no useful language to explain my thoughts and feelings. *"A border is where human personality expresses itself most fully, whether in harmony or in contradiction with itself."*[11] A lot of it I did not understand as a child, but I still trusted and had faith. *Haraam* ("forbidden") was another word. It was used in many instances, for saying something inappropriate, wasting food or not wanting to eat meat, or later, for wearing tight jeans or disobeying my elders. Added to these words was that my actions were being tallied by angels at all times. I could not look at angels as helpful. I felt watched. *Why did Allah need to watch me all the time?*

The silence, shame, guilt, and policing (from within and without) have all been agents of repression for me, and although I have come to know that Islam (as a religion) did not condone my repression, still its name was used to do so, and it came to represent that repression to me. *Regardless of the "lost" laws of Muslim women's rights in Islam, what I was living was what being a "Muslim" represented.* Only later was I able to see the larger *stories* (oral and written) of such things. But tell me, what kinds of strategies do eight- and ten-year-old Muslim girls use to (successfully) survive such things? As grown women, we can conceptualize strategies and attempt to take control (even with all the challenges, limitations, and consequences), but as young children we are at the complete mercy of our cultures, societies, families, schools/teachers, communities, nations, governments, economies, and environments. *What rights do children have in this world?*

Azza, you pointed out that there are some differences in our spaces and locations, and I wanted to contextualize on this point, because it sheds light on what Khanum talks about as "excavating our Islamic memories and the weight of these stories on our bodies." I too went to Qur'an school. We called it Sunday school because we went only on Sundays. (Or was it named such because we lived in a dominant, Anglo Christian environment?) My first experience, although very short-lived, was emblematic. It was at a new mosque that was predominately attended and founded by the Palestinian Muslims in our Southwest Side community. Before this new mosque, we had no place to worship as a community except for someone's house or a rented hall. One Sunday I recall my father talking with some of the "leadership" men; words were spoken, faces seemed stony—we never did return. At home I overheard him express to my mother his disappointment and reservations. I vaguely recall the mention of Saudi Arabia's support of the mosque and the limitations on the founders and community from ownership, from worship (practice), and learning the teachings of Islam. My father later registered us kids at a North Side mosque, where we drove an extra hour to and from—the lingering incense from the Juma, the long drive, and the country-western music and AM news my father played sometimes made me nauseous—*Memories of Sunday school evoke smells of Chicago neighborhoods: rolling down the window, watching the people-streets as we passed, anticipating a chance to get out of the car, Polish sausage (forbidden pig smelled good), Jewish kosher, soul food, roasted peanuts, and a three-scoop ice cream cone.*

At our second *new* Juma/Sunday school, I learned that Muslims were from all over the world and spoke different languages, had different customs and traditions, but worshipped one Allah (precisely because the Juma was made up of diverse peoples). After class I would go into the prayer hall and sneak in the men's section and find my father on the *sajadah* (prayer mat) in the front of the prayer hall. When I got to be older in age, I no longer had mobility or immunity to move back and forth to the men's and women's sections. I also grew bored of my studies. It started to feel like what you described, Azza, about memorizing surah. I didn't know what I was saying, and I was concerned with pronunciation (which I was awful at) and handling myself properly (it became increasingly difficult for me to cover my head and neck). I would come home and ask my mother (she rarely came to the Juma), who did not read (fluent) Arabic or English, what things meant or questions I had. Thus, my Islamic teachings and interests were very much woven and kept alive by women's Islam.

However, I was giddy that my Muslim classmates and their families were shades of brown, black, and white (and colors in between), and we called each other sister and brother and had a feeling of togetherness. I especially needed, appreciated, and cherished this space because I grew up in segregated, racialized Chicago—the '70s: The white, working-class community we lived in was in an uproar about mainstreaming civil rights legislation and policies. There were violent protests against "busing" in front of the secondary and elementary schools we attended. I was aware of (white) privilege, even though it took years to name whiteness (the mythical but very clear and real color line, and the social construction of race and its meaning, and a growing color-blind society that allows unexamined practices to reproduce and recycle white supremacy—subscribing people to categories that carry power, authority, status and mobility). I silently questioned why my parents wanted to live in such a community and how some of us could pass as white and others could not (light skin and hair seemed to be visible markers), and why we even attempted to. What was so special about being white?[12] Over and over, I was told throughout my childhood, and more so in tense circumstances, "Be on your best behavior, and do not give anyone reason to say anything bad about our people, our culture and *deen* ['religion']."

My own experiences of racism and Islamophobia were birthed through socio-political-historical background events that took place throughout my young growing life. Some of these events directly and indirectly seeped in—the UN's partitioning of Palestine; the creation of the state of Israel, and its relationship with the United States and Arab and Islamic worlds; the Vietnam War; the oil embargo; Watergate; "Palestinian terrorists" and the Munich Olympics; the ongoing Indian wars in the Americas; Wounded Knee lockdown and subsequent court trials of AIM (American Indian Movement); Black Panther and Puerto Rican activists; the Trail of Broken Treaties march to Washington, D.C.; U.S. prison uprisings and "reform"; the legalization of abortion; the (white) women's movement; the killing of a former Allende diplomat from Chile by a car bomb in Washington, D.C.; Lebanon's civil war; Black September; New York's LaGuardia airport bombings by Croatian nationalists; the "Spirit of '76" and American patriotism; the UN's condemning of South Africa's illegal occupation of Namibia (which the United States vetoed) and human rights abuses in the massacre of blacks in Soweto; Israel's conducting of its first nuclear tests in the Kalahari Desert (aided by South Africa); the Iranian revolution/"America Held Hostage" as the theme in the news media;[13] the Chicago Police Department's Red Squad files, subjecting our new mosques to attacks and harassment, visits from the police and FBI to our house/communities/mosques, propaganda and education (through educational text books, language, media imagery—TV, movies, radio, music, newspapers, social interactions, educators/ service providers, etc.); fights after school—"Go back to where you came from, you dirty *Ayrab*," a poke under my right eye with a pencil that breaks its tip in my skin, blood on my face, the doctor visit, the dark purple bruise that I have to wear, learning to fight and defend myself (and my younger brother). I still have the faint light blue lead mark underneath my right eye. How I kept unconsciously touching it many years later, as I watched on TV in horror as the twin towers collapsed, wondering who was involved and what U.S. Arab/Muslim (or look-alike) children and youth will possibly have to go through.

Although my father did not intend to do so, he indirectly taught me to question (man's) authority in Islam when we changed mosques/Sunday schools. And so I did question, much to my parents' disliking. I can recall being asked why I was so difficult and uncooperative. There was much to question, being a female spirit—the contradiction and double standards, both in my inside and outside worlds, were prevalent. I don't recall ever being in the right position to ask questions about things—there were always consequences and it was never a good time—*like the UN and the question of Palestine.*

Why do they "hate" us (women) so, we ask? Even with the advances and contributions women make, the sacrifices, the knowledge and work they produce, their value and worth to public and private life, why are they still so feared and so harshly and quickly judged? *What is at stake?* This judgment is not just reserved for people who identify as Muslims. What is revealed is a universal reality and understanding that women all over the world are deprived of some fundamental human rights and that this deprivation is not taken seriously— *Patriarchs and their systems are never fair to women and children; many times they are not even fair to themselves.* It becomes difficult to lay bare how (some) Muslim men can (sometimes rather easily but not simply) use religion, causing much harm and damage to the entire religion, putting millions who practice and identify in jeopardy, and how "American"[14] mainstream media/experts/ academics/people use but small fragments of the many facets of Islam—histories, social constructions, cultures, languages, politics/laws, economies, schools, art, literature, music—to do the same. How quickly by all sides it is reduced to binary ways of thinking and practicing. It is "interesting" how *counter-hegemonic* a Muslim women's narrative really is, and how it often (but not always) can bring about a remarkably universal solidarity among vast numbers of Muslims (men and women) to denounce her, punish her (if they can), put her in her place *self hatingmuslimgoodfornothing,* and how at the same time she counters the "gaze" and attempts to understand and locate her and even use her in recycled modern "Orientalism"[15] in the United States, Canada, and Europe. Each generation of women and girls will have to be part of this. It will not go away and we can't wait for political, legal, economic, and religious justice; we already can see how they are manipulated against us and misused to "protect" us (us=not just women).

My memories of my teenage years growing up in Palestine are but a time. Years have only separated me from them. *I take care not to romanticize.* One thing I recall is something you mentioned, Azza, about living among a majority of Muslims, and I will add Palestinians—the feelings one has and shares. For me it was the very first time, and I relished it and took refuge from "minority" and "the other opposing" status in the United States. Sure, I experienced some of the "talk" you mention, Khanum; the fact that we lived in close proximity and knew each other's business made people more concerned about talk and gossip. The village my parents are from is populated with Muslims and Christians living in coexistence, and my family had/has very close relations with many of the Christian families (especially in the United States). I wondered why Christian women from our village covered their heads, too, among other things. I asked one of my mom's childhood (Christian) friends this very question when we visited her. She smiled and laughed, patted my hand and said, "You Americans do not know much about us. What do they teach you over there?" Living in North America blurred my knowledge of these people and limited my understanding. They did not just belong to the exotic smells from the boxes and suitcases we received filled with goodies (one becomes partial to "home"-grown *zait,* *zaytoon,* and herbs), the letters in Arabic I could not read, or the "old country" folk who lived with no electricity, running water/indoor plumbing, shopping malls, potato chips or plastic wrap. I was immersed among them, their way of life, their cultures, traditions, religions, schools, languages, and lands. I saw my own mother "transformed"—she was back in her familiar setting, and it was visible—she glowed. She was "home" and among her people, as she would say. I fell in love with her (again). I no longer saw her just as I did in Chicago. "*I am a reflection of my mother's secret poetry as well as her hidden angers.*"[16] My young woman's eye opened wide, and I was grateful to have it come to bloom in the land of Palestine.

Maddy—Chicago

September 7, 2004, 10:38 PM

Dear Maddy and Khanum, sisters of my heart,

Maddy, while you experienced racism and Islamophobia from an early age, I grew up privileged, because I was a part of the Muslim majority in Malaysia (even though I was still a minority among the majority with regards to some of my views of Islam that do not subscribe to the mainstream ideas of the "appropriate" woman's place in Islam). I did not experience racism and Islamophobia until I came to live in the United States. I remember the unpleasant looks and stares that followed my sister (she wears the *hijab)* and me when we were out and about, especially after 9/11. I have witnessed the way some people talk to her, as if she is an imbecile, just because she chooses to wear the *hijab.* I have seen the dirty looks directed at her, and the comments and disgust that accompany those looks, while I can "pass" as an "anonymous" Muslim. However, "passing" comes with its own price. . . . I can remember so many incidents where I wanted to lash out to protect my sister against their racist gaze, but what language do I use for people who have such low regard for human differences? This also reminds me that I was not born a woman of color, but became a woman of color here in the United States, where I learned the peculiar brand of U.S. North American racism and its constricted boundaries of race.[17] I think the peculiarity of this particular brand of racism has become more prominent for Muslims, Arabs, and South Asians, and peoples of color post 9/11.

As I write, Islam and "Muslim" are continuously being characterized for us . . . unpatriotic, terrorist, anti-American, antidemocratic, anti–women's rights—the list goes on. As I write, occupation, genocide, torture, ethnic cleansing, war, and aggression are raging everywhere: from Sudan, Chechnya, Afghanistan, and Iraq to the occupied Palestinian territories. Abu Gharib, Jenin, Darfur—these places witnessed the lowest form of low human tolerance. The incidences of hate crimes against Muslims and people who are perceived to be Muslims have increased tremendously since that fateful day of September 11, 2001.[18] A story I read a while back keeps haunting me. It is one of the testimonies from the Human Rights Watch on hate crimes against Muslims:

> On morning of June 18, 2002, I went to a drugstore to pick up allergy medication. A woman who was angry that I had left one of my children in my car while I picked up the medication began berating me. She told me, "I've learned all about you people [Muslims] over the last ten months, and I don't trust a single damn one of you." I tried to move away from her, but the woman slammed me to the floor and began pulling at my *hijab*. I screamed at her to let me go, and that I was having trouble breathing, but the woman kept pulling on my *hijab*. In a panic, I pulled off my *hijab* in order to stop from choking. The woman then dragged me by my hair to the front of the store. The woman did not let me go until police arrived. My young children witnessed this sad event.[19]

The war on Muslim bodies and beliefs. Is this the America that immigrants from all over the world flock to in search of a better life? Is this the America that screams freedom, liberty, and justice for all? Is this the America that prides itself on its racial, ethnic, and religious tolerance? With the current political climate of xenophobia, and Islamophobia, on some days I do not even want to leave the sanctuary of my apartment. "*Us*" *vs.* "*them.*" An October 2004 poll recently released by the Council on American-Islamic Relations (CAIR), "Islam and Muslims: A Poll of American Public Opinion," indicates that "one in every four Americans believes a number of anti-Muslim stereotypes and negative images of Muslims are sixteen times more prevalent than positive ones."[20] In addition, the poll indicates that "half of all Americans believes that the Islamic faith encourages the oppression of women."[21] These days, by virtue of being "Muslim," I am fighting two battles at the same time: the internal/personal/familial/communal struggle and the external struggle that has left me drained emotionally, intellectually, and physically. Do I fight the internal struggle raging within me in the midst of the wars against my community?[22] Dare I bring gender into the frontier when my community is being harassed, humiliated, denied its freedom of worship, and detained without proper trials, in the name of national security? Should I leave my feminism until it is "safe" to speak of my aspirations for gender reform within Islamic thoughts and practices? "*Us vs. Us.*" Why does my struggle against sexism and patriarchal domination have to take a back seat, yet again? Feminism cannot take a back seat to anything! Where does the line of sexism begin and racism end?

Sometimes I wonder about the crisis facing Muslims and Islam in the age of globalized terror. Isn't the crisis partly a result of our own disregard for the true message and teachings of Islam, and of the numerous economic, social, and political problems raging in the *ummah?* Shouldn't the scrutiny on "what is wrong with Islam and Muslims" be turned inward? Isn't it time to stop blaming others for our shortcomings? Internal division is not unique to Islam, as other religions have their own struggles, but somehow Muslims ignore this division as if it were insignificant. Before 9/11, many American Muslims I know adopted a don't ask, don't tell attitude about Islam: *We are Muslims, but we do not need to educate you about our religion, or how Islam has contributed and can continue to contribute to the American society. As long as we can live our life quietly, we are content.* After 9/11, when the arrests of Muslims (and people perceived to be Muslims) became a common occurrence, the American Muslim communities panicked. *Now* we have to educate the American public about Islam and about Muslims. We need to educate others that our religion means peace. We are peaceful people. We believe in Jesus, too! Most Muslims have adopted a new slogan in the fight against terrorism: "Not in the Name of Islam." CAIR now has an online petition for people to correct misperceptions of Islam and the Islamic stance on the religiously motivated terror.[23] CAIR has also sponsored an Islam in America advertising campaign, one of the ads of which is on how Muslims respect and revere Jesus.[24] Better late than never, right? Since it took the horrific tragedy of 9/11 to jolt Muslim communities (worldwide, not just in the United States) out of their slumber, does that not tell us something about our communities and our interactions with Muslims and non-Muslims wherever we exist? Should we not self-interrogate how we treat other Muslims? Who has the right to speak about Islam? Who is not Muslim enough? Who is Muslim enough? Should we view a Muslim woman who does not choose to wear the *hijab* as less of a Muslim? Should we view people who are born Muslims as always better than converts to Islam? As much as Muslims would like to ignore it, race and race relations are also important divisive factors in Islam—to think about African American Muslims and the discrimination and prejudice they encounter when interacting with non–African American Muslim communities.

In addition, the issue of gender reform in Muslim societies is another topic that is generating an even bigger crisis within the *ummah*. From my own experiences, one of the major obstacles in the discourse of Muslim women's rights is the common perception that women's human rights are Western-imported values, therefore incompatible with Islam and local Muslim customs and traditions. People who advocate for gender reform in Muslim societies are, more often than not, accused of being "agents" of the corrupt "Western" world. Despite placing utmost emphasis on ways in which many Muslim/Islamic feminists argue for, and define, gender reform in an approach that does not align organic feminisms with secularists, religious extremists, and neocolonial relations of domination, most attempts fail to generate reform.

After 9/11, mosques across America scrambled to open their doors to non-Muslims (despite still discriminating against women praying alongside men) in the hope of salvaging the image of Islam and Muslims; Islam is promoted as a religion that does not condone terrorism, and Muslims are not terrorists but peace-loving, law-abiding citizens. Additionally, nonprofit Muslim organizations sprang up like mushrooms to defend and popularize Islam. Book after book has been produced attempting to explain 9/11, Muslims, Islam, and terrorism. More and more Muslims are now self-interrogating in order to answer questions about the crisis that has befallen them. So, should we be thankful for the irony of the wake-up call? Will Muslims wake up and *stay awake*? Will the collective progressive consciousness of the *ummah* change the face of Islam? How will women configure into changing the face of Islam? Can the "gatekeepers" of Islam accept a woman's self-assertion to (re)interpret the Qur'an? Is it so wrong/ sinful for a woman to demand to enter the mosque through the front door and pray alongside men? I am not a Muslim refusenik. I am simply a woman who is passionate about her faith and who wants to see it restored to what it should be. *Muslims are a part of the problem, and Muslims need to be a part of the solution.*

Azza—Los Angeles

September 11, 2004, 4:25 AM

Dear Azza and Maddy,

Azza, as I read your passionate words about the struggles of Muslim communities in an era of "globalized terror," about the dehumanizing representations of Muslim men and women strewn across the landscape, and the internal fractures and conflicts within the *ummah,* I reflect on my own disengagement from the larger world as of late. Denial—a luxury only some of us can afford—the privilege, perhaps, of living in the most powerful nation in the world. After reading your thoughts, I asked my mother whether she thinks global violence has reached unprecedented levels over the last few decades. She said she does not really think so, that it is just my eyes that have developed the ability to see. Even in this moment, the sound of my typing almost drowns out the murmur of Kerry and Bush's voices on television, engaged in serious political debate about the future of "our" country—the United States. Have either of you been listening? I tried to stop and listen, to be informed of what our leaders have to say to the American public, but these days I just have low tolerance for lies. Smooth, savvy words, earnest expressions, combed hair, shiny ties, the meticulously prepared and rehearsed rhythms of their speeches— sanitized violence is the term that comes to mind. Can the most expensive manicures clean up the blood underneath their nails?

They are sophisticated terrorists. The difference is that they wear suits and ties and speak good English, my father once said.

The BBC website popped up as I turned on the computer to write to you both, and I quickly glanced at the headlines. "*At least twelve people have been killed and seventeen others wounded in a U.S. air strike on the rebel-held city of Falluja in Iraq.*"

The report says that the U.S. military was targeting a hideout for militants.

Turns out the precision bomb was not really that precise, and so it accidentally struck a house where a wedding had just taken place. So the groom died hours after the wedding.[25] Good news is that the bride survived the blast. She only got injured. *A union in the midst of occupation.* A ceremony that began with blessings and song and dance and food and celebration ended in death. Bombs, masked in the language of freedom, forcing their way into homes of people, blowing up grooms and injuring brides (and sixteen more people who were celebrating the marriage), disrupting ceremonies—how very entitled of the U.S. military, don't you think?

There are a few headlines about Mr. Bigley of Liverpool, who was beheaded by his captors—the Tawhid and Jihad groups in Iraq. Prime Minister Blair expressed "utter revulsion" at the killing of Mr. Bigley.[26] The *freedom-loving* Americans accidentally blew up the groom. The *terrorists* beheaded Mr.Bigley, because that is just what they do. In this battle of good vs. evil, the evildoers are fighting against the freedom lovers. It is "us" vs. "them," the beheaders vs. precision-missile operators. They are jealous of "our" freedom. *You are either with us, or with the enemy.* But who is the "us," and who is the "enemy?" UNITED WE STAND, say the bumper stickers on the SUVs cruising up and down these six-lane freeways here in Los Angeles. United with who? Against who? Who are the "we?" Maddy, did you know which of the two you belonged to when the blood rushed down your cheek after you were stabbed by the child in your school? On how many more levels will this hate-filled logic manifest: a pencil, a missile, an entire military operation—isn't it enough? Are these not the very binary logics that dominant religious discourses are based on? Are these not the very logics that have been used to categorize us Muslims, Muslim women? Maddy, you wrote, "Why do they hate us (women) so?" Let me share with both of you an excerpt from a newspaper article:

In June 2003, members of Islamist groups in Lahore and Multan, Pakistan, smeared three billboards put up by multinational companies and carrying photographs of women. When interviewed by the press, a spokesperson for the group Shabab-e-Millat said, "These multinational companies want to promote obscenity, lewdness, and vulgarity by showing women in different poses. We will not let them do so."[27]

This incident took place four days after the North-West Frontier province

(NWFP) voted to implement Sharia law (Islamic law). A few days prior to this incident, Islamist groups in the NWFP gave the local government a deadline to remove all billboards bearing images of women on the streets of Peshawar. One of the spokespersons from this group made the following comment: "We will not allow the advertisers to dishonor our women by decorating our streets with their images."[28]

Whose women? Whose streets? Whose multinationals? Whose morality? Whose honor? Whose images? Whose bodies? Who decides who gets to view my body or not? Who are these men speaking on behalf of me? Jamaat-e-Islami write on their website:

> A Muslim woman may wear whatever she pleases in the presence of her husband and family or among women friends. But when she goes out or when men other than her husband or close family are present, she is expected to wear a dress that will cover all parts of her body, and that should not reveal the figure. This is in total contrast with Western fashions, which every now and then concentrate quite intentionally on exposing yet another erogenous zone to the public gaze! In the past few years, we have seen the rise and fall of the minidress, the micro skirt, the wet look, hot pants, the see-through, the topless, and other garments designed to display or emphasize the intimate parts of a woman's body.[29]

Azza and Maddy, I reel with anger as I read these statements. Who defines this Muslim woman? Does she exist solely in opposition to the Western "woman"? Why do the Jamaat-e-Islami spend an entire section defining, capturing, and confining our bodies against those of Western women? I refuse to be contained by their binaries.[30]

Are you with us or with the enemy? asks president Bush.

And my head spins.

Perhaps it is the insistence on clearly pulling out the good from the bad, the pure from the impure, the West from the East, that leaves me feeling alienated. No room for contradictions, no room for crossovers, no room for living and loving in the crevices, in the borderlands.[31] I seek solace when I think of the story of the eighth-century Sufi woman Rabia-al-Basra who, when seen by a number of Sufis walking with a bucket full of water in one hand and a burning torch in the other, was asked where she was headed. Her response was that she was going to light a fire in Paradise and to pour water onto Hell. Blurring the clear-cut lines between Heaven and Hell, us and them, East and West, *haram* and *halal*, miniskirts and *hijab*—doesn't that sound refreshing?

Missing you both,

Khanum—Los Angeles

September 15, 2004, 2:15 AM

Dear Khanum and Maddy,

Khanum, the story of Rabia al-Basra is indeed refreshing, and while we have that history to be content with, perhaps in our times, Rabia comes in a different form: comedians. Not just any comedians, but *Muslim female comedians!* Our very own contemporary Rabia. I remember reading the following quotation on the website of Shazia Mirza, a British Muslim female comedian, and laughing hysterically: "The Muslim vagina is like the Channel Tunnel: It's not just long and dark, but it also has a lot of Talibans trying to get into it."[32]

The war on our sexualities . . . Have any of you thought of your bodies as temples? Slipperiness. Touching. Taste. Hymen. Ornamentation. To be worshiped at any cost? Why do we never speak of sexuality so openly? Why is there an imaginary taboo when it comes to our bodies, and the pleasure they give us? Warriors. Inside. Location. Why are we not taught that to love our bodies is to love ourselves? Why were we taught that sexual pleasure is forbidden in Islam? Inflatable. Pure/Impure. Ambiguity. Protection. Why were we taught to be ashamed of our bodies and sexualities? Engulfing. Encompassing. Engrossing. After reaching puberty, I remember my mother telling me that my body was a "land" that needs to be "protected." As a "land," I can also be "plundered" by the right "owner" when the land is "ripe" for harvesting. I was constantly reminded that my post-pubescent body was no longer seen as a "body" attached to the biological body, but had been transferred into the physical-public body where concepts of family "honor and shame" marked my body. The same *"ayb"* you spoke of, Maddy. What were my strategies to counter the oppressive patriarchal ideologies that legitimize themselves through the use of religion? *Silence, guilt, and shame. Those elements still penetrate my body, piercing holes that bleed Muslimness with every beat of my heart.* How do I explain that my body is not a "land" that one can possess, protect, and plunder when the owner is unwilling? How do I struggle for self-ownership when my body is not my own, but the property of religion, family, and community?

Love happens when we least expect it. It catches us by surprise. It baffles us. It amuses us. It rejuvenates us. Above all, it teaches us the meaning of pain and pleasure. Of glory and agony. Why do we not talk about passionate love or passionately loving someone within the boundaries of Islam? We talk about passionately loving Allah. Don't Muslims think that Allah would want humans to experience the ultimate passionate love? After all, it has been revealed in the Qur'an: "And among His signs is, that He created for you mates from among yourselves, that you may dwell in tranquility with them, and He has put love and mercy between your hearts. Undoubtedly in these are signs for those who reflect." (Qur'an 30:21). What do we make of people who refuse to reflect on this? This is the part of Islam that I came into on my own. Nobody has ever taught me about this *ayah*. Islam of my upbringing has mostly been about crime and punishment. It is mostly about conformity. Mostly about going to *neraka jahanam* ("hell") for my "un-Islamic" ways (whatever that means). Mostly about how I will be crushed in my grave by two giant snakes (in addition to poisonous spiders and other creatures) if I purposely neglect my prayers.

I am tired of the war on my feelings—tired of *not* feeling and tired of surviving. I want to feel. I want to live. I want to feel without any restraint. Why do guilt and shame penetrate every inch of my being just because I am able to live, even for a split second? Why do horrific childhood stories of "bad Muslim girls" who will be tortured in *neraka jahanam* emerge when I transgress? *The saddest part about transgressing is that I cannot even transgress the imaginary boundaries and regulations in my imagination.* My inherited memories of Islam do not allow me to transgress these boundaries, even if there is no physical body to patrol these boundaries. They are ingrained, and internalized. I am not capable of transgressing my shame, my guilt, and my anger for transgressing. *I have transgressed, but I cannot come to terms with transgressing.* There can never be enough showers that I can take that will wash away the feelings that have sown themselves into my brown skin. There have been so many taboos and so much censorship in all our lives that it became surreal to have certain *real* experiences. . . . Even as I am writing this, I feel censored. Censored by the real and imagined gazes . . . I can feel *their gazes* on me . . . I do not have adequate language to describe my feelings . . . writing feels surreal . . . I am at war with my feelings, body, and sexuality.

Azza—Los Angeles

September 22, 2004, 1:15 AM

Dear Azza and Khanum,

Azza, you wrote, "Why do we never speak of sexuality so openly?" I wish I had the opportunity to do so, for I think I would have been better tooled to handle certain situations. Did I see my body as a temple? I was aware, through constant reinforcement, of what could happen to a young woman who was not careful with her body and protective of her sexuality (it happens even when you are), but I felt that the idea of "safety" and "for my own protection" was used against me. I was told that it was not me that they did not have faith or trust in, but others who would take away my/their honor (the fear of boys' and men's sexual privileges and the outer American culture that was in our dominant surroundings. They could control me and keep me "safe," but the latter they had no control over). When I lived in Palestine, my mother was not on me as much. In fact, I was fortunate to experience some of my teenage puberty in Ain Arik, a village north of Ramallah. I did not feel like they were watching me as much as my older sisters were watched in the United States. I felt I had more leverage in this capacity, but I was exposed to a new threat to my honor—the Israeli occupation. *One day on my way home from school, I was walking to the bus terminal (I usually walked with my sisters). A jeep filled with four soldiers stopped right in front of me on the sidewalk, blocking my path. One of them asked me if I had participated in the demonstration earlier at the Ramallah manara (in protest for a young student named Lena who had been killed, shot twice in the neck and once in the heart, by Israeli soldiers[33]); he went on to tell me (in English) if he ever saw me in a demonstration he would come back to my school (he could identify what school by my uniform), find me, and rape me. A shopkeeper and two women immediately gathered around me to inquire about what was going on; the soldiers yelled at them and left. I was embarrassed/humiliated/ashamed, scared and angry. I only told my best friend J about it. She told me she peed in her pants once when she had a similar encounter.* As I write this I feel censored, judged, and "suspected" of not being "objective." I feel at risk and vulnerable all over again. This too is another silent and dangerous war that I struggle and resist. As I became older, I saw how a woman's body was used as symbolic representation of her family, her people, her race, her land, her nation, her religion. How her gender and sexuality were not just hers but belonged to the greater public and the public of others. How the threat of sexual violence was/is used to put her in her place as a woman. I saw my own experience in a larger context of militarization of other past and present wars, occupations, police actions, and state/nation violence—Korea, Vietnam, Guatemala, El Salvador, South Africa, Sudan, Bosnia, Chechnya, and Iraq, to name only a few.[34]

Maddy—Chicago

September 25, 2004, 3:30 PM

Dear Azza and Maddy,

Did I ever think of my body as a temple? you asked. No, Azza and Maddy, not really. A few years ago I was sitting with four of my best friends in Pakistan, sharing memories of growing up as young girls in Lahore, when the topic of Qur'an teachers came up. As we exchanged stories, we discovered that three out of five of the women in the room had been molested by their *maulvis* as young girls. When sacred space reeks of such violations, how can little girls ever think about their bodies as temples? Azza, when I think of your *ustaz*, and Maddy, the painful story you shared about the soldiers who threatened to rape you, is it a surprise that shame would be so intimately familiar to all of us? When I shared the story of molesting *maulvis* with my mother, she said that this is precisely why she made sure that our Qur'an lessons were conducted in a physical space that was always in her view. She could look out the screened window and monitor the supposedly "pure space" within which we sat with our Maulvi Sahib and learned to read our Holy Book. It was her watchful eyes, her warrior gaze that spun a shield of protection around the bodies of her little girls.

Did I ever think of my body as a temple? My dear friends, I find myself skirting around this question. Dare we speak of our bodies out in the open like this?

Can we put our bodies up on display so openly and bring our intimate selves into visibility through our words without knowing whose eyes will feast on these exposures? I too feel this heavy censorship that sits in my bones, locks my tongue, makes me hit the backspace key on the keyboard after every other word. What about the eyes of the aunties? The talk of the people?

And so, once again, I excavate my stories and allow them to speak on my behalf. I wrap them close around me, my warm and comforting chador, protecting me from the piercing gaze of who knows who. . . .

"Girls do not wear makeup," my mother said. "You will have plenty of time to dress up once you are a woman. Girls should stay girls." These, I now realize, were her ways of protecting her four daughters from prematurely entering into full patriarchal public visibility. These were her strategies of keeping our budding sexualities invisible in order to keep us safe.

It was her hawklike gaze that kept "their" gazes in check by forming a thin protective film around my body. Comfortably existing beneath this sheet of invisibility, I grew up not quite knowing that I possessed a body, Azza and Maddy. But I could not hide forever, and, at some point, I too came into view—body and all. Womanhood did come, and brought with it uninvited advances, sideways glances, and entitled commentaries from strange men. At the age of eighteen, I moved from my beloved city Lahore, to Los Angeles. I went from being hidden behind an army of badass older women and sisters, from the comfort of all-women's spaces, from the comfort of sexual invisibility to stepping into full and distorted view as a young, exotic woman in the United States. One of my first awakenings came in the form of being exoticized/sexualized by a white man months after I had moved to the United States from Pakistan.

"I think you are beautiful. You would look great in a deep-pink swimsuit."

I almost slapped him. It was shocking to be confronted with this white American man, virtually unknown to me, who felt fully entitled to imagine and comment on my body. Clearly, the rules were different here, but his audacity had me enraged. *Who gave him the permission to imagine and comment on my eighteen-year-old brown body? Why would I want anyone to have the power to see me whenever they feel like it? What if I do not wish to be seen?*

Over the years, I have found myself in continual dance between strategic visibility and invisibility. Negotiating how and when I assert my presence, and when to become invisible. Lovingly and with rage, Azza and Maddy, I have continued to battle the fences, overstep the boundaries, (re)write the rules, fight with the *logon kee baaten* that reside in my own head. Subverting, challenging, escaping, resisting the confines of their minds. Shamelessly asserting my presence, living unapologetically, laughing—deep and loud and joyfully threatening, and then strategically retreating into invisibility when necessary. Dancing—arms, legs, hips flailing, pushing through the lines that demarcate "appropriate" moves from "inappropriate" moves. Moving to my own beat, I stay in motion to defy the metal cast that seeks to close in, capture, and imprison my body. A few nights ago a friend of mine looked at me sideways and commented: *"It cracks me up how you do your womanhood."* What do you mean, I said? *"Just the way you hold yourself, your tough demeanor, your resistance, your f-you attitude. You are still a big tomboy."* Defining the contours of my being has been a process.

I teach a course on Women's Studies and confront young students who feel that while some of my young women have achieved absolute equality here in the United States, it is "those" women *(meaning your women, Muslim women, veiled women, oppressed women, Afghan women, Third World women)* that need help. *It is them you should be teaching Women's Studies to, not us.* As I stand facing the classroom, directly in the path of these ethnocentric verbal missiles, every inch of my body feeling these piercingly racist gazes, I am reminded that no matter how I construct my syllabus, I am always being constructed by them, by these patronizing eyes that can only place me within the Orientalist constructions they have inherited. Imposed visibility can be as oppressive as imposed invisibility—especially when the terms of our visibility are not in our control. Sometimes, at these moments, I wish to retreat into invisibility, to protect myself from being consumed by their entitled gazes.

These are my negotiations. At thirty-two years of age, I continue to re-create my relationship to my body, and to the spaces through which it moves. After all, burqa or no burqa, the women that I come from did not silently make their ways through this world without making an impression on the landscapes through which they traveled. They, too, have negotiated all their lives, shifting between visibility and invisibility—depending on the context. So why shouldn't I?

Much love to you both,

Khanum—Los Angeles

September 29 2004, 12:43 AM

Dear Khanum and Maddy,

Turbulence/Confusion/Turmoil/Disorder/Instability/Chaos = Religion (as revealed vs. as practiced) = Faith (my beliefs vs. inherited beliefs) = Gender (woman/man/ vs. womanmanandrogynylesbianmalefemalegayqueer). Sexuality

(Taboos + Forbidden Fruits vs. Conformity) = Feminism (consciousness + action vs. misogyny + ignorance) = Allegiance (faith vs. blind faith) = Love (surviving vs. living). Despite the waves of turbulence that threaten to unleash themselves in my mind and body, my "Muslim" soul screams for acknowledgment. Bits of my fragmented self, dispersed over a wide landscape of unstable identities, struggle for recognition. If we as "Muslim" "women" do not rise up now and demand that our struggles for authenticity, legitimacy, gender reform in our respective societies be heard, and for our feminisms to be a normalcy within our communities, then when will the time be right? If xenophobia and Islamophobia are causing us to forsake our agenda of (re)claiming our identities and (re)defining our faith, when will we be able to assert ourselves? Sisters of my heart, the time is never right. . . . My soul cries for nourishment, for care, for understanding, for compassion, for solidarity. My soul cries for Islam. My soul cries for "us" "Muslim Women." My soul cries for my roots and my heritage. Above all, my soul cries for us to rise against the Islam that has always been defined for us by our families, communities, religious leaders, men, misogynists. . . . My soul cries for you comrades to take back Islam. I cannot let my Islam (no matter how we look at Islam, as a religion, a culture, a practice, spirituality, etc.) be defined for me. *My Islam must be mine.*

I must be true to what I believe in, and to what I believe Islam is capable of providing for me. I must rise, (re)discover, and restore Islam. I must rise against those who seek to enslave us with their orthodox interpretations and implementations of Islam. I must rise against harmful cultural traditions that have been disguised as and carried out under the banner of Islam. I must rise against those who violate my thoughts, feelings, body, and sexuality, be they real or imagined. I must rise against the recycled, contemporary, Orientalist romanticism that produces new images of "Muslim women" and represents the inferiority of the "other." I must rise against the historically inherited representations and images of Islam, which view culture and religion as static, and "Muslim women" as homogeneous. I must rise against representations of "Muslim women" that are linked to imageries and occurrences of violence, religious observances, and oppression, but rarely to women's professional lives, achievements, or resistance. I must rise to (re)claim what I have been borne into and, in the process of reclamation, I am (re)defining what it means to be a Muslim woman.

I realize that on the road to (re)defining our faith and identities, we will encounter many obstacles (perhaps some encouragements), and this quote from Audre Lorde will hopefully continue to inspire us as we struggle:

> Those of us who stand outside the circle of this society's definition of acceptable women; those of us who have been forged in the crucibles of difference—those of us who are poor, who are lesbians, who are Black, who are older [I'll add Muslim women] know that survival is not an academic skill. It is learning how to stand alone, unpopular and sometimes reviled, and how to make common cause with those others identified as outside the structures in order to define and seek a world in which we can all flourish. It is learning how to take our differences and make them strengths.[35]

Our resistance has made us different from our society's definition of acceptable women. By daring to remember, write, and question, we stand alone, unpopular and sometimes reviled by those who wish to keep us in the bondage of silence and oppression. By building solidarity through our different experiences, we are charting a struggle that turns differences into strengths. By challenging our communities to turn inward for answers and solutions, we hopefully will be able to define and seek a world in which we can all flourish. You asked in the very beginning, Maddy, "What brings us to this (white) page where we will turn oral talk into (black) written word, to be documented, processed, consumed, judged, and concluded?" What brought me to this (white) page is precisely that Muslim women are usually denied agency and ownership of the self; we have to be represented instead of representing ourselves; others must speak for us instead of us speaking for ourselves; we are asexual creatures, and even when we are perceived to be sexual, our sexualities are subject to others' desires. You also asked: "What is my hope in writing this?" My hope is that we continue to struggle, so we can live our lives for what they are worth and not merely survive them.

Azza—Los Angeles
October 5, 2004, 1:30 AM

Dear Azza and Maddy,
Why, I have wondered, has the Allah of my imagination always been so

fierce? So policelike? What stories have I been told, and how do I carry them? Can I, need I, extract the remnants of these pieces of stories that sit under my skin? And what do I do with these stories that continue to surface? I grew up in resistance to the Islam that was taught to me. I declared myself a nonbeliever and refused for years to wear the Allah pendant that my mother gave me around my neck. I fought the version of Islam I was surrounded by every step of the way; questioned why we need to read the Qur'an in Arabic; why we must pray even when we do not know the meanings of the words we recite; why we must not eat or drink during Ramadan even as we engaged in the most vicious, un-Islamic activity of backbiting; or why it is un-Islamic to wear a long skirt, whereas no one questioned the most see-through and skintight *kameezes* we wore; why dancing with cousins or learning to sing was "un-Islamic." Lately I am realizing how my much of my identity has been defined "in opposition to," and to be honest, I am beginning to feel a bit tired of constantly warring against. Isn't there some law of physics that says "bodies in motion stay in motion"? Well, Azza and Maddy, I am tired of being always "in motion against." When resistance becomes your norm, when it turns into a permanent way of being, where is the space to envision, to re-imagine, re-create?

Azza, I know that sometimes you feel frustrated when some random story kicks me off into one of my passionate outbursts, and I begin to spew out all kinds of criticisms of Islam in front of others, in front of non-Muslims, in front of academics and fellow students in our classrooms. I know it frustrates you when I throw these comments around callously. I know I should be more cautious. Sometimes after I have spoken, I too feel their pitiful gazes on me, and I feel naked, vulnerable, and protective of our Faith. I know that at times my anger confirms the images already etched into their minds—images of wounded Muslim women, struggling to recover from the brutal scars that our "barbaric" religion has left on our bodies, juxtaposed against their self-images of liberated womanhood. But, Azza, there *needs* to be space for our experiences to emerge, to be heard, and to be healed. Naming has allowed me to begin (re)building my relationship with Allah, and with Islam. I do not wish to hang on to anger. I do not wish to have my relationship with Islam be ridden with images of burning hair and flesh, with fear and guilt and shame written all through my body. *Logon kee baaten* and disciplinary stories dipped in Islam should not be the mediators between my female Muslim body and my Creator. I wish to be in my body lovingly, while simultaneously being in a loving relationship with Islam. I cannot, must not remain locked in opposition to hegemonic discourses. *The terms of this relationship have not been written by me. I wish to release myself from the clutches of these wars.*

Another lingering thought . . . For the first time in my life, I hear myself referring to myself as a Pakistani Muslim woman. Is it the context of Islamophobia that feeds my desire to connect with the *ummah?* Is it the imperialistic wars against Muslims that propel me to (re)create my own relationship with a religion I have personally been warring with? Could it be that false sense of unity that happens to communities under attack? Sometimes, I wonder.

Khanum—Los Angeles

October 10, 2004, 1:36 PM

My Dearest Sister Friends,

What a whirlwind. You are right, Azza and Khanum, about charting our struggles and narratives and turning our differences into strengths. I hope this journey will be useful to others in that it lends itself as living histories. One of my hopes in sharing my experiences with other women like yourselves is to move out of victim-injustices and move toward reconciliation and building quality coexistences. On restoring my faith in Islam, I do not feel that I need to take back or (re)claim it. My experiences have unsubscribed me from the desire or feeling of needing to belong and be accepted. I live/lived without it in many ways and it was/is during these times that I "expanded" and became more fully human—something I am not ashamed of. This is the location and space that I met you both in. *We are not separate from theory, and theory is not separate from us.* Some of us are locked in or out by *chance,* some by *choice,* others are on the fringes and marginalized (sometimes even violently persecuted), all of us in the *context*—wanting authority/control, justice, liberation, freedom, safety, and peace in our lives.

Another hope I have: That Arabs and Muslims who live/work in America, who find themselves under scrutiny and targeted by U.S. hegemony, institutions, and agencies, attempt to place their struggles and solutions in what the social historian Howard Zinn describes as the people's history of the United States. To not just simply identify with what is happening to their communities but to locate themselves in the larger ongoing historical oppression and scapegoating of others in the United States (i.e., to understand the historical injustice of the U.S. prison industrial complex now that they are in it). One can connect the dots and see how we indirectly and directly are oppressed and oppress others. Many people say America is the land of the free, where democracy reigns all over the nation.[36] I get headaches when I hear this—how people can be disconnected from the histories and lands of those dispossessed and annexed before us, the terrors, injustices, genocides, slaveries, and exploitations of peoples (including the poor of all backgrounds), and the ongoing manifested issues that stem from them in our current time. The complexity of American democracy is evident; UN world conferences on racism are places where on the one hand high-level American government officials did not participate or contribute (refused, actually), yet "other" Americans, in record numbers, did. I know to change things one must take a stand, get involved, be collective, create spaces, educate others and ourselves, participate in activism—taking risks and being vulnerable. But one must start from the conflicts, challenges, struggles, and victories from within. This is more powerful then electoral institutionalism, for it is invested in everyday peoples and can create widespread understandings that lead to critical reflection, action/change, and improvements. It is going to be a long battle, and I hope people find the strength to keep moving in transformative directions within their struggles and not "*living dead*" ones.

All my best and love to you both.

Maddy—Chicago

October 15, 2004, 1:26 AM

Identity

Hend Al-Mansour

merha lal dupatta

sarah abid husain

torn pieces of my *dupatta*[1]
are bound to
sufi shrines
my secrets are whispered
into every single
thread
i tie them securely
between a thousand patient prayers
so many colors
like butterflies
FREE
to flutter
in the wind.

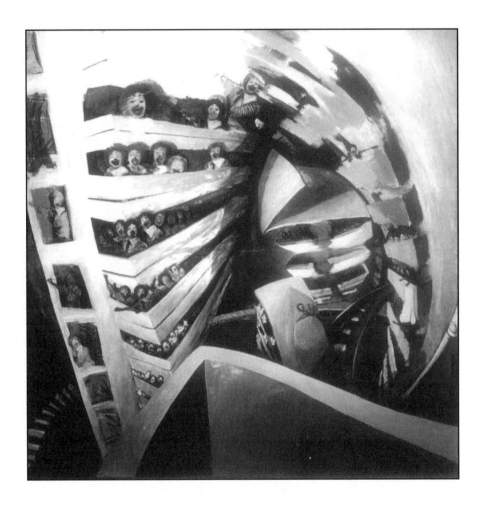

The Takeover

Asma Shikoh

Political Islam, Saudi Arabia, and the Five Pillars of Faith

Aisha Sattar

Declaration: We bear witness that there is no God but capitalism and that Bush is the last prophet.

Prayer: We pray five times daily, facing the Pentagon, the New House of Worship, built by Lockheed Martin and Boeing, dedicated to the worship of the one and only one God, capitalism.

Charity: This is incumbent on all, depending on collective guilt. We must provide food with bombs, camps to refugees (survival not guaranteed), irrespective of recipient's economic beliefs.

Fasting: For one month, from dawn to dusk, to recognize the plight of those less fortunate, we will engage in war with rogue states—no money shall pass the mouths of schools and hospitals.

Hajj: To invoke mercy and forgiveness for our socialist ways, we shall make pilgrimage to U.S. soil, funded by oil money, and observe a ritual of peace, which will henceforth be absolved upon return to native soil.

The Politics of Hajj

Aisha Sattar

My relationship with Islam has the motions of a boomerang—the circumstances of my life fling me far from the actual practice of Islam, yet I will always come whirling back to it and engage with it, each time delving a bit deeper. This motion is reflected in the verses of the Qur'an. Allah flings our attention to natural phenomena, as if pointing a divine finger and declaring "There is the proof of my existence—burning in the sun, coursing in your veins, rustling in tree leaves, drumming on your skin as the rain falls . . ." Nowhere is this more powerfully asserted than in the rituals of Hajj. The rituals, too, are reflective of natural phenomena and serve as a reminder of divine order. Circling the Ka'aba, I was reminded of planets orbiting the sun, electrons whirling around atoms, kept in place by an unseen force. I was delighted to find this movement on both grand and minute scales, with my own movement fitting somewhere in between. For a moment I felt the pulse of the universe, and then the realization that I was surrounded by two million people trying to be in the same place at the same time, violating the laws of physics, came crashing through my meditation and gave me a giant, global slap.

Perhaps it is my experience as a woman in a patriarchal world that has made me sensitive to the presence of contradictions. Perhaps it is my education at UC Berkeley that has drilled in my head the mantra of "race, class, and gender," so that no experience can be reflected on without these lenses. Despite efforts to submerge myself in the verses of the Qur'an or in the motions of prayer as I sat in the Ka'aba, I could not help but face the fact that my experience of Hajj was deeply gendered and affected by my class status.

Not observing purdah in the United States, my mother and I joked that our biggest jihad during Hajj had been keeping our hair covered properly. I had been warned beforehand of the self-appointed "purity" police, men and women who shout *"haram"* when a lock of your hair is accidentally seen. I was in no way prepared, however, for the selective use of *"haram."* While the purity police were quick to remind us that we were displeasing Allah and threatening the sanctity of the *masjid* by flashing our hair, they were silent on the obscene presence of malls and McDonald's lingering outside the gates of the Ka'aba. It became evident that it was much easier to subdue and control individual women than to struggle with the Goliath of globalization and commercialization.

Writing these thoughts, I am aware that I am walking a fine line between political criticism and blasphemy. In this essay, I am not questioning Hajj rather I am criticizing the Saudi government's management of Hajj. I explore how Hajj today is tied in with Saudi Arabia's political economy and larger global trends, and how the government's myopic focus on technical improvements, rather than on the spiritual dimensions of Hajj, undermines the beauty and power of the pilgrimage.

A feeling that permeates the whole journey is a sense of implosion, as if the corners of the earth had folded in on themselves. People of every ethnicity, race, and linguistic and national background converge in Mecca, united by purpose and faith. Trailing them are colorful and diverse histories mingling, overlapping, and resonating together in chorus. Every war you've ever read about in the newspaper, every headline detailing an event in some corner of the world, someone in this city has lived through it and could probably talk to you at length, if only you had the time and space to do it. Spanning five days, the Hajj rites are reflective of the nomadic lifestyles early Muslims lived. Moving en masse from city to city, two and a half million Muslims honor Islamic figures and perform religious rites at sites of historical significance each year.

In a sense, Hajj is a process of globalization that has been occurring for over fourteen centuries as diverse members of the global Muslim community, or *ummah*, congregate to share a spiritual and cultural experience. By drawing people from all regions of the world, Hajj creates the conditions for a vibrant exchange of ideas and material goods. Many pilgrims take the opportunity to sell items brought from home to fund part of their journey. In the past, people sold goods to raise funds for the journey back home and ended up trading styles and techniques in various arts and crafts, such as weaving, pottery, and calligraphy. A hajji from the Kashmir Valley, for example, could barter a rug for a wood carving by a hajji from West Africa. These items, carried back home, would then be admired, studied, copied, and modified by artisans, leading to a crosscultural exchange of art forms and designs.

Similarly, pilgrims engaged in intellectual dialogue and swapped religious, scientific, and literary texts. With Arabic as a common language for pilgrims,

Mecca and Medina served as educational centers for Islamic thinkers and scholars who came for Hajj and ended up staying to study with some of the most brilliant teachers and mentors in the world. Pilgrims had the opportunity for intellectual and spiritual growth as they came in direct contact with others from as far as South Asia and Africa. They shared, challenged, and developed ideas, opinions and theories.

In the past, the process of globalization in Hajj facilitated a healthy exchange of goods and ideas while creating a sacred space in which pilgrims could renounce the material world, if only temporarily. Today, capitalistic forces impinge on this space, evident not only in the extreme polarization of wealth and poverty, but also in the values that pilgrims bring with them, which influence how they perform the rituals. For example, I got the feeling that for many hajjis, going through the rituals was similar to checking off a to-do list. It was more important to get through and finish the rituals rather than to reflect on their deeper meanings and on the contexts that gave rise to them. It is this notion of doing as much as one can in the least amount of time, or productivity, that gives rise to disastrous events such as the annual stampedes.

It is these same forces that enable privilege, as defined by nationality, gender, and class status, to cut across the sacred and re-create hierarchies, ultimately overriding our common purpose. Those of us with American or British passports have access to the best housing, transportation, and food. My hotel in Mecca, a luxurious five star booked by my travel company, was a five-minute walk from the Ka'aba. In the campgrounds at Mina, the travel company provided gourmet meals three times a day in our large air-conditioned tents, which were covered with Persian carpets. I wasn't even used to this high standard of living at home! I felt more like an extravagant tourist rather than a humble pilgrim, especially when I stepped outside and witnessed thousands of people camping on the pebble-strewn streets without any tents or a stable source of food. People, many of them disabled and destitute, with young children, would spend the entire day on their prayer rugs, which were, in many cases, their sole possession. Back in our tents, food servers tossed approximately seven thousand meals a night in the garbage, while people scoured the streets for leftovers and scraps.

While I felt extremely grateful for having such a comfortable experience, I was also distressed because Persian rugs, unlimited cups of chai, and chicken *biryani* seemed like wasteful additions that served to reinforce our class status rather than cleanse us of the material world. My Muslim American identity, which put me in a precarious state in post-9/11 America, gave me a position of material power and privilege in Muslim countries, despite my gender. But my Muslim American identity also served to isolate me because the Saudi government, to ensure adequate living space for all hajjis, creates separate camps for each country or region. American and British citizens were in one camp, Pakistanis and Indians in another, and so on. While this was done for convenience, it also limited crosscultural exchange to places of worship, and the only people I was able to talk with were other women from the United States and the United Kingdom. Lacking was a sense of the global *ummah*, because even in the mosques people stayed locked within the groups they were camping with. My most meaningful exchanges occurred, surprisingly, in the bathrooms. Waiting in line, I talked to women from all over, everywhere from Trinidad and South Africa to Indonesia and the Phillippines. They were keen to strike up conversations, and the five minutes or so that we talked involved warm, lighthearted exchanges discussing the pilgrimage and our lives back home. Reluctant to go back to my tent after all the prayers had been read at night, I longed for a place where I could meet and talk with local and international pilgrims, reflect on Hajj and Islam, listen to lectures and readings by sheikhs and scholars, and discuss politics and events affecting Muslims worldwide. I wanted to share with others my brief but intense interaction with a refugee from Kashmir that I had met in the hills of Mount Uhud, where two women, Nusaybah and Umm Sulaym, had fought in a battle along with seventy men against those attempting to quell the growth of Islam.

On the second day of Hajj, standing in the Uhud hills listening to our sheikh relating various Islamic military victories and battles, my attention wandered to a Kashmiri woman standing close by. By this time I had seen thousands of war survivors from troubled countries such as Afghanistan, Somalia, and Sudan seeking temporary asylum in Saudi Arabia. She stood out because she was wearing a laminated card around her neck that gave her biographic details in English, much like a driver's license. I read on the card that she was from the Badgam district in Kashmir. Perhaps she wore this to facilitate interactions like the one I was having with her. Communicating with my broken Urdu, I understood that she had somehow escaped the conflict in Kashmir and was now living on the streets in Mecca, barely surviving on donations from the hajjis.

As she told me about her horrific experience in the conflict, I could hear the sheikh proudly relating a glorious battle tale in the background, but her story of loss and terror conveyed emotions and gendered insights of war missing from his. Due to my undergraduate research on women's agency in the Kashmir conflict, I was aware that war impacted women in an unequivocal manner, since they were the most disempowered members of Kashmiri society. The woman from Badgam had lost her entire family, which also meant that she had lost her only source of income—her husband. In addition, various militant groups had politicized Islam to gain power and had introduced militant and misogynistic practices. I wondered how she had managed to leave Kashmir, how long she had been in Saudi Arabia, and if she had come alone. Besides being Muslim, the only things I shared in common with the Kashmiri woman were that globalization had made it possible for us to be there at that moment and that patriarchal systems prevented us from practicing our religion and living our lives as we wished.

Malcolm X, upon reaching the Jeddah airport, was amazed to find that racist attitudes so prevalent in America had no bearing in the Muslim consciousness during Hajj. He encountered Arabs who would be considered white in America due to their light complexions, and they treated him with the utmost respect. More importantly, they admired and supported his struggle against racism at home. His Hajj experience and encounters with "white" Arabs were so powerful and positive that they changed his whole perception of the "white man." He began to realize that the term "white" as used in America was more than just the color of one's skin; it primarily referred to a whole set of racist attitudes and practices toward black people and non-whites. In Saudi Arabia, however, his interactions with men with white complexions were permeated with a sense of brotherhood.[1] Permeating his entire experience was a sense of brotherhood. And it was just that—a *brother*hood. He observed that he rarely saw women in public spaces. He said, "In Arabia, you could easily think there were no females."[2] It is this sense of invisibility, and by extension inferiority—in terms of politics, culture, and legislation—that permeated my experience and prevented me from feeling the spiritual elation that Malcolm X felt.

I was also surprised at the airport terminal in Jeddah when pilgrim guides referred to all of us, regardless of sex, as "hajjis." Having a minor obsession with words, I was delighted that there was no separation between the sexes rhetorically, and a part of me hoped that this pointed to a deeper equality. Yet, when it came to equality between the sexes, titles were as far as it went. Accessibility to the Prophet's mausoleum was limited to two hours in the morning on Tuesdays for women. Sometimes, through word of mouth, we heard that the mausoleum would be open for women for two hours on a random afternoon. Women would start the wait in the morning, and when the doors finally opened in the afternoon, there was a mad rush to the mausoleum, all pushing each other out of the way for a mere opportunity to lean up against the fence surrounding the mausoleum. While women make up approximately half of the hajjis, they do not have equal access to places of worship.

This limited accessibility sends out a sexist message: Women's presence at Hajj and their time are not as important or valuable as men's. Sexist attitudes also influence the degree of mobility women have during Hajj. In order to perform some of the rites and to move about from place to place during Hajj they need to be accompanied by a *mehram*, your husband if you are married, or a man you cannot marry, like your brother, if you are single. This practice provided protection to women in the early years of Islam when the journey took several months to complete, and they were at risk for being kidnapped, raped, or robbed by bandits or men in their party. Today it is archaic, since most women can travel long distances quite safely in short spans of time. I remember feeling exhausted at one point and sitting down next to a man that was not my *mehram* on the bus that would take us to the tents at Mina. A woman across from me protested, and I had to switch seats with my father for the twenty-minute trip. It was not moving to another seat that I minded, but the woman's narrow and rigid interpretation of the *mehram* concept.

Not only do such simplistic interpretations facilitate the institutionalization of inequality, they also give men a false sense of power, which they are quick to exert on women's bodies. The dress code takes on an inflated significance and becomes a means to control women's behavior. Nowhere in the Qur'an is it written that every single strand of a woman's hair must be covered. Lingering at a store counter outside the Prophet's *masjid* looking for scarves, I felt a hand push on my shoulder and a voice mumble something angrily to me in a language I didn't understand. I turned around and saw a man smoking a cigarette and pointing to my head to indicate that strands of my hair had escaped from my scarf. As he shook his head in contempt and repeated *"haram,"* clouds of secondhand smoke blew into my face. Only understanding the word *"haram,"*

I began to think about alcohol, premarital sex, gambling . . . things that could potentially have negative consequences in the long run. I balanced the effects of seeing a woman's hair against inhaling someone's secondhand smoke, and using my Islamic right of judgment, or *ijtehad,* decided that cigarette smoke was clearly the more evil of the two. In response, I mimicked the motion of smoking a cigarette and said *"haram"* a couple times to get my point across. He looked at me in confusion, and before he could register anger, I took the opportunity to walk away and disappear in the crowd.

As I walked back to the Grand Masjid, I started to think about my Hajj experience. The times when I had felt most present and at peace were in the valley of Mina, where we camped in large tents for three days. During these three days of the pilgrimage, the Prophet used to walk from tent to tent meeting hajjis and spreading the message of Islam by reciting various verses from the Qur'an. It was also during these days that the other women and I would lie out on blankets, undo our *hijabs,* share meals, and chat about our everyday lives. In an impromptu *halakah*, we would sit in circles, read, and discuss books on Islam, the sayings of the Prophet, and our Hajj experiences. Many of us had made a pact with ourselves before coming, that we would not focus on the sexism we knew we would encounter and instead concentrate on worship and our inner jihad. We had vowed not to talk about the imposed dress code or our limited accessibility, since friends and family members had warned us of these factors beforehand. We were guests in Saudi Arabia, and we had vowed to respect Saudi rules and ways of life for the time we were there. Yet, we were to discover, these ways of life were the very things that prevented us from meaningful worship.

Many women I spoke with felt disappointed about their accessibility to the Ka'aba. We had envisioned circling around the Ka'aba peacefully, contemplating Allah and existence, inspired by the devotion of the millions of pilgrims around us. Few of us had expected to be manhandled and pushed around by fervent men fighting for a chance to get closer to the Ka'aba. Pushing out whoever was in their path, regardless of their age or health condition. This equal-opportunity roughing was not only disrespectful, as men grabbed me wherever they pleased in an effort to get past me, but also disrupted worship. The circling, or *tawaaf,* began to feel more like a riot rather than a sacred ritual, forcing me to leave without finishing my *tawaaf* through the main gate, the King Abdul Aziz gate. I decided to complete the ritual later, at a more calm time.

Whenever I have experienced similar feelings of disappointment, generated by the gap between the actual practice of Islam and its guiding principles, I have always turned to the Qur'an. The Qur'an in Arabic, perfectly preserved in its original form due to the time and resources invested by the Saudi kingdom, is a considerable achievement. Some widely read English translations, in comparison, diminish the beauty and wisdom of the Qur'anic Arabic into crude propaganda against women and other religions. In my last-minute packing for Hajj, I had forgotten to slip a copy of the Qur'an in my carry-on. Sitting in the Grand Masjid, I wanted to use the time to read the Qur'an in Arabic and English. The two translations I've found to be most enriching and beautiful are the complete Yusuf Ali translations and the translation of select verses by Thomas Cleary. I went around to various bookstores in search of a good translation. I didn't expect to find the Thomas Cleary translation, and the Yusuf Ali encompassed several heavy volumes. So I bought the only English one I could find.

Flipping through the pages, I was dismayed to find that the translator had taken the liberty to put in his own biases. He had translated the text word for word, and then in parentheses he would "clarify" the verses. A typical verse would go something like this:

Prophet! Strive hard,
Against the Unbelievers
And the Hypocrites (Christians and Jews)
And be firm against them (Refrain from contact).

Having read the Yusuf Ali translation, a translation accepted and revered worldwide, I had never come across a passage that declared all Christians and Jews to be unfavorable and not worthy of interaction. The verses I had read expressed tolerance and acceptance toward people of the Book.

The verses on women were equally hateful. I felt hurt and outraged that the primary text upon which my beliefs rest, when translated, had been turned into a tool to spread anti-Christian, anti-Jewish, and anti-woman propoganda. I wondered, who were the imams and sheikhs responsible for these translations? What were their agendas, and what were their political allegiances? What kinds of relationships did they have with the women in their lives? Why was the role of women in Islamic history consistently downplayed? Why wasn't there a biography of the wives of the Prophet, who played a crucial role in the growth of Islam? Were there any translations by Muslim women? Most of the translations I had read provided a crude translation at best, because the translators failed to acknowledge the multiple levels of meaning in the Prophet's revelations. Hajj, after all, is a glorious show of multiplicity and design; it seems to highlight diversity. Due to the economy of the Arabic language, the passages of the Qur'an appear brief and simple, until one draws out the multiple meanings of each word. Upon close reading, it becomes evident that the informed reader can deduce many different interpretations from one passage, depending on how one translates each word. This flexibility and depth is the cornerstone of Islam; it provides the critical thought and guidance that can lead to a spiritually based activism against the structures of Western imperialism, not the shot-in-the-dark approach practiced by some fundamentalist clerics against certain Western customs.

For me Hajj didn't end when I left the borders of Saudi Arabia. The journey has continued, as I am still processing and reflecting on the place of Islam in my everyday life. While Hajj officials must be commended for making massive technical improvements, they fail to ensure that the Hajj is equally meaningful and accessible to men and women. Instead of promoting equality as stated in Islam, they perpetuate sexist attitudes. As airport officials at Jeddah stamped my passport for exit, they gave me a "gift for the female pilgrim" encased in a pink package. Inside was a guide for women on how to live the proper Islamic lifestyle. Rather than outlining our rights within Islam and discussing models created by strong and bold women like the wives of the Prophet, this "guide" informed me on how to live according to the whims of overbearing men. A passage on sexual relations advised that whenever a man wants to have intercourse with his wife, she must submit, regardless of how she feels at the time. An "authentic hadith," or saying of the Prophet, quoted to support this view gave the example that even if a woman is busy riding a camel at the time that her husband wants her, she must satisfy him. Perhaps this is an actual hadith, but missing is the context within which the Prophet uttered those words.

Written in a panicky tone, the booklet is more a diatribe against Westernization than a guide. Rather than focusing on economic imperialism by Western countries, the author focuses on the "evil ways" of individual Western women and warns against mimicking their behavior. The author advises Muslim women not to pluck their eyebrows or cut their hair short, as this is what Western women do and is therefore evil. He finds justification for this in the aesthetic sensibilities of one man, the Prophet Mohammed, who preferred his wives to have long hair, or so some Islamic historians believe. By obsessing over the female body, these various forms of sexist propaganda not only circumscribe the scope of femininity, they also divert attention from critical problems in the practice of Islam, and its troubled relationship with the United States and other economic powers.

Anxious about the possibility of the U.S. invasion of Iraq during Hajj this year, I felt that my physical appearance at this time was the least of my concerns. While the purpose of the journey is spiritual, Hajj is inevitably tied in with global politics. Malcolm X realized the immense possibilities present in Hajj for making important political connections and fostering new, radical thinking based in spirituality. He recollected that during Hajj, and the time spent in Africa, he never missed an opportunity to speak the truth about the indignities black men in America faced on a day-to-day basis.[3] It was in Hajj that Malcolm X formed the conviction that he had to connect his struggle against racism at home with the anticolonial struggles of African peoples around the globe.

Only with this kind of unity could African Americans and Africans in Africa dismantle the imperial white power structure. In Ghana, and in other African countries he visited after Hajj, he made this point quite powerfully. He recognized the positive impact that the twenty-two million African Americans living in the United States could have on African politics. In turn, African nations could exert diplomatic power to combat racism in America. According to X, ultimately Africans had to unite with African Americans because racist regimes around the globe, such as South Africa, depended on support from the United States. For him it meant, "Until you expose the man in Washington, D.C., you haven't accomplished anything."[4] Malcolm X was speaking of Pan-Africanism. Leaning against a cool marble column of the Grand Mosque, mesmerized by the circular, rainbow movement of millions of hajjis, I envisioned a global alliance based on a Muslim identity that would be political, cultural, and spiritual.

Already having to deal with complications caused by health, travel, and overcrowding, the Saudi government attempts to keep Hajj apolitical, and therefore calmer, by banning pilgrims from carrying or distributing political materials. This is a reaction to Iranian pilgrims who attempted to politicize

Hajj with demonstrations and dissemination of political materials. In a demonstration that evolved into a riot several years ago, around four hundred persons were killed. Pilgrims today are warned in a public statement that "some of the Muslims who come to perform the pilgrimage carry, with good intention as we believe, booklets, photographs, and pamphlets that are for political, propaganda, or ideological purposes in a way that contradicts the noble goals of the Pilgrimage. The Ministry of the Interior would like to draw attention to the fact that carrying such things is absolutely prohibited and make it clear that violators of the regulations will be severely punished and deported."[5]

Ironically, the Saudi government does not follow its own regulations, because it uses the Hajj to promote its own particular brand of sexual politics. The temptation to use Hajj as a political forum is enormous: There is not only an audience of two million, but also people are watching on televisions around the world. Back in my hotel room, I watched the Bush administration on BBC casually ignore the United Nations and resistance worldwide in its zeal to bomb Iraq and secure oil interests. Seeing millions pour through the wide esplanades of the Grand Mosque, it was clear that Hajj had created the conditions for possibly the largest and most powerful protest against the war in the Muslim world. This rare show of global unity could serve as an intimidating check on U.S. power and a possible catalyst to stop the war before it started. Another motivation to protest was that if a war with Iraq did start during Hajj, this could incite major riots in Mecca and Medina and lead to the deaths of hundreds of thousands of people.

My Hajj might not have been the meditative journey I was expecting, but it was a spiritual catalyst. Having encountered sexist propaganda and attitudes, I am motivated to learn more about Islam and the Middle East, to read the Hadith, reread the translations available, and reach my own conclusions. Hajj has embedded in me the notion that a political life guided by the principles of Islam can lead to radical thinking, action, and transformation, as it did with Malcolm X. More than anything, Hajj has made me want to live and practice the Islam of Khadija, a strong-minded woman who married the Prophet, saw his truth, and became the first convert of Islam.

Magnetism

Leila Montour

i.
Driving down Federal
once more,
passing that sign

Mecca Tavern
A seedy brick building
at the crossroads of a highway
and my thoughts.

ii.
Flip through a dictionary:
1. A place that is regarded as the
center of an activity
or interest.
2. A city in Saudi Arabia
near the coast of the Red Sea.
The holiest city of Islam
and a pilgrimage site for
all devout believers of the faith.
Population: 689,010.

iii.
Instructions:
Pass, turning left or around
or right.
Headlights glare
and surround a maypole.

Make pilgrimage
to this box, to answer that
pull,
to home in on that object
of distillation.

Wait through the hours
in dry heat on a plain,
pelt a solidified pillar
with stones, and call it
Shaytan.
And cheeks pressed
to concrete,
complete the ritual of slaughter.

Pull into driveways,
or run to a hill.
Return seven times.
And drink this liquid
with no knowledge of
sweet springs.

iv.
Feel the magnetic center
calling them back to
a sign.

JIHAD

Aiesha "Ansaro Bah" Balde

"Marry women of your choice, two or three, or four . . ."
Surah An-Nisaa 4:3

The pain is raw, gaping wide
A missing limb, almost.
A woman's jihad. Be patient.
Be constant. Have faith.
To love for another as
You have yourself.
There it is. Here it is.
Hide the pain, the mask on.
Alhamdullilah. A mujahideen,
Soldier of Allah . . . evoking strength.
The cause first, the personal last.
My sister to you I give.
For me, a jeweled wound,
To gape at and wonder . . .

Double Edge of Scimitar

Saba Razvi

Trim your beard
a little bit shorter this time,
haaji, so your wife doesn't
smell the other woman,
still young enough to
water like a peach,
still innocent enough to think
your attentions
will lead her ascent to heavens
beyond your *hafiz* flesh.
And don't forget to shower
before you step
onto the newly swept floor,
past the table laid out
with your wife's delicate
touch spread banquet-wide
and festive
because she knows it
isn't her you're gracing these nights,
you quick as the binding needle,
swift as the unbinding knife,
her unstitched
warmth too familiar and still
not tight enough to hold
away the clenching of a fist.
Remember, she'll lie
still as a floorboard, for you,
all the dusty creaks you expect,
but, no, don't
stay long or she will notice

other splinters, hardened
in your tauter muscles.
Better to leave her
unrewarded, contemplating her errors,
the barren hollow inside the waist,
how much more compliant she should be.

MYWESTERNFREEDOM

Amitis Motevalli

Haram! Haram! Haram!

Anida Yoeu Esguerra

for Abidah Ali

She is known by many names across many continents, but we simply knew her as Mey. My grandmother—the great spoiler of American assimilation—the premier customer of *halal* meats—the champion of daily prayers—the keeper of the ways of the properly performed *wudu*—the reciter of random stories and even more random Qur'anic passages. She *is* the circle of elders—a circle of One. She is the supreme storyteller of terrifying parables about the apocalyptic Day of Judgment—the ultimate converter of the curious infidels—the defender of premarital virginity—the advocate of the *hijab*—the preserver of long sleeves and even longer hemlines—the barber of firstborn babies. She is the gatekeeper of wholesome traditional values for Muslim families stuck in a hedonist consumer culture.

My grandmother was indeed no ordinary immigrant woman. She was the grand mama of us all! Mey was the matriarch who choked our childhood into a dichotomy of *haram* or *halal*, the forbidden and the permissible. Allah never sent a messenger more frightening and disciplined than my grandmother, a stout Thai woman who stood at four foot eleven with silver-streaked hair. She was an aging woman with a noticeably short torso and breasts sunken down to her waist. Grandma was plump with stories, while her grandchildren were ripe with fears. She would always scare us into being "better" Muslims. Grandma convinced me at ten years old that if I didn't eat all the rice on my plate, each uneaten white grain would rise on the Day of Judgment to testify against me. Their testimonies, numbering in the thousands, would send me straight to hell, and even my own mother wouldn't be able to save me. After all, it was *haram* to throw away food.

No one ever wanted to disappoint Mey. None of us ever wanted to do anything wrong according to her Shariah. Every summer we learned to read the Qur'an. She taught us Arabic and threatened us with hellfire if we did anything sinful. One hour a day for five days a week, sometimes longer if we didn't get the lesson exactly right. And if we did, she wasn't afraid to hit us—either with her knuckles or with the long metal part of a fly swatter. Mey wanted us to learn our lessons, both in Arabic and in life. According to grandma, life was very simple. Things, people, places, actions were either *haram* or *halal!*

She'd tell us, "Pork—*haram!* Shorts, miniskirts, sleeveless shirts, tight jeans—all *haram!* Hair dye—*haram!* Perms—very *haram!* [But henna was okay because it was natural.] Swimsuits—*haram!* Two-piece bikinis—super *haram!*" Grandma expected us to be fully clothed in loose, lint-attracting fabrics at public pools and beaches. She believed there was nothing shameful in going to the beach on a sweaty summer day fully clothed. After all, the other half-naked Americans were all *haram!* If we didn't pray—*haram!* Watching too much TV—*haram!* Dancing—*haram!* MTV—*haram!* Cyndi Lauper—*haram!* Madonna—very *haram!* Rock and roll music—the gateway to *haram*-ness! Smoking—*haram!* Drugs—*haram!* Boys—*haram!* Dating boys—*haram!* Kissing boys—*haram!* Sex before marriage—*haram!* Kinky sex even when married—*haram! HARAM! HARAM! HARAM!*

We felt suffocated. We couldn't do anything growing up. Having fun seemed like it would be *haram!* Mey drew her lines between the *haram* and the *halal* very sternly and clearly. For example, beef hot dogs sold by Muslim butchers— *halal!* A McDonald's garden salad without the bacon bits—also *halal!* Good pious Muslim VIRGIN girls who pray five times a day, who marry good Muslim VIRGIN boys who have memorized the entire Qur'an—VERY *HALAL!*

shimul blossom

Sarwat Rumi

i am not
a shimul blossom transplanted
here   coerced to struggle to thrive
in this   dry   winterland.

tropical wetlands color the blood
that runs through these veins   deep red
under brown rivermud skin

but the rains of north america
make long bengali hair brittle
suck the vital glow from her surface
so that the bright hues of her
saris and *salwaar kameez*
seem lurid in the gray light of this world.

always displaced.
here i am Other
                foreign.
there i am Other
                bideshi.
always displaced.

one foot in this land
the other in another
an ocean stretched between.
six yards of brown red yellow silk
expand taut as strained tendons
reaching to connect
the bindi shining on my motherland's horizon

to the cold sunsets of this waitingplace
locked in winter twilight.

i am more than bridge
more than six yards of brown silkskin
stretched tighter than a drum.
i was meant for more than this
slow   ripping   apart.

Shades of a Barbed Wire

Sarah Husain

You are lying on your bed for over ten years,
now. Praying by gestures, by signs, by your
eyes, internally, by the rhythm of your voice
disconnected from your bones and its movements.
> *(Stiffening joints only harden convictions,*
> *it seems, the more disjointed they get the stronger a faith becomes.)*

I can picture you. Shutting your eyes tight
when you heard, she's married a Hindu!
And in the next room a TV running loud
sounds off another war.   Tight.

This time on the west side of the border
more bombs have rained than water
the scorched earth hides from the sun
beneath the only shade—the barbed wire,
separating one more side from
the other.

She's married a Hindu!
Continents away. You don't want to hear.
You shut tight. Your eyes. Your ears.
As you lie on your bed. Feeling helpless.
Believing. Could this really be
your punishment? Married a Hindu!
You turn your face the other way. Away
from a world in which you live. Lie. Half.
Plunged in. Dreaming of another half,
some promise away, for over ten years, now.
Every muscle stiff. Joints tight against joints
unable to move.

A beggar outside tired of asking with pennies
in hand. Takes his shadow and turns a corner,
and the sun burns another day.

You lying there on a straw bed.   Eyes. Tight.
Shut.   Would rather not hear. The war. The fight.
For what? And him?

War Stories

Jawahara K. Saidullah

War has been a constant backdrop in my life. My mother was nine years old when Rangoon was bombed by Japan during World War II. She and her family fled to India on the last boat that left the harbor without being bombed. I knew her stories by heart, and I asked her to tell them to me over and over again.

I had nightmares. I never told her about them because I didn't want the stories to stop. In my dreams, I would see the laughing faces of pilots as they dove over crowds, spraying them with bullets, so close they could see their victims fall. I could see the outer shells of buildings peeled away, insides exposed, like dollhouses. People dead in the street, limbs blown apart, blood, sadness, and desperation scattered in the dust.

Safe in my cocooned life, trapped in the immediacy of a child's tunnel vision, I told myself that wars were in the past. Then I learned otherwise. I told myself that wars happened in places far away. But living as I did in India, with the periodic escalations of conflict between my country and Pakistan, belied that assumption too.

How do I define war? How do I redefine it? Is that even possible? For years war has been the fear that follows my mother, even into her later years. Fear that blossoms like daisy cutters in my dreams. It is being violently uprooted from long-held anchors like home, family, city, nation, and comfort. It is the understanding that places that were havens can become killing grounds, in an instant. Wars don't even have to be fought between countries. They are fought within them, between people who live side by side. They can be fought between strangers or between brothers. Wars unleash machines of destruction from afar like mega video games. You can look straight into the eyes of your killer, and he can feel the warmth of your blood on his hands before you die. War has to be felt and experienced. And it still might never make sense. Living in a culture and in a time where war is part of the constant narrative, it is no wonder that its stories haunt me, though I am lucky enough never to have experienced it firsthand.

COLD WAR

I grew up during the Cold War, in India, when the world was divided into two blocs, the faraway, enigmatic, capitalistic United States and our comrades in the nearby U.S.S.R. On the personal front as well, I lived my life in the uneasy truce of a no-man's-land; in the inside world and the outside one. In the inside world, I was a Muslim. On the outside, I was a member of a young, secular country.

I kept my first *roza* at nine and finished reading the Qur'an when I was thirteen, even though I did not understand a single word of Arabic. We celebrated Eid and Bakr-Eid; I wore *ghararas* at weddings, greeted people with *as salaam alaykum,* and attended *milad-un-nabis.* Those are the definitions I think of when I think of my life as a Muslim.

My family was proud to be termed progressive. No woman in my family had worn the burqa in over two generations. My mother had a bachelor's degree in math at a time when most women did not finish high school. She had studied in a Christian school and traveled the world. We did not pray every day, except during Ramzan and for the two major festivals. My family believed in and talked about the precious secularism of India and was proud of its participation in the struggle for Indian independence.

Still, something made me hide my Qur'an lessons from my friends at the convent where I studied. I reveled in my less-than-usual first name because it was not typically Muslim. I was flattered when someone would say, "Really? You're a Muslim. You don't look Muslim." I did not stop to think what a Muslim looked like. I was just glad I did not look like one. Without being taught, I learned that being Muslim was my dirty little secret.

I hid my family's taboos. Despite our non-Muslim friends, my parents' dabbling in the trendy transcendental meditation movement, the Buddha that sat in the drawing room (a direct violation of the Islamic prohibition of statues), there were some cardinal rules. In some ways we lived a schizophrenic existence, the Muslim self in the larger non-Muslim world. The media, history books, even overheard conversations made me aware that being a Muslim was not something to be proud of, nothing to flaunt. At home I lived comfortably, not having to think of the two parts of my identity, my dual role. Until I started growing up.

Though I might have friends of other religions, I was told there could be no marriage between us. Even though I could not understand Arabic, the old *maulvi sahib* came to teach me to read the Qur'an, and my parents made the necessity of this very clear. While a Muslim man could legally marry an *ahl-ay-kitab,* or person of the book (Christians and Jews), a Muslim woman had to marry a Muslim. Neither Muslim men nor women could marry a Hindu, the predominant people around us. This was the one unpardonable offense, marrying a polytheist. That was the one thing, my mother warned, that could make my parents disown me.

My mother told me the story of someone she knew in Allahabad. An only daughter adored by her father, this young woman fell in love with and married a Hindu classmate. Her family disowned her. Some years later, when her father died, he left instructions that she not be allowed to look upon his dead body. She was not allowed into the house. So, she sat at the roadside, outside her childhood home, sobbing, unable to see her father one last time. This was told to me as a great example of principles. Even love—the love of a parent for a child—fails when confronted with what is wrong. The wrong of a Muslim woman marrying a Hindu man.

So, while I played with Holi colors, said the Lord's Prayer in school, wore skirts and jeans, and called myself a secular, enlightened Muslim, I lived within these constraints. I fervently prayed to Allah that he not let me fall in love with a Hindu boy. My faith was strong then. I had not yet started to question it, and I would pray often. I ruthlessly killed my crushes and tried to become a good Muslim girl. I was a good Muslim girl. This was my own no-man's-land. I navigated its battlefields, still ignorant that I was already a foot soldier in a war.

THE FIRST VOLLEY

Cold wars have a tendency to unfreeze. There were times I came face to face with my Muslim identity and the war in which I was engaged. I could not look away.

Even behind the walls of St. Mary's Convent, tucked away from the rest of Allahabad, some things penetrated. An assembly in the middle of the day was always the herald of breaking news. There are riots in town, we were informed. We had to go home. Parents were calling, and there was already a line of cars, scooters, and motorcycles gunning their engines outside the high gates. I went home with my father, driving through the eerily deserted streets of my usually bustling town.

While the city labored under curfew, our lives in the mixed part of town were largely uneventful. However, I had a persistent nightmare culled from stories I read in the newspaper and tales that filtered in from places in the old city.

I am standing in our little study. From behind the frosted doors, I see a strange red-gold glow. I am cold in my cotton nightie, and I want my father to stay away from the front door because I've heard they kill the men first. The bell rings, and I am compelled to answer.

With torches blazing, the men standing before me are covered in blood. One of them waves a bloody scythe toward me as he asks, "What's your name?"

"Jawahara."

"Father's name. Father's name. Quick. Quick."

"Said . . . ullah," I say, and I feel hot pee slide down my leg. Their laughter is deafening, and I feel a deep cold settle within me.

The scythe arcs toward me, and I wake up. I had become aware of my Muslim fears and had imbibed the lesson that I deserve what I get. I was suspect, a violent terrorist, even in my own eyes. This is what the outside world told me.

Later I learned of a family friend, a Muslim, newly married, whose father was a sitting judge of the high court at the time. His scooter was stopped by a group of rioters and police. They asked him his name. He gave it, but before he could say anything else, they beat him up badly. A couple of the policemen hit his breastbone repeatedly with their rifle butts. His breastbone was fractured, his ribs shattered. Luckily, he did not die, though he was left to do just that in one of the gutters.

As the curfew lifted, other stories filtered in. A young Hindu man was hacked to pieces and thrown inside an open manhole in a Muslim area. Burning Muslim hutments illuminated the sky in reds and golds for miles around. The riots ran their course over the next week or so. I added the stories of this war within me. I still do. I simultaneously felt fear and guilt.

I felt different, somehow, when I returned to school. The teachers, my parents, the newspapers all said the right things.

Politicians manipulating people.

We've lived in harmony for so long.

These are not people from our well-meshed community where Hindus and Muslims have lived for generations.

No one acknowledged that slowly a movement was being born that would come to fruition in the late '80s and early '90s. Centuries of unresolved issues, pushed under the surface, real and imagined hurts, were emerging from the depths, propelled by rage and vengeance.

I grew up during the Doordarshan TV days in India. For every major religious holiday and especially during riots, there were the endlessly repeated skits on communal harmony. Muslims and Hindus visiting each other, smiling, laughing, eating *siwai* on Eid, bursting crackers on Diwali, everyone dancing the *bhangra* for Holi. We are all brothers and sisters, they informed me.

But even brothers and sisters have issues with each other, I said silently. *Even they get angry and vengeful.* I kept my thoughts to myself.

To me, these skits were like desperate surgeons performing cosmetic surgery on a structure whose skeleton was decaying. Hindus, Muslims, and others in India have real grievances and hatreds against each other; they have prejudices. Yet, instead of having open debates and frank conversations in a safe environment, we, all of us, lived in a constructed *siwai*-eating, cracker-bursting, *bhangra* world where we had always gotten along and should continue to do so.

Violence, unfortunately, is the volcano that erupts when the pressure of aligning reality with unrealistic images collide at regular intervals. Tamping down on these issues, ignoring them, just makes the hatred fester and explode into violence sooner or later.

My ambivalence about my own identity became even more crystallized during this time. I was a Muslim. A cow-eating, bloodthirsty, backward, hated Muslim. No one had to spell it out to me. I know that my friend, Soma, whose lunch I shared, and who licked the one ice cream bar we shared, was different, very different from me. I knew she was different. An idol worshipper, someone less evolved than me, a monotheist, because she needed a physical statue to pray to her god. Krishna was a promiscuous playboy. Shiva was a drug addict. These were her gods. Hindus drank cow piss and sprinkled it in their kitchens. I didn't stop to examine if any of this made sense, if any of it was just ignorant, simplistic wordplay, a collection of negative stereotypes. What had clearly swung into focus was that we were different. Very different. Yet both of us living in a time and place where differences were not to be talked about. So we pushed them deep down, internalizing our thoughts. We truly became part of a society that told us that acknowledging our prejudices was harmful and pretending we were all the same was the thing to do. Life settled down and the cold war resumed.

SECOND VOLLEY

In 1992 I visited Allahabad from where I studied in Kentucky. I was buying a brownish gold nail polish—Tips 'n' Toes—from Pandora's Box, one of the most popular cosmetics and knick-knack shops in the Civil Lines shopping area.

Some kind of electricity pulsed through the whole Civil Lines. *Clack, clack, clack!* Shutters crashed down. The shopkeeper told me to come back later. Then he hesitated and told me not to go home, just yet. To wait with him, the other worker, and with two young girls who had been looking at some cosmetics. The shopkeeper's name was Khalid, a young bearded man with a crocheted cap. He ran Pandora's Box. He knew I was Muslim since my family and I had shopped there for years. We had just never seen each other as anything more than shopkeeper and customer.

"*Babari masjid*," he mouthed silently to me. I was stunned, though not surprised. *Kar sevaks*, here in Allahabad, in Civil Lines! We weren't sure what to do. All I knew was that we were two Muslims, subtly acknowledging our identity to each other, each with the same fear. Despite our differences, we bonded because of this identity.

A roaring wave could be heard from afar. Khalid dropped the shutters, leaving just enough room at the bottom so that he could lift it up from the inside when it was safe to do so. He switched off the lights to make the store look deserted. All of us huddled together in the darkness, trying not to draw attention to ourselves. We peered through the gap between the shutters and the ground, and through a small window on one side. I had never felt more alone. What would I really say if they confronted me and asked my name? In my jeans and light pink lipstick I did not fit the stereotypical mold of a Muslim. Would I be able to lie? Or would some misguided sense of bravery prevail?

It was a sea of saffron. The kar sevaks, fresh and invigorated from the enthusiasm of the successful demolition of the mosque in Ayodhya, had come to town, swaggering with the euphoria of their success. I berated myself. Why the heck did I have to come out today?

They converged around the Ganga statue that sits in the big turnaround in the middle of the Civil Lines. Water flowed in a steady stream from the pot Ganga holds at her waist. It flowed and splashed against the full skirt of her *ghagra*, stone pleats frozen in an invisible wind.

They were young, these men, with their saffron headbands and *kurtas*, triangular flags held aloft. They were drunk with victory, ecstatically maniacal, and I shook with fear as I contemplated what would happen if we were discovered.

A cold blanket, icy on a hot day, was draped over me, and I tried to focus on making my breathing silent, on making my body shrink into the rough-textured wall against which I crouched.

The leader spoke in pure, Sanskritic Hindi. I don't remember what he said, but after smashing up the one shop that had been too slow in closing up, they moved on. A too-calm hush descended as the rest of us made our way home.

These things happened in the old city, in Chowk and Atala and Himmatganj. Not in genteel Civil Lines, where we lived, the mixed, cosmopolitan part of town. But there they were, *kar sevaks* marching through my turf as I watched in silence and fear. It was a defining moment, this ecotone, this clashing of worlds, and it was a permanent change. The war was at my doorstep.

FINAL VOLLEY

When I was twenty-seven, I decided to marry my boyfriend. I had struggled against falling in love with him, but I had failed. Throughout our relationship, I was aware of one thing: He is a Hindu. Well, at least, he was born one, though he had officially renounced his religion in court, as a teenager at the height of the Ratha Yatra fever. Whatever he was, it did not change the fact that I was Muslim. And I knew I was in for the battle of my life.

Despite the fact that I lived in Lexington, Kentucky, away from the wars being fought in India, I came up against the enemy within: My own family. The same family that had been proud and accepting of my lone travels in the Himalayas, my backpacking trips, my outspoken nature. My father wrote that I was dead to him. Me, his favorite, the youngest, the one who had rarely been punished. My mother tried to blackmail me, telling me it would kill my father, reminding me of his bad heart. I remembered the woman in Allahabad who was not able to attend her father's funeral.

I was told my marriage would not be legal in the eyes of Allah. Perhaps I should talk to my fiancé about converting to Islam. That would make it all right, would save the day. I stood my ground. If he respected me enough not to ask me to convert, how could I insult his beliefs, his background, and ask him to convert? Just to marry me.

There was another enemy. Myself. Even though I remained adamant, I had doubts. Was I strong enough to withstand this family pressure? Would I really be able to walk away from them, if it came to that? Perhaps to never see them again? To never be a part of the messiness that defines my relationships with them. Maybe I had been given too much freedom? Was I really sinning? Living with a man, in an unsanctioned marriage? Everything I had been taught about Islam came back to haunt me. Yet, some force propelled me. Perhaps it was mere stubbornness. Maybe it was something else, something more.

I got married. My mother was in the same town but did not attend the simple, legal ceremony. I was married in the eyes of the law. I was a fornicator according to the laws of Islam.

A decade later, I remain a part of my family. After two years of not talking to me, even my father came around. Four years ago, he hosted a party—a belated wedding reception—at our home in Allahabad. A cease-fire.

SURRENDER

What is my identity? I am a lapsed Indian Muslim who feels no obligatory love for an amorphous *ummah*. To tell the truth, a large gathering of Muslims, or any religious group, scares me more than anything else. I cannot relate to them, to their unquestioning faith, their beliefs, their practices, their single-minded devotion. A part of me is envious of anyone who has faith to fall back on. For I have none left. I have been at war with some of the core teachings of Islam. I am against most of its laws. What was revolutionary fourteen hundred years ago is severely archaic today. Islam and Muslims need to change.

I may no longer be a religious Muslim, though I describe myself as an ethno-cultural and social Indian Muslim. I relate to Muslim art and culture, to Urdu poetry and writing and etiquette. Being Muslim, for me, at this stage of my life, is not necessarily tied to Islam. It is a state of confusion, but I am comfortable in it for now. I can call myself whatever I want. It will never change the fact that I am a Muslim. And that we are in the middle of a war, a real war.

This current American war machine, chewing up resources, truth, money, and people, terrifies me. I am angry that there is a war that my tax dollars are paying for. A war that is killing Muslims.

Goosebumps rise when I hear stories from Afghanistan and the death toll from Iraq. I am enraged at the complacency of the people of the United States who are so naive as to allow themselves to be willfully misled and not even care that they had been lied to. Do they care that thousands of people are dying in their name, paid for by their tax dollars? Are the dead in Iraq really human to them?

I ask myself if I would feel any different if Iraq and Afghanistan were not Muslim countries. Perhaps if they weren't, they would not have been attacked? I may not pray to Allah anymore, but I can still relate to what it feels like to be a Muslim in this polarized world. I know what it feels like to feel guilty for no reason, no fault of my own. I cannot imagine what it feels like to have your country invaded, your family decimated, your life ravaged.

Do I feel this as a Muslim? Or just as a human being? I am not sure I will ever know the answer to this question.

Is this current war a clash of civilizations? A war of cultures and religions? Is this really the new crusade? What is my role in it? I can understand why fundamentalism is growing. When you are under attack and your place in the world is threatened, fundamentalism and violence are unfortunately the only things left.

War is what lives within me. On one side I am Indian, American, female. On the other I am a lapsed Muslim, but a Muslim nevertheless. That is an immutable fact I cannot escape even if I wanted to. War remains the constant backdrop of my life. I try to navigate past virtual minefields and feel simultaneously lucky and guilty that I am not the target of real bombs and night raids. I live with the fact that I live in a country that inspires fear and hatred among my fellow Muslims around the world.

At the end of it all, death and destruction are the lasting legacies of war. And nothing is left but painful memories and stories.

Train Dyptich, Gujrat/New York

Maryum Saifee

This image was created in the aftermath of the communal carnage in
Gujrat. I chose a photograph of a train in Gujrat in particular to symbolize
the Godhra train incident that sparked widespread anit-Muslim riots.
The U.S. train is meant to symbolize the flow of funding to Hindu
fundamentalist groups carrying out the violence by non-resident
Indians, including those residing in the United States.
—Maryum Saifee

Holy Land

Saba Razvi

Inside every field of sunflowers, one
can find a field of suns—and so
every
soldier fights for something noble.
But
in each free movement by a one,
is the slavery of another. One
head held high only
because another is bowed
to give it light—a shadow anchors
every stem.
   Nothing can exist
except in absolutes.

Every east must be another's west.

The lines we carve on maps, mortal
   as skin.
Each split hemisphere will open
like a sliced sun.
One half falling,
held half dripping
down the grasping hand.
    Nothing
left to balance the scale.
     Instead,
we make fences of bone,
their gardens mark the weight of air.

Karachi, Pakistan

Aisha Sattar

Nestled cozily but tightly
between China and Iran,
I can hardly turn my head east or west—
wearing blinders and earplugs
seeing straight ahead a silent
seething ocean, holding monsoons
in its right hand, tidal waves in its left.

I turn inside myself, fingering
mango trees, picking caries—
sour and green.
I smooth down dark soil, braiding
cotton seeds in rows. Pouring
wet thick rain, moistening dry patches.

I trim myself down, clipping off
Bangladesh, all with blinders,
now cracking, so those dark orange
and purple rays of the Iranian sun
creep in and crouch on my irises.
All with earplugs, now wearing away,
so those faint strains of Chinese
mandolin tiptoe in and tremble
on my eardrums.

Mother says it's been too long
and enrolls me into the world.

Welcome to Peshawar

Maliha Masood

Peshawar is perhaps one of the few cities in Pakistan that can make even a Pakistani feel like a foreigner. To most liberal urbanites, the mere mention of the city immediately conjures images of people speaking Pashto in male-dominated public spheres, a conservative society bordering on the ultrareligious, and traditional tribal values enslaving women. Definitely no place for an uninitiated female to be traveling on her own, more so if she is unfamiliar with Pashto, the local language, and newly arrived in the country after twenty-one years.

I was issued strict warnings in Islamabad about the perils of going to Peshawar alone. Just two weeks ago, the ruling MMA coalition and its bearded mullahs had scored victory by passing the Shariat bill, calling for rigorous, allegedly Islamic standards imposed on society. While a few enraged youths were tearing down billboards advertising women and their adornments (while ignoring similar images of men), these were mostly isolated cases that were heavily exaggerated by both the local and foreign press as standard practice. A pervading sense of fear and mistrust had tainted the North-West Frontier province into an even wilder and more lawless place, made even worse by the recent Islamist victory.

"You are only asking for trouble if you go there at this time," asserted my friend Nasir with his typical know-it-all attitude.

"How do you know?" I retorted. "You can't just form sweeping impressions about a place and its people by reading news stories in *DAWN* and watching BBC World. When was the last time you were in Peshawar?" I scoffed rhetorically, knowing he hadn't recently stepped foot in the city about which he claimed to know so much.

It was easy to be discouraged when it came to traveling alone in Pakistan as a woman. Though the country had developed an extensive network of buses and public transport to get around to virtually any town on the map, it was a system reserved primarily for men. Female travelers required a male companion for "protection"; going without an appropriate chaperone was considered virtually impossible, an assumption I found extremely difficult to swallow. The fact that I was neither a complete foreigner nor 100 percent local made matters more complicated. I couldn't get away with breaching cultural protocols against solo travel that don't seem to apply to the odd Western tourist, who is not supposed to know anything about such things, nor did I want to be bound by those same protocols and lose my cherished independence. It was interesting to gauge local reaction to my seemingly abnormal desire to travel. The prevailing attitude was, "Sorry, but this is Pakistan; you cannot wander around alone here. It simply isn't done." Then there were those who regarded me as an "eccentric," encouraging me to be one with the common folks by relying on public transport and, of course, riding on top of buses for the best views.

I was sorely disappointed. For the first time in my life, I gave up and resigned myself to forgo the spirit of adventure and discovery integral to my travels—at least in Pakistan. But the more I suppressed the urge to set myself loose on the road, the more it grated my nerves, until I was seething in anger for surrendering so easily. It made no sense that because of public opinion I could be deprived of the right to see my native country just because of my gender. They seemed to have forgotten that danger is not something that screams to you from afar. It occurred to me that one of the reasons for the country's stagnation is the overwhelming need to steer to the status quo, no matter how outdated and ridiculous. Thinking in black and white is, after all, a national obsession. No wonder most people didn't know how to respond to a Pakistani-born, American-raised liberal with a vaguely foreign face, intent on discovering the "real" Pakistan on her own. I was a walking contradiction for all practical purposes, but I no longer cared.

It would be fun to challenge stereotypes and widen perceptions long lurking under the guise of "cultural norms." If this society chose to cling to narrow-minded, discriminatory attitudes, that was their problem, not mine. I knew that as long as I exercised common sense, dressed appropriately, and held on to my faith, I would be fine. My old self-confidence rushed back. It impelled me to follow my heart and find out for myself what it was really like to travel alone in Pakistan as a woman, even to places deemed "dangerous." No doubt, I was about to take a calculated risk, but one that had occupied a force of its own. The call of the open road was blaring like a foghorn.

Much to my surprise, women in Peshawar were not covered from head to toe, or even wearing the face veil, or *niqab,* as I had commonly seen in Islamabad. They simply wore lightweight, pastel-colored chadors or draped a large *dupatta* around their heads and upper bodies. I had definitely gone overboard, donning a tight maroon headscarf and a heavy beige shawl on a sweltering forty-five-degree Celsius day. My thin cotton *shalwar kameez* was drenched in sweat, and I had to wear my extra-large shawl toga-style to avoid tripping over its ends.

Despite the cumbersome layers of clothing, the maddening heat, and the complete foreignness of my surroundings, a surge of excitement coursed through my veins as I started wandering by myself in the old city, camera hidden under the voluminous folds of my garments. Not once did I encounter any problems with the local men. In fact they got quite a kick out of seeing a lonesome girl madly clicking away at ancient, decaying buildings and rickety doors.

It was back. That familiar sense of adventure had definitely resurfaced with vengeance after all that suppression in the seemingly modern capital, and I literally skipped my way through the narrow alleys of *kisakahani* or the old storytellers' bazaar of Peshawar. It being Sunday, most of the shops were closed, and my presence was all the more conspicuous. However, the attention I received was mere curiosity, not hostility, and the most refreshing aspect of it was the way people handled their natural inquisitiveness about seeing a stranger in their midst.

They would simply come up to me and ask who I was and where I came from. The camera was a dead giveaway of my tourist status. But instead of driving a wedge, it helped to break the ice, and before I knew it, a small boy led me by the hand to show me around the neighborhood. He instantly picked up on my fondness for rotting old houses and took me to some real gems. Nowadays, they serve as tiny ateliers for tailors, bookbinders, and weavers, or crammed with a family of ten in one room. Clearly the utility principle was more important than preserving the intricate wooden carvings, fading arabesque paintings, and imagined opulence of what once was.

"Now I show you Dilip Kumar's house," announced my guide, referring to the famous Indian actor who at one time had lived in Peshawar's old *havelis*. I trotted behind, enjoying the simple friendliness so easily encountered just by virtue of being out and about. Where were the dangers, the harassment that so-called "knowledgeable" folks had warned me about? What was most interesting was the subtle acknowledgment I received from men wherever I strolled by; whether it was a courteous nod or a warm *salam*. This was quite unlike my experience in Islamabad, where men at best simply pretend that women do not exist or at worst leer like hungry wolves as if they have never seen the female species before.

In Peshawar, I was treated more as a person first, someone who had just as much right to occupy public space and was graciously welcomed on top of it all. Every time I passed shopkeepers sitting inside half-shuttered shops, eating lunch or sharing a cup of tea with friends, they would turn their heads and look toward me with interest, slightly puzzled at my hard-to-place looks. Not once did I ever feel degraded or humiliated simply because I was a woman walking in the old bazaar. In fact, I often detected a hint of admiration and even a gleam of adventure in the male eyes that scanned my every move and gesture.

Eight hours of exploring the old city unscathed and unharmed proved to me that the Peshawaris were more human, civilized, and liberal than the stuffy urbanites of Islamabad, Lahore, and Karachi. I knew then that I had scored a small victory by turning upside down the stereotypically backward profile of Peshawar that the so-called progressive denizens both inside and outside Pakistan would find hard to believe. But this was only the first of richer ironies to come in the Frontier land.

JinnahtoSanders

Asma Shikoh

Sari Blouse

Salimah Valiani

Sari blouse
Some 40 years old
Each time
I wear you
I wear you out
Your sparkling bits
Chipping-off
With moves of my body
Leaving
Glue marks like rust
On glass-nylon[1]

I can't remember
How many times
You were worn
Back then
It was
Before I was born
But in those times
There was Pride
Gleaming through
Your transparent sleeves
Dignity
Like the bow
Clasping the point
Of your V-back
And the accomplished originality
Of placing
Bit by bit
Sparkling specks

In shapes of bows
On front and back
Bringing out the life
Of a black sari
Worn out of a requirement
Of love

And yet
That black glass-nylon sari
Was not quite
In line
With the chilling black burkha[2]
Required
By the Ishnashari[3] clan
Of an Ishnashari lover
Of an Ismaili[4] lover.
Still
It worked
It was accepted
And that was because of pride
Pride in being one's self
And that was the accomplishment
Of my path-breaking Aunt
Killed so young
Driving her car
Between Jinja and Kampala
43 years ago.
Your black glass sari
And glimmering blouse
I wear them
Like as if I knew you
Wear them out
Like as if you had lived.

Infinite and Everywhere! My Kaleidoscopic Identity

Mansha Parven Mirza

All I know is Love,
             And I find my heart Infinite
                              And Everywhere!
—*Hafiz, Sufi poet*

I like the idea of our hearts and minds being infinite and open to encompassing, absorbing, and reflecting our world in all its multiplicity. In fact I'm tempted to be venturous and extend Hafiz's verse on infinity and all its implications to the concept of identity. At this point, I'm reminded of an apocryphal story I came across about Vedantic Scholar Adi Shankaracharya.[1] Hearing a knock at his door one day, Shankara asked, "Who's there?" When his visitor replied, "It is I," Shankara is supposed to have retorted, "If this 'I' is so dear to you, then expand it to infinity, or else get rid of it altogether!"

Hmmm . . . a Vedantic scholar and a fourteenth-century Sufi poet cited in close juxtaposition; I must be South Asian, or somewhere thereof. At the risk of playing into stereotypes, I would say yes, I am South Asian . . . that and more, much more. Which is precisely why the idea of the "I" being laden with boundless possibilities appeals to me so much. My personal affinity for a conceptualization of identity that has an inherently amorphous and elastic trajectory stems from the syncretism that has defined my life so far.

I was born to a Muslim father and a Hindu mother in Bombay, a metropolis that is ample testimony of the breathtaking multiplicity of my country of birth. My father was born and raised in Lucknow, India, while my mother's family migrated (read: fled) to India from what is now Pakistan. I feel it important to include that last bit of information to my birth history, to underscore how national boundaries drawn on religious grounds are often rendered futile in preventing the mixings and crossings of cultures. However, delving too much into nationcentric politics would be digressing from the point I'm trying to make here—that multicultural and multireligious affiliations have been an inceptional part of my identity.

My mother embraced Islam after marriage but never gave up Hinduism. She would pray five times a day and fast during the month of Ramadan, and she even performed the Hajj with my father while at the same time celebrating the birth of Lord Krishna with her maiden family. With both my parents coming from large extended families (though my mother's family size beats my father's hands down), spending religious holidays with the whole family (on each side) was customary for us. My childhood memories are laced with marking down our calendars for Eid, Diwali, Mohurram, and Holi.[2] My fastidious father would insist on turning the entire household upside down for weeks in preparation for the Eid and Diwali festivities. My sister and I of course looked forward to both. Although it may seem trivial to adults, for children, one of the biggest plus points of being bicultural is you always get double the amount of goodies—*eidi* during Eid and *kharchi* during Diwali,[3] henna tattoos adorning our palms during Eid and fire sparklers in our hands during Diwali. Gosh, our lives rocked!

But there were tough choices to make, too. Every few years, Mohurram would coincide with Diwali. My sister and I always sulked when that happened. We knew that then our family would have to choose between celebrating Diwali and mourning the martyrdom of Imam Hussain (a.s.), and we knew also that our father would invariably choose the latter for the family. The sulking, however, would eventually give way to a religious ardor of a different kind as we engaged ourselves in reciting *nohas*[4] and beating our chests with fervor to mourn the hardships faced by Imam Hussain (a.s.) and his clan on the battlegrounds of Karbala thousands of years ago. Soon it would be time to foreground our Hindu identities again as we would set off with our Hindu cousins and aunts to the holy city of Hardwar along the banks of the river Ganges for our once-in-five-years soul-purifying ablution.

This is what it was like growing up in a bicultural/bireligious household. Several times in the day (and I admit, I skipped at times) I would unfold my prayer mat, position it toward Mecca, and bow down to touch with my forehead the little piece of clay with Arabic inscriptions. Then on the weekends, off I would go to the Ganesha temple with my maternal grandmother, adorning the elephant god with flowers and saffron, and getting blessings and offerings in turn from the resident priest.

Many people, particularly those of us raised in any of the Abrahamic faiths, might cringe at the mere thought of living such a dual life. The Abrahamic faiths inculcate in followers a sense of religious exclusivity that posits our respective religions as the final word on matters of ultimate truth, and one that perceives other belief paradigms as untrue and invalid. As a result, we come to think of all of mankind in terms of binaries, where one can fall either in the category of believer or nonbeliever. On the other hand, polytheistic religions like Hinduism (the one I am most familiar with) do not espouse any exclusive version of the truth and as a result are more tolerant of pluralism. And by pluralism I do not mean mere respect for cultural differences, but an appreciation of the possibility of multiple truths.

Quite understandably, therefore, many average Hindus I've met are more accepting of pluralism, while many average Muslims (including moderate ones) seem to have adopted a dichotomous way of thought whereby you can either be Muslim or the non-Muslim "Other," and never, I repeat for emphasis *never* both. Unbeknownst to myself, therefore, I was simultaneously embodying both and relishing every minute of it. And then one day, though a little prematurely, came the moment of reckoning.

While my father never tried to stop us from going to Hindu temples, he never stepped inside one himself. As a kid I never understood why. Now I know exactly why. He was a Muslim, and while he respected the non-Muslim "Other," he chose to never cross the boundary to the other side, even for a few minutes at a time. But like I said, he never imposed that choice on us until . . .

One day my maternal grandmother gifted me a tiny *puja* set—an assortment of Hindu worship items—complete with a little steel lamp and a tiny clay Ganesha[5] idol. Periodically I would take out the *puja* set from my toy basket, arrange all the tiny bowls and the lamp on a plate, and pretend to go through the whole gamut of adorning the idol with saffron and flowers, just like I'd watched my maternal grandmother do so many times. My father ambled in on one of my pretend-play ceremonies and asked me to wrap up and get rid of my precious set. I protested. "It's either the *puja* set or the Quran, you'll have to decide," he said. At eight years old, I was too young to decide. I was also fickle; moving on to another pretend game seemed more reasonable than bickering with my father. I promptly put away my *puja* set and never played with it again.

Little did I realize that at several points in my life, I would be presented with the choice between adhering to the Muslim way of life and pursuing other interests like taking *kathak*[6] dancing lessons, for instance, like it was impossible to pursue both. It was always my decision and not one that was imposed on me, but nonetheless I had to choose. I chose to go without the dancing lessons. Besides, graduate school was beckoning, and there was so much more to do (I guess fickle-mindedness persists well beyond age eight).

There were other things happening, too, around this time that made me consciously reflect on my Muslim identity for the first time. Every time I found myself in a predominantly Muslim setting (for example, being around our Muslim family and friends or attending a religious sermon), I felt like I was being judged. I felt like I was being tested for my degree of "Muslimness," if there ever was such a word, and unfortunately for me, I always failed the test. I also knew why I always failed the test: It was because of my Hindu blood. Nobody said it in so many words, but I could sense that. If I didn't dress in Islamic attire, I wasn't Muslim enough, and that was probably because of my mother's influence. If my Arabic pronunciations weren't correct, it was my mother's influence again (by the way, Arabic is neither my mother nor my father tongue). If I did not know enough about Islam, it was because my mother was born a *kafir*[7] (notwithstanding the fact that every time I read the Quran, it was in a language I did not understand). If I questioned my Arabic tutor (who taught me only to read Arabic and never to decipher it myself) about Quranic teachings that relegated women and other religious minorities to a secondary status, I was turning into a *kafir* myself. If I took a stance against the destruction of the Bamiyan Buddhas by so-called Muslims, I was defecting to my mother's idol-worshipping side. In retrospect, I think these happenings had been occurring insidiously all my life; it's just that as an eighteen-year-old, I couldn't suppress the feelings they invoked in my mind anymore.

To say that I felt unwelcome in the Muslim community would be too simplistic a description of what I was experiencing. It was as though my acceptance within the Muslim community were contingent on my relinquishing of another community that was so close to my heart. My Hindu culture wasn't the only thing I was expected to relinquish to be a "true" Muslim. I was also expected to give up being the critically thinking woman that I was aspiring to be. To be able to stake claim to a Muslim identity, I had to first stop asking questions about Islam's potential fallibility on certain issues. . . . I had to stop "thinking" about the faith whose "faithful" elite I wanted to gain acceptance with—sounds paradoxical, doesn't it? But that's the way it was, and I became very disillusioned with Islam and my Muslim community. This brings me to the most turbulent part of my story—my gradual drifting away from Islam.

It was September of 2002 when I left Bombay to pursue graduate studies in the United States. This was a year after the September 11 attacks in New York, and international perceptions of Islam and Muslims had changed for the worse. Unlike many Muslims, who were embittered that their religion had been "hijacked" by extremists, I felt more than embittered. In a strange way, I felt guilty and responsible for what had happened, and most of this guilt was my own and not induced by popular media or non-Muslim reactions. Perhaps I shouldn't have stopped asking the critical questions about Islam that I used to. Perhaps if we had all been asking critical questions of our faith and its various interpretations, we wouldn't have reached a stage where we were witnessing Islam being reduced from what should have been a dynamic, evolving, religion to a static object, vulnerable to narrow-minded interpretation by a handful of zealots. I don't mean to say we were all responsible for what happened. What I'm saying is that we didn't do much to stop it from happening, either. Like the non-Muslim world, we too turned our backs and closed our eyes to what many of us agree is a contemptuous use of religion to justify questionable ends. Like everyone else, we too alienated the "hijackers" and let them get on with their mission without questioning or engaging in dialogue, education, and perhaps even reform.

While on the one hand, I wanted to immerse myself in religious reform, on the other hand, I wanted to steer clear. I started to fear that the global Muslim community was becoming dominated by views that defined how to be a Muslim in very narrow and extreme terms. And within such a community, I started to fear there would be very little room for people like me, the "me" who embodied both the Muslim and the non-Muslim "Other."

Being thousands of miles away from my own Muslim community back home, I now had to find and forge ties with a similar diasporic community in the United States. I never took the initiative. For reasons unfathomable to myself, I started downplaying my identity as a Muslim woman. Not only did I stay away from Muslim communities and other young Muslim students on campus, I also became cautious about revealing my religious identity, unless it became absolutely necessary to do so. Having been christened with a first name that's hard to associate with a particular religious group, I let people think what they wanted. Most people presumed that I was Indian and therefore Hindu. The numerous Ganesha idols that adorned the walls of my apartment only corroborated that idea. My prayer mat, of course, was stashed away into the deeper recesses of my bedside bureau. I still rolled it out every day but never in front of visitors. When anyone offered me food or drink during Ramadan, I made up one silly excuse after another. I mourned the martyrdom of Imam Hussain (a.s.) and his clan alone within the confines of my bedroom. It was a well-kept secret all right, but for how long?

It wasn't long before I realized that what I was trying to pull off was a phenomenon labeled "trying to pass" or "passing." I was pursuing a doctoral degree in disability studies, and through some of the literature I was exposed to during the course of my studies, I learned about the practice of "passing." "Passing" refers to the phenomenon in which people with disabilities attempt to hide/downplay their impairments to pass off as able-bodied.[8] I too was trying to pass; the only difference was that while people with disabilities "try to pass" because of societal pressure to conform to the "normal," I, on the other hand, was doing so because of both lack of societal acceptance for who I was and my own intrinsic uncertainty about who I wanted to be. Did I want to be Muslim, or did I want to be the non-Muslim "Other"? It had to be one or the other, remember, no matter how badly I wanted to be both.

To complicate matters, I soon met and fell in love with a Christian man (like I did not have enough religious diversity in my life already!). Being religious more in spirit than in community himself, he saw through my "passing" act. Of course I initially denied ever "trying to pass" deliberately, but being the persistent man that he is, he not only got me to realize what I was doing, but he even encouraged me to question why I was doing it. In the course of our numerous conversations about faith, religion, and their metaphorical and literal interpretations, I began to recognize that sooner or later, I would need to reconcile my Muslim faith with the important life decisions I was making. In choosing to explore a relationship out of wedlock with a Non-Muslim man, I was not only exercising my personal autonomy as an adult woman but also expressing my female sexuality—both forbidden by my Muslim culture.[9] Wait a minute; did I say I was seeking to reconcile my Muslim faith with these seemingly radical decisions I was making? Was reconciliation even possible? The way I knew it, I would have to pick one over the other. Reconciliation was out of the question; or was it really?

Call it serendipity or a subconscious will of the mind; I was inspired to negotiate these difficult questions by exploring the writings of two female Muslim authors that I happened to chance upon in my quest for answers. One of these writers is Ismat Chughtai, author of several works of fiction, born in early twentieth-century India. Rather precocious for the times she lived in, Chughtai's stories were grounded within a feminist philosophy and championed the cause of gender equality and sexual liberation for women in South Asia.[10] However, I was personally drawn toward the works of Chughtai not so much for her feminist leanings but for her own pluralistic identity. Born to a Shi'a Muslim father and a Sunni Muslim mother, she followed both sects of Islam at the same time. In fact, it gets even better. She would also unabashedly visit Hindu temples and recite Sanskrit verses invoking praise for the temple idols, all this while proudly claiming the identity of a Muslim woman (albeit to the chagrin of many in her community). Lesson learned—if she could do it nearly two generations ago, I could certainly do it today.

The second author I mentioned above is more contemporary and to some extent more rebellious in her writing. Irshad Manji is a proud lesbian Muslim woman. (Wow, that these four expressions could be used in concurrence with one another was a revelation to me!) She is a writer and TV show host who talks and writes extensively about the need for critical thinking and religious reform within Islam.[11] Where Chughtai explores the contentions between Muslim culture and personal autonomy and sexual liberation for women through many of her stories, Manji takes these contentions a step further. She openly challenges Muslims all over the world to move beyond merely repeating what the Quran says by rote and to instead engage in critically analyzing Quranic teachings and what it means to be a Muslim. Like many other female religious scholars, she exhorts all Muslims to engage Quranic teachings at an intellectual level and in a way that is equally empowering and respectful to men, women, sexual minorities, and non-Muslims alike. Lesson learned—think outside the box.

The powerful works of these two writers have encouraged me to conceptualize my identity beyond a binary logic that polarizes the Muslim against the Non-Muslim "Other" and beyond stereotypical ideas that posit modernity as polemical to the Muslim way of life. I feel empowered by the thought that I can be both Muslim and Hindu, that I can embrace my Muslim culture and still be an independent and liberated woman, and that all these facets of my identity are both intermixed and compatible. In this endeavor, I'm immensely helped by the concept of liminality,[12] which suggests a third means of thought and understanding without presupposing binarism. The concept of liminality thus explains the valid existence of a multiple subjectivity; it is therefore possible to be both Hindu and Muslim at the same time, because the two are not binary opposites. Besides, examined in this way, identity is rendered not fixed but rather fluid and constituted in processes at multiple sites with endless possibilities.

> And I find my heart Infinite
> *And Everywhere!*

At last, Hafiz's words ring true. At last I feel comfortable and empowered with my identity. It isn't monolithic . . . never was. It comprises multiple strands—Indian, woman, Muslim, Hindu. Do all of these strands come together to form a unified system, or do they contribute commensurate or hierarchical portions to my identity? Neither! Rather I live these multiple strands in a chaotic simultaneity, and this chaos, as I have come to accept, now constitutes the essence of my identity. This chaos makes me what Latin American feminist writer Gloria Anzaldúa calls a "multiple subject"; it renders me the capacity to mediate between worlds and as Anzaldúa puts it, is a precondition for social transformation.[13]

My liminal identity may trouble some purists, but it is one that will not only survive but also thrive in a globalizing world characterized by cultural mixings and crossings. For those who cannot deal with the likes of me, tough luck! I'm here to stay, and this time I won't drift away.

four:

RE-CLAIMING OUR BODIES/ RE-CLAIMING OUR SEXUALITIES

Through Me the Prophet Speaks

Amitis Motevalli

And Ain't I a Muslima?

Halimah Abdullah

In image-driven American culture, the icon of the veiled, almond-eyed Muslima steeped in her own private melancholy is a persistent phantom. She haunts the pages of newspapers and magazines, the wasteland of made-for-television movies, and the screens of well-intentioned documentaries. For the Western media consumer, she is the dusky-skinned beauty with the exotic, polysyllabic name who is in desperate need of salvation. She is always Middle Eastern. She always speaks Arabic. She is eternally oppressed.

Evidence of these views is in the deluge of biopics, articles, and narratives that flooded the American market in the months after the September 11 attacks. Stories about women fleeing Sharia with babes born out of wedlock in their arms. Stories about brave teachers who expose their students to banned literary works. Stories about mothers who sacrifice their sons to "extremist" causes. Westerners hungrily sought out these tales, because they were strange and foreign and yet somehow comforting, in that they reaffirmed the perception of the pathos-filled "other." To be sure, most of these stories contain a degree of veracity that cannot and should not be denied. The sexual, intellectual, and cultural oppression of women is a global pandemic; one that seems more pervasive in some cultures than others. However, the voracious appetite for all things Muslim (and therefore mysterious) also speaks to the American zeitgeist.

Americans revel in unveiling and conquering the unknown . . . just as long as the discovery reinforces preconceived notions.

In the subsequent rush to report on that unknown, we American Muslimas writing for the mainstream media (whose cultural "otherness" was previously relegated to a blip on our publications' diversity rosters) suddenly found ourselves quite popular. *Explain yourselves to us,* our editors asked. Often what they meant was: *Tell us something new, but tell us something we already know.* As a result, opportunities to craft pieces with greater cultural depth remain lost. Instead, storytelling continues to trend toward suggesting that most Muslimas are shrouded in some mysterious, untold past: an oppressive childhood, an abusive husband, the desire to flee arcane cultural laws. These paternalistic attitudes are insidious and leave little room for deviation. Indeed, those ideas are forced on even those for whom this ready-made backstory is a fiction.

"True" Muslimas are never lesbian, African American, Latina, Chinese, enlightened converts, happy about wearing *hijab,* unhappy about wearing *hijab,* intellectually or sexually liberated, comfortable with men, raised in American ghettos, or politically active for some cause other than feminism. True Muslimas are never individuals.

Even among Muslims, the experiences of these other Muslimas are deemed invalid. Their status is less than the *hijab*-wearing, Arabic-speaking, Middle Eastern variety because of course these others do not understand "true" Islam. In many American cities, mosques are often self-segregated along racial lines. Far too often, African American and Latino Muslims worship in *masjids* in the hoods and barrios, and Middle Eastern and Southeast Asian Muslims worship in suburban enclaves. One of the saddest symbols of this perpetual undercurrent of inferiority is the African American Muslimas who attend mosques where they are in the minority but relegate themselves to the backroom roles of child caretaker during Jummah services.

We the diverse sisterhood of Muslimas must wage war against such damaging typecasting. We live a multitude of both shared and distinct experiences—each one valid and worth telling. However, if those tales are ever to be heard, both we and the mainstream media must acknowledge and insist upon a broader understanding of cultural verisimilitude.

The truth of my existence rests somewhere between my mission to help deepen my own and readers' cultural understanding of the faith of my childhood and the disapproving looks from my mother's *hijab*-clad associates. I feel ever keenly a type of double consciousness as a writer, a member of the mainstream media, a womanist, and a woman who grew up Muslim in the deep South. This position provides a unique vantage point when writing about matters of faith and culture. Yet, the very nature of writing is that of separate observer. I stand in the bittersweet doorway between the interior and the exterior, unwilling to move in either direction. I know what each room contains, and I choose both and neither.

Recently, an editor at a well-known religion publication called and asked if I was interested in a part-time position editing a section on Islamic issues. She prefaced the conversation by asking, "We know you grew up Muslim, but are you still Muslim?"

I remember thinking: *How do I explain my soul's ache whenever the* adhan's *call echoes out over my bustling Brooklyn neighborhood? How do I describe the* iftars *of my Gulf Coast childhood—meals of dates, cheeses, red velvet cake, and gumbo. Would you even understand if I told you that bits of Quranic passages work their way into my waking moments and fill me with such a longing that I almost always weep? How do I explain that though I officially left the faith ten years ago over issues of cultural gender practices, Islam has left an indelible mark on my heart and psyche.* Islam is my mother, and I am ever her child.

But I edited my own story and simply replied: "Culturally I will always consider myself a Muslim. And as a former religion reporter for *Newsday* and a woman who was raised Orthodox Muslim, I am very familiar with both the nuances of the faith and the tenets of journalism."

The editor chuckled, admitted she'd struggled with gender inequalities in how her own Christian denomination is practiced. She shared that though she edits articles on Christianity, she is not the typical Christian.

Then she asked me to help her find a Muslim to edit the section.

I must admit, I look on with no small amount of wry amusement when my white colleagues or associates in the mainstream media or associates try to unravel my family's Islamic history. I say white because people of color almost never question my identity. The barrage of questions is scripted. The queries are often an attempt to unlock the unknown, to conquer the truth about the Black girl with the funny name. "That's an Arabic name, isn't it?" "Where were you born?" "So, were you raised Muslim?" "When did your parents convert?" They listen only long enough for confirmation of the story they already know. This is usually followed by some smug revelation of racial, religious, or cultural trivia.

Translation: *See, I do know your people.*

I once attended an outdoor reggae concert with a fellow rebel Muslima and a Jewish friend of ours. As we grooved and swayed to the steel pan beats, the young man turned and asked if I knew that my ankh earrings were un-Islamic because they are idols. He made no comment about my Muslima friend's low-cut top or skintight jeans. What bothered me was not his misunderstanding of the ankh's cultural and personal significance. What bothered me was that my friend felt more comfortable educating me about "true" Islam, because as an African American woman I must clearly have a weaker understanding than our Pakistani American friend. In his defense, he later recognized the ignorance of his statement and apologized profusely. I respect his willingness to examine his own cultural bias.

Not everyone is as willing to admit such things. When my Muslima credentials are questioned, I often think about Sojourner Truth's address at the 1851 Women's Convention in Akron, Ohio. When the reality of Truth's experience was overlooked, the former slave, abolitionist, and suffragist insisted, "And ain't I a Woman?"

I am an African American woman who was raised Orthodox Muslim in Alabama's Gulf Coast. My *"as'salam alaikums"* rang out with a deep Southern drawl. As a child, I committed to memory Quranic verse, literary prose, and hip-hop lyrics and recited them all with the same joyous fervor. I've spent a lifetime trying to reconcile cultural gender discrimination practiced under the banner of Islam. I've been physically, emotionally, and sexually abused and ostracized from my family for daring to speak out against these issues. I reject the mantle of tragic victimhood. I am a survivor.

And ain't I a Muslima?

Tayyibah Taylor and Marlina Soerakoesoemah's *AZIZAH* magazine chronicles the lives of convict convert, teenage, Japanese, Puerto Rican, Sudanese, and a multihued host of other Muslimas. They celebrate each other through poetry, prose, and song. By gathering together to discuss their common faith and their varied visions.

And ain't they Muslimas?

A friend of mine is a gay spoken word artist who gathers atop New York City rooftops to pray and discuss Hadith with like-minded women.

And ain't she a Muslima?

My younger sisters read Quranic Arabic fluently—Southern accents and all. They are a popular, giggly cadre of flag girls; volleyball, basketball, and track stars; pageant contestants; and stylish sorority girls.

And ain't they Muslimas?

A few years ago, I began writing a memoir chronicling my upbringing as a member of the first generation of African Americans raised Orthodox Muslim. The draft sputtered and was clunky in places. I struggled with how to best direct the flow of storytelling, but it was as if I was trying too hard to shape the backstory. As one editor kindly put it before rejecting the work, "I wish Halimah would just tell the story the way it happened."

I've thought a lot about that comment over the years. Journalists are thick-skinned by training; however, of the hundreds of critiques I've received in my career, that comment cut the deepest. Perhaps it was because the overriding themes in my work have always dealt with telling individual truths. Perhaps it was because as an abuse survivor and a member of various groups I have always felt as if others have tried to force ready-made stories upon me. Or perhaps it was because that editor sensed that I was standing in the doorway between observer and participant. Her admonishment was a clarion call that I have since taken up and now pass on.

Tell your stories, my Muslima sisters. Tell them loud and tell them true.

Chand Raat: Eid ul Fitr

Saba Razvi

Greensweet
henna in sugar-oil and eucalyptus,
I trace
in hair-thin coils,
along my upturned paling palms.

Beneath this
bouquet of temporary futures,
twined with blossoms opening in my night,
your own
wishes—palmlined map
to the walls of the city inside my breath.
These worldly wishes in red, drying lines—
only complements.

I go tonight,
not to the bridal chamber of a man,
but to the thinnest crescent of a moon.
Hear these, my bangles, Beloved.
Here, these my knees—cracking—
on which I kneel toward
the Easterly.

I have left it behind, Beloved.

The laughter of carnival
in the distance,
a bright-lit bazaar,
shop-keepers selling sandalwood or myrrh,

rock-sugar candy,
beads on which to count Your name.

It is enough
for me—
these knuckles: an abacus under thin skin,
a carpet of green grass blades,
the nightbirds in the wind—
and in the wind,
tendrils of my hair lifting off my nape.

Light rising from resting in contours everywhere.

Iqra

Fatima Qurayshi

Your eyes, the only allowance
you offer the world, with a laugh
and say, *"So I can see it as it sees
itself!"*

Draped from head to toe,
a black shadow, without
the world's form, a woman!
With thick *kajol.*

Your purdah, Iqra,
is deeper than the red sea
through which you transplant
artillery, make love to women
no man can reap.

Rapture

Samira Abbassy

the str8 path: a coming out sequence

Tina Zaman

there is no such thing as a breakdown

only crisis long in making
await peace inside hollow body
the superficies of hers

depression does not exist
just weakness in solitude's face
ways she welcomes into escape
white open room
space

there is no such thing as your face
outside memory you are immaterial
unheard

YOU ARE ONE OF MY WARS

white. oblivious. comfortable. and blonde.
she erupts when my Brown mouth opens
i disrupt everything she thinks/ she knows
wake up woman
i won't fight all your wars

JUST LET ME TRUST

myself
my body

colored guilt makes both mother
and female lover impossible
i will not feel guilty
will not feel ugly for loving her
fucking her
this guilt is un-natural.
& the shame that never comes

but the ugliness does
coming out coming away

their str8 is supreme
natural as his lies that tear us
from our bodies

female skin, breasts, wombs
men's most useful myths

TOWARD A CLOSURE & AN OPENING

is leaving ever worth eternal exile
oneway expressway to outsider status

i'm your terrorist

Brown and angry
better fence your whitegirls in
i'm coming to claim
what's mine

erect gates to deter me
but i got bombs, millions of missiles
your white daddy bought me

i'm coming inside

MY PUSSY TASTES LIKE GINGER

to him
my breath dark cardamom

exotic unknowable unknown me
pressed beneath his ivory

her handsome face

lingers
skin of palest gold
bleeds categories like
Brown bodies leak red
whose order/ whose power
her bodily script a
contradiction-mixture
we read faces. skins
stories of difference we believe

GLIMPSING THE ORIENT IN HER EYES

i follow her with my own
to conquer the colored continent
of her body

tempo sumisse

le temps qui soumet
le moment qui ne se termine jamais
she leaves the room and i am

now, here
single Brown face among pale ten
or seven

time which resists change
which itself cannot be trans
formed
cannot submit

ignorant time.

ISLAM OF YOUR DREAMS

dark religion, dark peoples
mystical backward exotic

resisting your bloody/ white empire
eastern echoes purchased, taken

you may call it your own
islam

monolithic black stone
for worship
Brown face in your mind when
i say islam

another tool for you
to speak for me

when i say islam meditate
on your ignorance

remind yourself to step down

to be silent
when we say islam

THESE MARGINS ARE NEVER TRANQUIL

soundless suffering of daily holocausts
trained torturers/ show your bruises

jugun ianfu
we fill military brothels
are stolen dalaga

silenced screaming female bodies

SOMEONE'S SILENCED VOICE

to her own spoken words

she keeps talking
silencing

TRYING TO ESCAPE YOU
Erlinda
don't want to see you because
i am you

mother
exploited dejected
sun after moon after sun
& for my freedom
endless trek toward retirement
may never come/ despite

scores of un(der)paid years

you have worked for my freedom

thirdworldfeminist
our struggle came long before
those white women's words

daily dare of survival
destroyed by labor to unleash
your daughters

i, with my libraries
pianos in seas
dreaming toward degrees
my luxuries, not yours
my victories
that belong to the Brown
of your flesh
that breadth of suffering
that i must claim

& like ivory pillars beneath my feet
my mother's bones nourish

Circumventing Circumcisions

Salimah Valiani

Her lips were tight.
Never parting
too wide
for too many words
or too wide a kiss.
"If you are sex-y"
she said
"they can never de-sex you."
Her lips
plum-full.
But pursed.

Because of the migration
she could now
spare her daughter
the ritual.
Her daughter:
lips free
legs fast
eyes wide
speaking early
in many tongues.
But she felt
she could not
shepherd
her daughter
the way her mother had shepherded her.

The migration
was mitigating
but left her ashore.
Her longings
had become foreign.
Her life,
a stranger.
How to phonate,
to be erect
in a new place
of different constraints?

Her mother arrived
another face,
another frame,

the wars back home intensifying.
Progeny and territory.
Flesh and hunger.
Meat and potatoes.
Her mother cut,
she cooked,
her daughter consumed
persevering   resurging   retreating
the sepia-flow unsealable—

You can't bleed the life from woman.

home in one piece

chompa rahman

if you met me, and i were to tell you that i'm from bangladesh, you might show a little surprise. i don't look totally bengali and in fact have been mistaken for an ethiopian on numerous occasions. i also don't dress in traditional bengali clothing in any way, except that i'll wear the hell out of some sandals whenever the weather permits. if i were to say i'm a bengali muslim, you might be a little less surprised, since about 83 percent of bangladesh's population is composed of muslims. so if you knew where bangladesh is, you'd probably know to make that connection.

but how about if i were to say . . .

"hi, my name is chompa and i'm a bengali muslim lesbian."

surely you don't hear that often. . . ? it's not that we don't exist, as i am living proof that we do. it's just that most of us are either still in the closet or living on the down low. and i have to admit, all three of these identities combined tend to create a pretty big bang. of course, that's not all i am, but it's certainly a measurable chunk of my mental and physical makeup, and i personally embrace all three of my identities equally and happily.

i was born in bangladesh, embraced islam in my early teens, and somewhere in my midtwenties discovered my homosexuality. i'm in my early thirties now, and i've come to understand that while these three important identities bring me immense joy, they also carry with them a fair share of pain. not in an everyday life sort of way, but in that they impose certain limitations on my ability to make future plans, one of which involves moving back to bangladesh at some point . . . for a little while.

"hi, i'm chompa . . . and i'm a bengali muslim lesbian."

what if i were to rearrange the sequence? like, say "lesbian" first to get it out of the way or at least hide it somewhere in the middle? or maybe put emphasis on "muslim" by saying it before bengali? i mean, what's stopping me from making my identity a little more palatable for the masses? a little sugarcoating, a little stroking, a little . . . oh, i don't know, less shocking?

nah . . .

i definitely consider myself bengali first. there's no doubt in my mind about that. i'm a *daalpuri-*, *chotpoti-fuchka-*, *murgi'r thorkari–*, *begun bhaji–*, *aam bhortha–*, *kamranga-*, *laddu¹*-lovin' kinda girl. and i like *everything* spicy.

i don't, however, fuck with *shutki*.

but before i go on any further, allow me to clarify my position: i love my country, i love my heritage, and i love being bengali. i spent my formative teenage years in bangladesh and despite the usual growing pains, i have to say, it did this body (and mind) good. at the age of three, my family and i left bangladesh to move to maryland, so my parents could pursue their academics. after spending several years there, my parents finished what they came to do, and we all moved back home. i was nine and i truly believe that i was in the right place at the right time, because back then, in bangladesh, it was a great time to be a kid. i look back on it tenderly and have absolutely no regrets (except maybe a particular hairstyle circa 1987). i was given the opportunity to submerge myself in the culture, know my extended family, develop fantastic relationships with schoolmates, and i did it all.

it wasn't easy at first. as a nine-year-old moving back from maryland to dhaka in the early '80s, i experienced a severe case of culture shock. i mean, come on, no english-language pop radio? no kit kat chocolate bars? no video arcades to play pac-man? it was my worst nightmare, and i secretly wished that eventually i would return to the states for college, and all would be right with the world. it didn't help that i didn't speak the language very well. i mean, my parents spoke a combination of bangla and english at home, so both my sister and i learned to speak very basic broken bangla, but i really learned the language once i started school in dhaka.

i also finally got to meet all twenty-eight of my first cousins from the twelve uncles and aunts on both sides of my family, many of whom i actually like and became friends with. but who knew that my family in dhaka was so big? who knew that they would also be so anxious to meet their tomboyish, shy little cousin? i had no idea. but i definitely felt the love, and it made the culture shock a little easier to handle.

i suppose what i didn't realize until later was that moving back to dhaka would really set the stage for my blossoming as a bengali.

"amar naam chompa. ami bangali"²

if the saying is true that home is where the heart is, then i must conclude that my heart is in bangladesh. i was fortunate to be able to come to the states for college, as it wasn't easy on my parents financially. but once i was done, i got so used to my independence and carefree lifestyle that i never bothered to leave. fourteen years later, i'm still here, and i'm starting to wonder if i've been wasting precious time trying to find my life's work in a country that i struggle to call home. so, lately i've really been contemplating a move back to the homeland. back to desh. but now that i'm faced with the reality of such a decision, i sometimes wonder if i will ever really, truly, be comfortable again living in dhaka. i go home to visit every year to see my family. but will i ever be able to pack up my life and settle down there? i don't know. and really, this wasn't much of an issue before. after i finished college, i figured i'd settle down in the states for the rest of my life. it was almost a no-brainer. i didn't think i'd ever want to go back home for any extended period of time, because i was happy with the life i'd made for myself in the states and couldn't fathom giving it up. but things changed. i've changed. as i've gotten older, my priorities have changed. i've always missed my family deeply, but i realize now more than ever that their presence is not guaranteed. every time i go home to visit, i notice that my parents are getting older, and their passing is an issue that has become deeply ingrained in my conscience. i recognize more and more that my desire to spend time with them while i still can easily trumps the conveniences i've allowed myself to be spoiled by here in the states.

but the reality of my living in bangladesh is no joke. sure, monthlong vacations are standard for me, but anything more than that? it's difficult to say. admittedly, part of the beauty of these trips is that i get to come back to *my* life, *my* space, *my* private little haven in minneapolis where i can be me twenty-four hours a day. but i realize that the only real difference between having that haven in bangladesh versus the states is that living alone in the great big united states allows for quite a bit of anonymity. i'm not likely to run into a relative while standing at the bus stop smoking a cigarette, or have a friend of my dad's spot me having dinner at a romantic restaurant with another woman. i'm not worried about making sure no one's looking when i lean over to kiss a girl, or hold her hand. i mean, living in the states certainly doesn't offer a special asylum for homosexuals, but the anonymity factor does provide for some relief, something that i don't think i'd find in bangladesh without having to resort to living in absolute secrecy. i am a lesbian no matter where i am; it's just that in bangladesh i'm constantly reminded of the uniqueness of my lifestyle, and heterosexuality is sort of on a plate served right next to the rice. so really, it isn't so much about the place than it is the privacy. the fact that i can literally do as i please without having to worry about what my family or other people would think makes for a less stressful and more carefree life.

from as far back as i can remember, my appearance, behavior, and general disposition were all pretty sexually ambiguous. i remember as a child never wanting to play with dolls, and being fascinated with lego sets. i remember playing baseball and running and jumping and doing "boyish" things while the girls played hopscotch and jump rope and other "girly" things. as far as i was concerned, i was a boy. you couldn't convince me otherwise. the funny thing is, my parents didn't seem to really take notice of my socially odd behavior and cooperated with me effortlessly. mom knew not to buy me frilly pink dresses, and dad knew that i'd always be up to go see a baseball game. i think that they were actually okay with my taking on the persona of their son. i think that they thought it was cute and harmless and even now when they tell stories about the time i wore a three-piece suit and tie to my kindergarten graduation ceremony, they laugh until their bellies ache. and i love them for that, and i can respect the fact that they gave in to my childish fantasies of being a boy.

bengali society, however, is not as welcoming of my sexual ambiguity. walking down the streets of dhaka, i get catcalls from men across the street asking me if i'm a boy or a girl. it's rather uncomfortable, period, when you get unwanted comments from people you don't even know. on several occasions, while i was in a car waiting for traffic to clear panhandlers came up to my window pleading to me as a *bhaiya* ("brother") first and then changing to *apa* ("sister") once they realized i was a girl.

"hi, i'm chompa. i'm a lesbian."

in a perfect world, i wouldn't have to worry about being a lesbian in dhaka. there would be no need for categorization, everyone would be accepting of all people, and life would just go on.

frankly, i really wouldn't give a flying shit who knew about my sexuality. but it's obviously not a perfect world, and the reality of my sexual preference and how it affects the rest of my life is far too complex and important to disregard. especially because i am bengali, and even more so because i am muslim.

"i'm chompa . . . and uh . . . i'm a dyke."

i guess i'm just not sure how to eliminate the shock value of living in bangladesh as an out lesbian. i certainly don't want the attention. nor do i care to elicit any animosity. i just want it out there, in the hopes that it'll make some things a little easier and possibly preclude infinite careless assumptions and questions. i mean, it borders on ridiculous how some of my bengali relatives and friends are always forthright with their questions about boyfriends and marriage, right after they tell you that you've gained weight. most of the time, i manage to ward them off with shrugs while they silently pity me for being dark skinned and boyish. but it absolutely horrifies them that i'm still single. they wonder if there's something wrong with me (outside of the dark thing and the boyish thing), but eventually trail off the conversation with serious offers to look for men on my behalf, which i politely decline, and they unwillingly oblige.

it was easier in the beginning, because i was still young, and i would use my youth as an excuse. but now? now i'm thirty-two! i'm well done. charbroiled.

for all intents and purposes, i consider myself a spiritual muslim. though many "real" muslims will undoubtedly argue that because i am homosexual, i cannot possibly be a muslim, since the qur'an supposedly prohibits same sex relations. well, that's their problem, not mine. to be totally honest, i understand my religion based on what i consider to be its truest, most simplistic form. some "rules" i embrace, others i do not. if they don't make sense to me, then i don't believe them. if they do, then i abide. or at least try to.

i do, however, drink occasionally, and i do smoke. and i do thoroughly enjoy a premarital roll in the hay every now and again, with the right woman of course. but do all of these things really make me a bad muslim? doesn't it count that i'm also a compassionate, caring, thoughtful, respectful, sensitive human being (with a bitchy side as well that i try to keep under wraps)? wouldn't it be worse if i were praying five times a day, fasting and whatnot, but then being mean to, or even beating, my wife? or going to work every day to make astounding profits off dirt cheap labor? or causing other people harm by gossiping about them and ruining their privacy? or starting wars that serve absolutely no purpose, simply because i have the power to do so? surely there are a million other more horrible things in the world than being a smoking, drinking, good-time-having lesbian!

the point is that my islam is between me and my god.

together we've established a healthy, calm, we-all-know-who's-boss relationship. i know the difference between good and bad. my parents and my own personal experiences taught me well in that department. i'm one of the most harmless people i know. let's face it, there are just too many underlying pretenses within islamic practice that really do fuck women over. and the thing about it is that i really, truly do not believe that god *ever* intended for women to be oppressed. *man* did. and if i truly believe that, then i must also believe that god never intended for *any* group of people to be oppressed, whether it be because of race, sexual identity, class, you name it.

*"amar naam chompa. ami ek jon bangali musulmaan _____."*³

in hindsight, i can safely look back on several women that i've "admired" throughout my teens and beyond and know that they were actually crushes. and i'm not talking about girls who i thought were pretty or had style. these were women who i felt an unexplainable affinity toward. women i was drawn to and wanted to get to know better. but it never occurred to me, at the time, that there was anything romantic/sexual about it. i suppose if i were to shuffle through my brain vigorously, i might come up with an explanation along the lines of social conditioning. after all, bangladesh offers an über-heterosexual environment. come to think of it, there isn't even a word for lesbian in the bengali language. there are negative slang terms for transvestites and overly "effeminate" men, but i've never, ever come across an official bengali word used to describe a homosexual, let alone a lesbian.

from what i hear, i was more fortunate than most when i discovered my sexuality. it was at a restaurant when i was in my midtwenties where i met a woman who literally and figuratively turned me on from the inside out. upon discovering my new feelings, i almost felt as though i had been denied something my entire life. it wasn't a horrifying experience for me; in fact it was more of an awakening. i felt like my vision of life expanded from a ninety-degree view to one eighty in a matter of moments, and i welcomed it with open arms. it was almost as if overnight, my whole life made sense to me and some of the pieces of my life's puzzle began coming together in a way that forced me to be introspective all of a sudden.

but once i figured out how it all fit into my life, i became much more comfortable with my being. a lot of my social demons disappeared, and i no longer felt the need or desire to explain myself, my attitudes, my appearance, or my quirks to anyone.

through my entire adult life prior to this discovery, i felt extremely awkward in my own skin. i never quite fit in with the masses, and now i know why. i have always been different and will probably always be, but my difference is an asset now, not a hindrance. and i revel in it.

i came out to ma during one of her visits to minneapolis a couple of years ago. she came at a time when i was living with my female lover. it helped that we lived in a two-bedroom apartment, so at first we played it off as though we were roommates. but that got really tricky and just got in the way. i couldn't keep track of all the lies anymore, and it interfered with my ability to enjoy my mother's visit. so i finally told her, amid conversation about a friend of mine who recently had a baby. of course conversations like that always result in what i like to call "spotlight chompa" moments: "so what about you, chompa? will you ever settle down and get married?" ma asked.

the stress of telling ma the truth had been brewing inside of me all day, and so when i reacted with an almost-instant welling of tears, i knew it was time to make my confession. it was as if my heart jumped out of its cage to plead to ma for her understanding and frankly, she handled it the best way she knew how. in the span of about ten seconds, her facial expressions changed twelve times, and then she finally cried. she asked god what she did wrong and why did she send me to america and how could this happen to her. it was the saddest yet most precious moment of my life, because in the end, after some explaining, she hugged me really tight and said that she would always love me no matter what. supposedly she waited a few years until she was pretty sure this wasn't just a phase before telling daddy recently. i haven't seen him since he heard the news, but we talk on the phone as though nothing has changed. he tells me how much he loves me and misses me, especially during *iftar*[4] while eating *piyaju*[5] or during the summer while eating mangoes. but as far as the lesbian "thing" goes, he never brings it up and i dare not.

if i were to go home for anything more than a vacation, i would have to live a life of secrecy or celibacy, or both. the alternative would be to just disregard everyone and everything near and dear to me and overtly establish my now-exaggerated rebel status. the cost is, at times, astounding. at least in my head. my parents just wouldn't know what to say to people. they'd be humiliated and ashamed and mortified if they had to live through a scandal like that. it's one thing for me to live far away and do what i do in the privacy of my faraway life, but it's entirely different to actually live an "out" life in dhaka. i can just picture word spreading like a verbal virus among relatives and friends i know, and even some i don't. but the association isn't hard to establish. someone in dhaka's "english medium" or "westernized" social party circle knows someone whose sister's husband's brother used to go to high school with someone i know. and somehow it all stays relevant.

so the question then becomes, am i unconditionally ready to sacrifice an integral part of my being, my existence, my passion, my life, to allow my parents to save face?

absolutely.

i've come to the decision that i will do it. though it's inherently unfair and not necessarily the way i want to live my life, i would do it for my family because they are that important to me. it's unfortunate that such a sacrifice needs to be made in order for me, simply, to spend time with my family. deep down inside, i wish it weren't so. i wish i could just go to dhaka and continue to be me and flirt with girls and go out on dates without having to hide everything from everyone. i want to be able to live my life without the constant pressure of getting married to a man. maybe i want to fall in love with a bengali woman and speak to her in bangla and live happily ever after in bangladesh, after having traveled the world. and i want it all. why can't i have it? the truth is, even if i did live an out life in dhaka, it wouldn't necessarily be easy. it's not like there's an open lesbian community that everyone knows about. it's not like i could just go to a party, meet a beautiful woman, and expect her to want to come home (to my parents' house, no less) with me. in fact, the last time i was home, i did meet a stunningly beautiful bengali woman at a party, and i flirted with her all night long. people don't believe me when i tell them that she flirted right back, but it didn't matter because in the end i found out that she was engaged and soon to be married. that's the sort of thing that gives me a reality check in terms of what it would be like to live in dhaka, out or not.

the bottom line is that some sort of sacrifice is due on my part. whether i choose to do it or not depends entirely upon the experiences i will encounter. but going into it, i know I must be prepared for the worst. despite everything, it's tremendously important that i spend quality time with my parents before something horrible happens and i get that phone call i've been dreading my entire adult life while living thousands of miles away from them.

ma came to visit me in minneapolis this past summer and stayed for a month. she told me that she's proud of me and everything i've accomplished here. she sees me now as a well-rounded, stable, sensible person who manages to take care of herself in this lonely land of opportunity. and while she better understands my sexuality, she also feels tremendously emotional about my living alone. she wonders how i cope when i'm ill or when i feel lonely. she wishes i were a better cook, so i could feed myself well instead of eating unhealthy american food. she wishes i had more money saved up in case of an emergency and wonders if i'll ever find someone to settle down with, man or woman. well, the truth is that even though i think i wouldn't trade the world for the independence i've achieved, i do often wish that my family were closer to me. i don't want to live the rest of my life alone, but at the same time i also can't fathom giving up my independence. at some point, however, i had to weigh the scales and figure out what's more important to me. my religion, my culture, and my sexuality are all extremely important to me, but my family easily tops that list.

so, even though most muslims wouldn't consider me a muslim, and bengalis become easily confused by my "boyish," "western" appearance, and i may very well be forced into celibacy for a while, i know what i have to do. i can't live my life expecting to fit in everywhere because i can only be me. i have to make my surroundings fit in with me. so, if after spending several months or years in bangladesh i find that i'm unhappy or unfulfilled, i can always move back to the states. but, at the very least, i have to give it a shot, because if i don't, i may regret it later. so i suppose at this point it's just a matter of having enough time to get my shit together, save some money, and buy a one-way ticket home. it may take a while for all this to come to fruition, and i'll probably go back and forth about it in my head until i finally do it. but once i get on the plane, i'll be reciting the arabic surahs[6] I learned and chanting *"la ilaha illa allah muhammad-ur rasul allah"[7]* to calm my nerves during takeoff, turbulence, and landing.

"hi, my name is chompa. i'm a toking, smoking, drinking, pool-playing, gambling, peace-loving, concertgoing, good-time-having, bengali muslim lesbian fool!"

Geneology of Hussein

Samira Abbassy

My Name Is Munerah

Munerah Ahmed

My name is Munerah. No, I don't have a nickname. Thank you, but if it's so pretty, why were you asking if I have a nickname? Let's be honest, you were hoping I had a nickname so you wouldn't have to work too hard to remember my real name. It's too ethnic to remember, too foreign. But to me, Jennifer sounds just as ethnic. Actually, I've never thought of changing my name. Why should I have to change my name, my identity, my history? So it can be easier for you?

Don't worry about that. I really don't care if you say it incorrectly or if it ends up sounding Caucasianized. All I care is that you try. That you validate me for who I am and not for what I should be. No matter how long I've been in this country, my name is and will always be Munerah. I don't have to be a Britney or an Elaine to be an American. By the way, those names aren't American; they're European. And as you can tell, I'm not European.

I'm not Spanish. I'm Arab, actually Yemeni. Yemeni is someone from Yemen. It's in the Middle East. No, it's not near Iraq; we're south of Saudi Arabia. Yes, I am a Muslim. What are you?

What do you mean, have I ever seen my mother's face? No, not everyone covers up their face. And if they did, it's only for the outside. Do you really think they walk around like that when they're at home? I don't wear "that thing" around my hair, because it's my own choice. *Why not?* I think that you know the difference between what people are supposed to do and what they actually do. Look at it like this: Aren't Catholics not supposed to have sex before marriage? And are you telling me you're still a virgin? You smirk like it's a stupid question, but I wish you could see how stupid some of your questions are. I know there's no such thing as a stupid question, but could you try to use the same standards for me that you use for yourself? You're not the perfect Catholic; why should I be the perfect Muslim?

I *am* a real Muslim. I don't know what you're talking about. Who are those kinds of Muslims that you're talking about?

How can you tell I'm liberated? Because I speak English? Well, thank you, I've only lived here for most of my life; your English is good as well. Oh, because

I don't wear the *hijab*, which is what that *thing* is called. Do you really think that everyone who wears the *hijab* is imprisoned at home or completely oppressed or can't walk alone outside? No, America isn't the only place she can. My sister wears it, and I'd like to see someone try to mess with her. I am so sick of all this focus on this one stupid piece of cloth. It doesn't matter what we wear.

You're saying I'm not a real Muslim. Other Muslims say I'm not a real Muslim. They say it for the same reason you said it, because they think I'm Westernized. And you know what, Muslims aren't even supposed to say shit like that. Only God can tell what's in our hearts. I don't mean to get snappy at you. Listen, all I'm saying is that it doesn't matter how we dress or what we wear.

I know there's a lot of fucked-up shit in that part of the world. Clothing is the least of our worries. How about we focus on having the right to go to school, to have good healthcare, to be able to take care of ourselves and decide what we want to do with our bodies and our lives. You have to admit, that's not so different from this part of the world, is it? We don't have to look all the way over there to find real fucked-up shit, do we now?

The Veil, My Body

Nor Faridah Abdul Manaf

It's just a piece of cloth
It rocks the world
It shapes a civilization
A civilization misread

It's trapping, says the untutored
It's oppressing, echoes the unlearned

The veil is my body
The veil is also my mind
The veil defines my cultural identity
The veil is who I am

Your slurs and instructions
That I rip it off my head
Is a rape of my body
An invasion of my land

It's just a piece of cloth
But after Palestine, Iraq, Afghanistan, Maluku, Kosovo
This is all I have.

The Scarf

Z. Gabriel Arkles

I was raised as a Muslim girl, but I rejected my faith around five years ago, not long before I realized I was a transsexual man. When I think about going back to Islam, I automatically think about wearing a scarf over my hair again. I feel a sense of loss when I realize that would be less appropriate, now that I live as my true gender. To me wearing a scarf was a symbol of being Muslim—the external expression of my religious beliefs.

When most people asked me why Muslim women wore a scarf, I explained that I knew of four general reasons. One was that Islam enjoins modesty on both genders, and that some people think that keeping hair covered is an important part of modesty. (That was not my reason. I took the duty of modesty seriously and, to that end, never wore anything that would show my legs or shoulders. Showing my hair didn't seem immodest to me in my culture.) Another was that some people understood the Qu'ran to command women to cover their hair, the reason for which was to show one's willingness to obey God's command. (That also was not my reason. I had seen the verses people quoted as the command and was unimpressed. If I had seen an *ayah* ["verse"] saying, "Women should cover their hair in public," I would have believed it.) The third was a mystical Sufi explanation I had heard in my mosque, stating that there was a spiritual *arsh*, or opening, on the top of the head, and that it benefited both men and women to keep it covered from the world. (That also was not my reason. I did not understand it.)

The fourth reason I mentioned was to declare oneself publicly as a Muslim, to show pride in one's faith. I had wanted to wear a scarf for this reason long before I actually did. In the beginning I wouldn't allow myself to do it because I felt the motivation was too secular, too full of anger: anger at the classmates who kicked me and asked me if I bowed down to a black rock; anger at the teacher who said all Muslims were raised by the sword to slaughter infidels; anger at the camp counselor who told me she loved me but that I would burn in Hell; anger at the social studies textbook that called Jesus inspired and magnanimous, but that called Muhammad (s.a.w.) a nut who stole his ideas from Judaism; anger at the threats to my mosque after the 1993 World Trade Center bombing. It was a motive aimed outward, toward the world, rather than inward, toward a spiritual journey to submission to God. When I finally did begin to wear the scarf, it was in college, primarily as an external reminder for staying on the straight path, but I only told close friends that reason.

At the time, I was going to school at a Methodist-affiliated secular school in Lynchburg, Virginia, a community dominated by the money and personality of Jerry Falwell. Raised in Philadelphia suburbs, I was no stranger to being one of the only Muslims in a Christian-dominated community, but in Lynchburg the atmosphere was even thicker with right-wing Christian morality. There were no more than ten Jewish or Muslim students in my college. My friends and I almost got used to being asked if Jesus was our savior when we went out to buy groceries. When other gay rights activists and I asked the City Council to add sexual orientation to their nondiscrimination law, the members quoted the Bible to us.

Each fall semester in the college chorus, all of our music was Christian, all of our performances in honor of Christmas, and our biggest performance in a church. When the one atheist singer, the one Jewish singer, and I complained, the choir director invited us not to sing songs we felt uncomfortable with, which meant not singing at all. When some witches started at my school my junior year and held rituals, a student from Falwell's university spied on them and wrote an outraged newspaper article and letter to the Methodist clergy, sparking some outcry. The pagans' fliers were vandalized almost as often as the queer student group's fliers were. The fliers of the Christian student groups, which were at times aggressively proselytizing, were never vandalized.

Because I am white, no one took me to be a Muslim unless I told them. Wearing the scarf, though, saved me the effort. Walking in that community as an out Muslim was an act of defiance, similar to walking hand in hand with my girlfriend. I loved making that statement, even though I did not enjoy the attention. People pointed, stared, laughed, gossiped. People hassled me. People asked me ignorant questions. People warned me that I might be attacked, that I should take off the scarf for my own safety.

My French instructor assumed I began wearing the scarf because of a discussion the previous week that left me furious. We had read an article about a 1994 directive in France that prohibited public school students from wearing anything religious to school. The justification was that Christian students were assaulting Muslims and Jews. These assaults were linked to increased tension surrounding West African immigration to France. Supporters of the directive argued that making the students' differences less visible would help protect them. The article had interviews with Muslim girls who were faced with the decision of violating a command from God or not going back to high school and who chose not to go back. The students and the instructors in my French class, all Christians, could see the French government's point of view, with calm and objectivity.

For me, it was impossible to be calm in a discussion of this intense policing of French Muslim women's bodies and attempted erasing of their identities, supposedly for their own good. I also could not ignore a connection I felt with my own experiences. I remembered how I had to pretend to eat lunch every day in the cafeteria of my public school during Ramadan so the cafeteria workers wouldn't find out I was fasting and take me to the principal's office. I remembered my cheeks burning as I wore leggings under the biggest pair of gym shorts that would fit me, doing my best to avoid immodesty and avoid a failing grade in PE at the same time.

A few weeks after that discussion, I showed up to French class wearing a scarf. It was not for that reason, but I did not mind that my class took it as a statement.

This year, I fasted during Ramadan again for the first time in five years. I feel closer to reaching a point where I can bring Islam back into my life with integrity, in a way that works with my politics and identities. And again, I think of the scarf with some yearning.

I stormed out of my childhood mosque the day the imam gave a *khutba* that blamed male sexual assault on female immodesty. Holding men and women to different standards of modesty is a form of sexism rampant in Muslim (and other) communities. One way many Islamic, male-dominated societies exercise control over women is through violent control over the way women cover their bodies. I know all of these things, but still non-Muslim use of the scarf or the veil as a synonym and a symbol for Muslim male oppression of Muslim women troubles me. Sexism, misogyny, and patriarchy go far deeper and express themselves in far more ways than codes of modesty alone. The scarf is far more than a symbol of male supremacy alone.

It is the only article of "women's" clothing that I have missed wearing.

Silent Protest

Shadi Eskandani

"I need to cut my hair. It's been so long since my last cut."

"I thought you were growing it out. I like it long; it suits you."

"Well, actually, I was thinking of shaving it all off. You know, a new start."

It is cold, the almost-winter cold of a Toronto mid-October. We are standing across the street from the Israeli consulate, doing the usual weekly thing— peacefully protesting the occupation of Palestine by the Israeli state. Our group's weekly silent vigils have become routine for a few of the dedicated members. We usually stand there, all eight of us, holding our sign, MUSLIM WOMEN AGAINST THE ISRAELI OCCUPATION, while slipping into conversation with one another, forgetting to maintain the one hour of silence.

"Did you hear about Ahmad's family in the West Bank?"

"No, what happened?"

"Well, they bulldozed their house to build a new settlement. The family has nowhere to go, so they're staying with Mahmoud's family."

"Hey, does anyone know the details of Sahar's U.S. border story?"

"Not details, but I heard they kept her for nine and a half hours and harassed her. I mean, they were asking her personal stuff, like her sex life! They told her that it was a good thing our men kept us covered! Can you believe it?"

"Those assholes! I would have let them have it!"

"What did she do about it? She has a Canadian passport. She's a *Canadian* for crying out loud! Can't she do something?"

"What could she do? Apparently, she's totally traumatized and can't talk about the incident. And besides, she is put on some list where she has to check in with U.S. officials every time she enters and leaves the country."

"Yeah, she doesn't want to bring on any more trouble. She doesn't want to risk making things difficult for her family. Her family has to travel to Iran and the United States often."

We stand there, breathing in the cold, crisp air, trying to stay warm. Across the street from us we can see security guards in the building. They are looking over at us and rapidly taking down notes on their pads of paper. I look over to my right and notice a man and woman approaching us. From the stiff, mechanical movement of their bodies, it is obvious they are cops.

"Hi there! My name is Officer Gordon, and this is my partner, Officer Holmes. We thought we'd come by and introduce ourselves. We are the new RCMP officers who will be checking up on you ladies from now on."

He lets out a chuckle, overamused by his own enthusiasm.

"Nice to meet you. It's great to see police officers in solidarity with the cause."

"Why don't you grab a sign and come stand with us?" says Latifeh as she quickly turns around and continues her conversation with Hamida. The rest of us do the same.

"So as I was saying, I really want to shave my head."

"Don't be ridiculous, that is going to look horrible."

"You'll do it, regret it, and then want to hide your shiny, bald head from everyone!"

"Maybe then you'll be forced to *hejab* to save yourself from the humiliation!"

"*Hejab?* Never. I'll leave that to you two. But this time next week, mark my words, I will be bald."

I stand there, listening to Hamida and Sara argue over whose head will look better shaved, while watching officer Gordon converse with some of the other women. Officer Holmes stands there, all quiet, obviously lacking the exuberance of her partner. Or perhaps she feels uncomfortable among a group of politicized and outspoken Muslim women. Maybe she feels threatened in our space, this space of Otherness, which we have reclaimed and redefined. This space to where she clearly does not belong.

"Well, ladies, it was nice meeting you all, so same time next week? Alright then."

At this point, all eight of us stop our conversations and look over at the two officers as Hamida says, "Thanks for dropping by. This week we were discussing hairstyles, but you should definitely come by next week. We'll be talking about manicures and pedicures."

The officers leave. We go back to our conversations. I look from the corner of my eye and watch the officers cross the street and enter the building where the consulate is. They, along with the security guards, look over at us and begin scribbling on their pads of paper. I wonder what they are writing about us.

Who's Got Us?

Anida Yoeu Esguerra

who's got us when we fall?
who will be there to catch us
when the sky becomes too heavy to hold up
when we slip away as obscure phantoms
souls too thickly burdened to stand up tall
who will break our fall?

what of my sisters—the shadow walkers?
the women who resist beneath cotton cloaks
black slits designed to fit a woman's eyes
but with holes too small to see the sky.
when chador is no longer a choice,
there is no modesty in fear.
so the women lock fists in a secret circle
with Allah trapped in their throats.
they rely on a rotating council of resistance
if one sister stumbles the others will catch her.

generals command soldiers,
"wars are won when the hearts of women crumble!"
they fear women nations
who sew our seeds for 7 legacies
like our mothers
secretly stashing their dreams in the hope chest of history
knowing that space and time will unfold them
my mouth is the cosmos opened up for interpretation
swallowing me into a nocturnal hole
and i struggle to climb out
to see my mother and the women before me.
i see the sisters who speak with silent mother tongues

and mothers whose tongues tied/twisted in silence
as we unlearn the wrongs
and rites of passages not our own.

we are "too much woman" they tell us
compared to models, emaciated paper ghosts
fragmented scares and stares—pasted glossy clippings.
our sistergirls—painted living dolls behind pupil casings
lips sewn shut like dusty raggedy anns.

we share ducts of salty sea foam tears
and fears plucked from hysteria
we give birth to dicks who prick with privilege
spit from lips that drip with love
and *still* allow strangers
to steal our kisses at random moments.

we are the women whose
hearts are strung on fishline poles
esteems kicked to the curb
as street lamps dim and flicker like distant memories.

so who's got us?
who will catch us when we fall?
sometimes, i see myself
diving off the edge of my own heart.
tall grasses sway in the field
like a million open arms waiting to catch me.
sometimes i dream me drowning—
a current sucks me through a cave of my cracked open chest
the she within stares back at me—
the darker thin skinned woman whispers,
"you must learn to survive yourself"

when i awake— i   am   left   alone.
so who's got us?
when Allah and angels and ancestors all turn their backs
when we are each other's worst rivals
what becomes of the everyday mothers and sisters
with deadpan faces that bind our living histories?

i have seen our women survive each other
cradling cups of tears in a circle of fears
mature salty puddles fused into fuel
forging salvation in arm linked huddles
chanting, "fuck the bullshit and fuck the suffering"
and waiting for the rest of the world to catch us.

i have watched our women catch each other.
we are the neo feminists with borrowed souls
constantly evolving ourselves past
the post modern trap holes.
we streak our strands resilient shades
and wear lipstick on occasions when
a shade of rouge makes life a little more vibrant.
we revoke the laws that feed the frenzy
to bind our feet
and defy scriptures—"fanatic" excuses
for a religious patriarchy.
fundamentals are foundations
God is not a man!
we snatch back our ovaries
keep our children close
we remember to mouth our names even in silence
and dare to define ourselves beyond our own imagination.

sister / woman—
spread your wings across the horizon
take flight past the heavens
and we will catch each other when we fall.

How to Solve the Problem

Salma Arastu

AFTERWORD

miriam cooke

Sarah Husain has assembled a remarkable collection of poems, essays, and stories that open up the lives of Muslim women around the world, but especially in post-9/11 America. Whether they were born in Afghanistan or Pakistan, in Palestine or Iran, or in the United States, these transnational feminists are intensely aware of the connections between their experiences and those of Muslim women elsewhere. Many are becoming aware of themselves as Muslim women for the first time.

These radical writings form bridges across the world, linking the Palestinian suicide bomber to relatives in its diasporas and the confused American girl working out how to act and dress in an America grown fearful of veils with a Pakistani situating herself in a society unfriendly to women with too-large ambitions. They tell of lives dedicated to the struggle for peace, even when that goal seems most remote. Age-old anxieties are juxtaposed with twenty-first-century challenges and fears in an anthology that is ever attentive to the connections between gender, religious, political, and ethnic identities.

Voices of Resistance interrogates all acts of violence, whether committed by Muslims in the name of a distorted Islam, or against Muslims and wrapped in the language of self-defense, or against women on behalf of a misogynistic understanding of the religion. Shahrzad Naficy enters the tortured mind of an Afghan girl whose mother the Taliban have just murdered and whose sister they have raped. The details are graphic and yet surprisingly lyrical. The reader feels the numbness of shock and disbelief.

Each writer is aware of multiple threats to her right to enjoy the same privileges as her brother in Islam and her non-Muslim sister. Many of the writers practice what I have elsewhere called multiple critique, a self-positioning with like-minded others against those who would deny them their rights as women and as Muslims.[1] Each knows that she risks falling between the cracks of the various communities in which she wants to belong, and so each attack on her integrity, whether political, religious, or sexual, is resisted with the ardor of the soldier at the front. No matter the risk of censure and the accusations of cultural betrayal, each writer knows that negative practices must be resisted. In 2006, Muslim women's bodies have indeed become "a site of multiple wars and struggles," as Husain puts it, and these authors are eloquent in asserting their Allah-given right to define themselves, their desires, their fears, and their hopes.

The Euro-American vilification of Muslims that became so widespread after the September 11, 2001, terrorist attacks on the World Trade Center in New York and the Pentagon in Washington, D.C., haunts the volume. Each selection resists the ways in which Muslims are reduced to a single core identity and calls for an understanding of the variety and richness of women's lives in the Muslim world. There is a vivid awareness of discrimination in the United States that connects Muslim women's struggles for recognition and dignity with those of African Americans in the civil rights movement of the 1960s. Some of the writings are clearly addressed to a non-Muslim reader, but some target Muslims who systematically deprive women of their religiously sanctioned rights.

Each writer must be considered a *mujahida,* a struggler in the path of truth and justice. The word *mujahida* is an active participle that comes from the Arabic word "jihad," meaning spiritual struggle for improvement of the self and of society. In rare cases, "jihad" refers to war when a Muslim community is under threat and must fight to protect itself. A woman's jihad, to use Ansaro Bah's term from her poem "Jihad," contains what some might consider to be two contradictions: women and war, feminism and Islam. The dichotomized projection of these pairs has been constitutive of a hierarchical worldview that valorizes masculinity in the secular and sacred realms, and then trivializes all that pertains to women.

Women and war for some is an oxymoron, for others, like the *Voices of Resistance* contributors, the concept entails a "vital intervention in today's discourse on war, peace, sexuality, religion, politics, civil rights, humanitarianism, activism, and art," to quote Husain's introduction. The oxymoron view generally prevails through a gendered partitioning of space. Women are here and war is there, and that is how we know what is going on where. To connect women and war, however, is not an oxymoron. It is a challenge to military discourse, threatening some accepted structures, like "men and the front," and "women and the home," and revealing the stakes in maintaining this myth.

Many argue that the other dichotomy, feminism and Islam, is irresolvable, because patriarchal Islam and gendered politics on behalf of women's rights are incompatible. Even Muslim women committed to gender justice may subscribe to such a view.[2] Pointing to scriptural prescriptions that seem to affirm women's essential inferiority, they scoff at "apologists" who try to reclaim a gender-just Islam from the clutches of misogynist interpreters. Since the late 1980s, however, scholars have been revealing the compatibility of Islam and feminism and the strategic effectiveness of thinking them together.[3] The idea of women's jihad brings these apparent paradoxes together.

The *Voices of Resistance* poets, essayists, and storytellers know that women have engaged in spiritual but also military strife even before the seventh century, when the Arabian Muhammad became the Prophet of Islam. Some mention the struggles of Hagar, Abraham's concubine and the mother of Ismail, whom Muslims consider their ancestor. Then, there was Muhammad's first wife, Khadija, whose affirmation of her husband in his new and difficult role was pivotal in the development of the young Muslim community. His granddaughter Zainab is acknowledged for her courage in the face of the tyrant Yazid and for her exemplary behavior on the Karbala battlefield. The mystic saint Rabia has inspired generations of women, including the authors in this volume.

Women who write about women who denounce fighting are not necessarily advocating pacifism, the stereotype of inherently peace-loving women. Rather, they are calling for more effective ways to wage a just war. A community that is oppressed or that is internally oppressive demands action for change. Algerians fighting the French in the middle of the twentieth century, like Palestinians today trying to shake off the Israeli occupation of their lands, need everyone, men *and* women, to participate in the struggle.

Since the 1980s, some Muslim women have joined in a jihad that opposes the evil manifestations of what Islamists are calling the current *jahiliya*, an expression that refers back to the eponymous age of ignorance and depravity that preceded Islam. Ironically, both Islamists and some Islamic feminists are invoking this *jahiliya* as emblematic of primordial chaos that must be confronted and overcome. In this new jihad, women may be fighting with or against the men in their community.

Jihad does not preclude conventional fighting, *qital,* for the Qur'an does call for it as well as for spiritual struggle.[4] In Surat al-Baqara, the second chapter of the Qur'an, men and women are told that they must fight, however loathsome fighting might be to them: "Fighting is written for you even though you hate it. But it may well be that you hate what is good for you and that you love what is bad for you. God is the one who knows and not you" (Qur'an 2:216).

This is the verse that the Saudi preacher Fatima Umar Naseef quotes in the "Right to Participate in Jihad" section of a chapter devoted to women's political rights in Islam.[5] She elaborates on the meanings attached to jihad for women. Even though some say that it is "without fighting," should infidels invade Dar al-Islam, "all inhabitants of this country should go out and fight the enemy. Indeed, it is *unlawful* for anyone to refrain from fighting." Women, children and slaves must fight even if without their husbands', fathers', or owners' permission.[6] Naseef is careful to show that she has not exercised undue license in her reading of the Qur'an by quoting from the Egyptian scholar Sayyid Qutb, a prominent spokesman for radical Islam, who had asserted in the 1960s that, like the seventh-century women surrounding the Prophet, modern Muslim women should be mobilized for jihad in cases of emergency.

During the state of emergency that war creates, individuals must choose not only appropriate behaviors but also the people to whom they will turn as the appropriate authorities in their lives. In the war to advance God's reign on earth, norms are even more dispensable than they are during ordinary wars. It is God, not the father, who is now the senior authority in the family, and God's law supersedes that of the father when the *umma*, the Islamic community, is in danger. Naseef's advocacy of total mobilization and the resultant transgression of hierarchical norms is striking, especially when articulated by a highly respected woman scholar.

Jihad provides the rhetoric and virtual reality of war within contemporary Muslim societies where religious language and symbols have such power. To argue the religious right of women to go to war is to frame the struggle for women's rights within the deeply moral language and rituals of Islam. So widespread is the appeal of jihad as a morally justified struggle that it has spread to the Internet. Articles on the laudable precedents of early *mujahidat* have proliferated since the late 1990s.

Husain is right to point out that Muslim women today are fighting all over the world, some as victims and some as victimizers. In a world dominated by George W. Bush's war on terror, some find no solution other than a suicide that, however terrible it may be, may help avenge injustice: "I am no angel," writes the poet

Bushra Rehman, "and won't be until the fuse is lit." Husain knows how important it is to talk about all these forms of violence so that their acknowledgment may lead to their eradication.

Nothing is too sacred for these *mujahidat* to tackle. Ramadan is a time of fasting and ritual cleanliness, but that state of purification, some protest, may not be available to women. Aisha Sattar criticizes the Saudis for institutionalizing inequality during the Hajj, the great annual pilgrimage that brings together millions of Muslims for the most important ritual in their lives. The standard take on the Hajj is that it is the one time that men and women are truly equal, as they circumambulate the Kaaba dressed alike in the seamless white cloth. Yet Sattar questions this view, based on her own experience. She exposes the blatant misogyny of some men and talks openly about her own defiance of some of their most objectionable actions. Malcolm X may have felt deep solidarity with his Muslim brothers, she writes, but that was just it: He felt welcomed and accepted by Muslim men in a way that a Muslim woman does not.

It is the information revolution that has enabled some of the most powerful exchanges and coalitions among Muslim women across continents. Voices from Asia and Africa come together on the Internet to question interpretations of the Qur'an and the Traditions[7] that have long disadvantaged women. Passionate about their faith and affirming their reverence for the scriptures of Islam, they call for new, enlightened understandings of the scriptures' meanings so that the religion will fulfill its promise to bring a better life to all regardless of gender, race, or class.

The confluence of these voices from the far-flung corners of the globe amplifies local issues and reassures women that their concerns are not individual and exceptional but rather shared among millions. Between July 10 and October 15, 2004, Azza, Khanum, and Maddy, sitting alone in Chicago, Los Angeles, and Cairo, communicated openly and frankly in a way that might have proven difficult had they been together in one of the women's homes. Their three-month-long email conversation included in this volume gives the impression of listening in on private conversations.

Some selections are so outspoken and daring that they feel like confidences shared with a friend; it is as though the reader were being made privy to angers and anxieties too great to be shared with just anyone. Although they know that their criticism of behaviors and practices prevalent in Muslim communities may be condemned, these *mujahidat* have nonetheless decided to share with us the most intimate details of their struggles in the hopes that such acts of daring and defiance might change a world too violent to be lived in. Azza writes, "By daring to remember, write, and question, we stand alone, unpopular, and sometimes reviled by those who wish to keep us in the bondage of silence and oppression. By building solidarity through our different experiences, we are charting a struggle that turns differences into strengths."

Voices of Resistance is a collection of writings that will be used in the classroom, but it is also an activist manual. It is about Muslim women's problems yesterday and today, and it is also about their hopes for tomorrow and how these hopes might be realized. Each woman has contributed her piece in a puzzle that perplexes Muslims and non-Muslims alike: How can we make a difference in a world spinning out of control? How can we take on the leviathan of religion and yet hope to pursue spiritual paths of our own?

The women in this collection write so that their voices will be directly heard and their histories will be correctly known; they write to retain control over their writings and their bodies. They write to assert their identities and rights as women and as Muslims. They write to demand an Islamic practice that considers men and women to be equals. They write to change the world. Tender as a mother's tears, beautiful as butterflies fluttering above Ground Zero, yet also raging at injustice and tyranny, these are very brave writings; braver, I suspect, than most of us will ever have to be.

miriam cooke *is professor of Arabic literature and culture at Duke University and past president of the Association of Middle Eastern Women's Studies. Her first book explores the life of Yahya Haqqi, one of Egypt's leading writers of the twentieth century. Subsequently, her writings focus on the intersection of gender and war in modern Arabic literature. She is the author of* War's Other Voices: Women Writers on the Lebanese Civil War *(Cambridge University Press),* Women and the War Story *(University of California Press), and* Women Claim Islam: Creating Islamic Feminism through Literature *(Routledge). Her most recent book, coedited with Bruce Lawrence, is a volume of essays entitled* Muslim Networks from Hajj to Hip Hop *(University of North Carolina Press).*

ENDNOTES

INTRODUCTION

1. This definition was translated by Marmaduke Pickthall and taken from Wikipedia: http://en.wikipedia.org/wiki/Al-Alaq.

2. Collections of writings by women of color that have been crucial in the formation of the aesthetics and politics of this collection include: *This Bridge Called My Back; Making Face, Making Soul/Haciendo Caras; Blood into Ink; Colonize This! Young Women of Color on Today's Feminism; Third World Women and the Politics of Feminism; Feminist Genealogies, Colonial Legacies, Democratic Futures; Postcolonial, Queer: Theoretical Intersections; Our Feet Walk the Sky: Women of the South Asian Diaspora;* and *Writing Self, Writing Nation.*

3. See Audre Lorde, "The Master's Tools Will Never Dismantle the Master's House," *This Bridge Called My Back,* ed. by Cherrie Moraga and Gloria Anzaldúa (Women of Color Press, 1984).

4. See Pam Morris, *The Bakhtin Reader: Selected Writings of Bakhtin, Medvedev, Voloshinov* (London and New York: St. Martin's Press, 1994): 245–52.

5. Although this term has had a long history in the Western imagination as a repressive and controlling space where women are imprisoned, so to speak, here the term is also used as a positive space. A space in which we have to learn and exchange with our mothers, sisters, grandmothers, and daughters. . . .

6. See Zohra Saed's poem "Answering . . ."

7. All human rights organizations evacuated Afghanistan when the United States announced it was going to begin bombing in 2001. The important question to ask is what if these organizations that have been working for decades in this devastated and war-torn country refused to evacuate? Can humanitarianism actually move to stop and deter a crisis rather than simply provide sympathy and charity?

8. A Fortune 100 U.S. corporation, the Caterpillar Inc. sells their militarized

D-9 bulldozers to the Israeli state, which uses them to demolish Palestinian homes and land. It was by the "Made in the U.S.A." CAT bulldozer that activist Rachel Corrie was crushed and killed.

9. See Michael Kaufman, "The World: Film Studies; What Does the Pentagon See in *Battle of Algiers?*" *The New York Times* (September 7, 2003).

10. Forbidden, unkosher, full of sin.

11. See M. Jacqui Alexander and Chandra Talpade Mohanty, "Introduction: Geneologies, Legacies, Movements." *Feminist Geneologies, Colonial Legacies, Democratic Futures* (New York: Routledge, 1997): xiv.

ON OCCUPATION AND RESISTANCE: TWO IRAQI WOMEN SPEAK OUT

1. This piece originally appeared under the title "Voices of Resistance: Two Iraqi Women Speak Out" in the newsletter of the Women's Studies Program at the University of California, Los Angeles, and in the *Middle East Women's Studies Review* (vol. 18 nos. 3 & 4, 2004). We have reworked the title for this publication.

2. "U.S. Military Quizzed on Iraq Press," *BBC News* (December 2, 2005), http://news.bbc.co.uk/1/hi/world/middle_east/4492768.stm.

3. See Anissa Hélie, "The U.S. Occupation and Rising Religious Extremism: The Double Threat to Women in Iraq." *PeaceWomen* (June 2005), Women's International League for Peace and Freedom, www.peacewomen.org/news/iraq/june05/doublethreat.htm.

4. "Iraq: Focus on Increasing Cases of Abused Women," WLUML (September 10, 2005), www.wluml.org/english/newsfulltxt.shtml?cmd[157]=x-157-380183.

5. See Anissa Hélie, "The U.S. Occupation and Rising Religious Extremism," *PeaceWomen*.

6. See Rubina Saigol, "Militarisation, Nation and Gender: Women's Bodies as Arenas of Violent Conflict," *Women and Sexuality in Muslim Societies,* ed. by Pinar Ilkkaracan (Istanbul, Turkey: Women for Women's Human Rights, 2005): 107.

FOR FAROUK ABDEL-MUHTI

1. Farouk Abdel-Muhti was a Palestinian refugee living in the United States for more than thirty years. He began working on WBAI's morning program called "Wake-Up Call" in March 2002 and a month later, on April 26, 2002, he was detained on immigration charges. For more than two years he was transferred from one facility to another. He was kept in solitary confinement and faced harsh interrogation, often being denied food, without ever being charged of any crime. He bravely organized other detainees, while in prison, against their mistreatment. He was released on April 12, 2004, and died three months later after speaking at the Ethical Society in Philadelphia.

DHIKR—

1. See Agha Shahid Ali, "Farewell," *The Country Without a Post Office* (New York: W.W. Norton and Co., 1997): 21.

2. For forty-five minutes on December 6, 1989, an enraged gunman roamed the corridors of Montreal's École Polytechnique and killed fourteen women. Marc Lepine, twenty-five, separated the men from the women, and before opening fire on the classroom of female engineering students he screamed, "I hate feminists." Almost immediately, the Montreal Massacre became a galvanizing moment in which mourning turned into outrage about all violence against women. From CBC archives: http://archives.cbc.ca/IDD-1-70-398/disasters_tragedies/montreal_massacre/.

3. See Jalal al-din Rumi, *Mystical Poems of Rumi*, translated from the Persian by A. J. Arberry (Chicago: University of Chicago Press, 1968): 153.

ANSWERING

1. Based on a series of Shirin Neshat's photography of Iranian women entitled *"Women of Allah: Secret Identities."* Interview with Neshat by Anne Doran, *Grand Street* 62, 1997.

APRIL 1978

1. "Daoud Khan" is the name used in Afghanistan. He is also referred to as "Daoud-e-Diwana" which means "Daoud the Crazy," a name that the Communists gave him after they killed him and massacred his family.

RED CLAY WOMEN

1. Muslim prayer for the dead, in Arabic: From the divine we come, and to the divine we must return.

YIMBERZAL

1. The first flower of the Kashmiri spring and Kashmiri poetic symbol of spiritual and physical rebirth.
2. Long, canoe-shaped paddleboat used for taxi, commerce, and leisure upon Dal Lake.
3. Kashmir Valley's beautiful glassy lake and a World Heritage Site, a major tourist attraction known for its houseboats, floating gardens, lotus flowers, and surrounding Himalayan foothills. Today, pollution, development, and general overuse threaten to further shrink and shallow the Dal.

BLACK WIDOW

1. Major Rehman is the Army Officer accused of raping a woman and her ten-year-old daughter in Badra Payeen, Handwara in Kupwara district of North Kashmir in early November 2004.
2. Hazratbal Mosque in Srinagar—the most important Muslim shrine of Kashmir. Situated on the west bank of Dal Lake opposite Nishat Bagh, the shrine's importance lies in the fact that it houses the Moi-e-Muqaddas ("The Sacred Hair") of the Prophet Muhammad. The shrine is known by many names, including Hazratbal, Assar-e-Sharif, Madinat-Us-Sani, and Dargah Sharief.

TONGUE TIED WITH CANCER WARS

1. Meaning an "evening."
2. Eyeliner.

YA SIN

1. Surah 36 of the Qu'ran establishes a firm foundation of faith and brings to witness visible signs of the unlimited power of Allah.
2. A small clay brazier held in a wicker basket. In the winter it is filled with burning coal and held underneath the *pheron* (woolen overcoat) close to the body. A source of warmth for one or two people.

GOD GAVE ME TWO CHILDREN

1. January 14, 2004, a Palestinian mother of two blew herself up at the main border crossing between Israel and the Gaza Strip. She is said to be the first Hamas bomber that was a mother.

RHUNG

1. Color.
2. The Five Daily Prayers of Muslims.
3. In the name of Allah, the most Gracious, the most Merciful.

COLLATERAL DAMAGE

1. Hazrat Zainab was the granddaughter of Prophet Muhammad and a witness at the historic Battle of Karbala, where her entire family was martyred. She led the people of Kufa to avenge the death of her brother Imam Hussein. Many people follow her courage and teachings till this day.
2. Friday prayer.
3. Evening prayer.
4. *Khajol,* eyeliner.
5. Mourning, grief—a ritual performed by Shia muslims during the month of Moharram.
6. Martyred.
7. Burial prayer.

THE IMMORTALITY OF "TRIBUTE IN LIGHT"

1. On the six-month anniversary of the WTC attacks, New York City paid tribute to those killed by erecting two lights at the site of the twin towers.

VIOLENCE, REVOLUTION, AND TERRORISM

1. See "Critique of Violence," *Walter Benjamin: Selected Writings, Volume One* (Harvard University Press: 1996).

OUR MEMORIES OF ISLAM

1. This is a complex statement that I cannot explain in a few sentences. I understand and know it was painful for them, too.

2. Fawziya Abu Khalid quoted in *The Literature of Modern Arabia: An Anthology*, ed. by Salma Khadra Jayussi (New York: Routledge, 1988): 134.

3. A few examples: 1) Shortly after September 11, 2001, someone in my apartment complex shoves in my mailbox a ripped-out page of a hunting magazine with a circled picture of a man dressed in camouflage, center stage, taking aim with his rifle. 2) Here in Chicago some of the public schools that service communities of low income (immigrants, relocated refugees, African Americans, to name a few of the most affected) opened the 2004 school year with their schools either turned into military academies or "destined/planned" to. In the words of a protesting sophomore at Senn High School, "We need to learn how to read and write, not how to shoot guns." (Quoted in Jesse Sharkey's "Get the Military Out Of Our Schools": 2004). 3) There are hundreds of newly installed cameras in public facilities and streets in the downtown area where I work. In response to questions and concerns about the violation of privacy and rights of citizens, Mayor Daley commented in a press conference that the people of Chicago should not feel that way, rather they should think about it in terms of having more "police eyes" to serve and protect the city.

4. Excerpt from June Jordan, "Poem About My Rights," *Lyrical Campaigns* (United Kingdom: Virago Press, 1989): 103–104.

5. See Lisa Suheir Majaj, "Introduction," *Nadia, Captive of Hope: Memoir of an Arab Woman* by Fay Afaf Kanafani (New York: M.E. Sharpe, Inc., 1999): xiii.

6. I borrow miriam cooke's definition of feminism, whereby it is a "state of consciousness, each reflecting women's understanding of themselves and their situation as related to their social and biological condition. Thus, defined, feminism is not bound to one culture or another." See miriam cooke, *Women Claim Islam: Creating Islamic Feminism Through Literature* (New York: Routledge, 2000): x.

7. See Fatima Mernissi, "The Muslim Concept of Active Women's Sexuality," *Women and Sexualities in Muslim Societies* ed. by Pinar Ilkkaracan (Istanbul, Turkey: Women for Women's Human Rights, 2001).

8. Email communication between Azza Basarudin and Maddy Mohammed, "The Nile Beckons . . ." (August, 2004).

9. Lo! Men who surrender unto Allah, and women who surrender, and men who believe and women who believe . . . and men who remember

Allah much and women who remember—Allah hath prepared for them forgiveness and a vast reward (Al-Ahzab 33:35).

10. See Adrienne Rich, "When We Dead Awaken: Writing as Re-Vision," *On Lies, Secrets and Silence* (New York: Norton, 1971).

11. Quoted from Jean Genet, *Prisoner of Love* (New York: New York Review of Books, 1986): 170.

12. See David R. Roedgier, *The Wages of Whiteness: Race and the Making of the American Working Class* (London and New York: Verso, 1991); Peggy McIntosh, "White Privilege: Unpacking the Invisible Knapsack" (1989); Richard Dyer, *White* (London and New York: Routledge, 1997).

13. See Edward Said, *Covering Islam: How the Media and the Experts Determine How We see the Rest of the World* (New York: Pantheon Books, 1981).

14. I try to avoid words like "West" or "American" for I know how complex these meanings are, just as I know that "Muslim" or the "East" are also complex words used to lump peoples and cultures and religions together with little understanding.

15. I borrow this word from Edward Said.

16. See Audre Lorde.

17. See Chandra Talpade Mohanty and M. Jacqui Alexander, "Introduction: Genealogies, Legacies, Movements," *Feminist Genealogies, Colonial Legacies, Democratic Future* (New York: Routledge, 1997): xiv.

18. See "We Are Not the Enemy: Hate Crimes Against Muslims, Arabs, and Those Perceived to be Arab or Muslims after September 11, 2001," Human Rights Report (Vol. 14, No. 6, November 2002).

19. Ibid.

20. See www.cair-net.org/downloads/pollresults.ppt for poll results.

21. Ibid.

22. I borrow from Benedict Anderson's notion of "imagined communities" to indicate my solidarity with the situation of Muslim Americans in the era post-9/11. The Muslim community is imagined, because while members will never know most of their fellow-members, in the minds of each member lives the image of their unity. This community is also imagined because it is conceived as a horizontal comradeship. See Benedict Anderson, *Imagined Communities: Reflections On The Origin and Spread of Nationalism* (London and New York: Verso, 1991).

23. For more information on this campaign, visit CAIR at www.cair-net.org.

24. This advertising campaign was created by CAIR's Southern California's office. The ad reads: "Like Christians, Muslims respect and revere Jesus. Islam teaches that Jesus is one of the greatest of God's prophets and messengers to humankind. Like Christians, every day, over 1.3 billion Muslims strive to live by his teachings of love, peace, and forgiveness. Those teachings, which have become universal values, remind us that all of us, Christians, Muslims, Jews, and all others have more in common than we think."

25. See http://news.bbc.co.uk/1/hi/world/middle_east/3725760.html.

26. Ibid.

27. See "Pakistan Islamists' Posters Threat," BBC News (June 6, 2003), www. news.bbc.co.uk.

28. See "Islamists Set Government a Deadline to Remove 'Un-Islamic' Ads," *Deutsche Press-Agentur* (May 24, 2003).

29. See http://www.jamaat.org/islam/WomanDress.html.

30. See www.jamaat.org/islam/WomanDress.html.

31. See Gloria Anzaldúa, *Borderlands/La Frontera* (San Francisco: Aunt Lute Books, 1999).

32. See Ayesha Javed Akram, "A First For Pakistan," *Friday Times Pakistan* (November 2002), www.shaziamirza.org/press/pr_fridaytimesnov02.htm.

33. For further details of the 1981 murder of Lena see the documentary *Occupied Palestine* by David Koff (1987).

34. For further exploration see Cynthia Enloe 1983, 1993, 2000, 2001; Meredith Turshen & Clotilide Twagiramariya 1998; Ji-Yeon Yuh 2002; Simona Sharon 1994.

35. See Audre Lorde, "The Master's Tools Will Never Dismantle the Master's House," *Sister Outsider* (Berkeley, CA: The Crossing Press): 112.

36. It does, but it is specifically "American" democracy and freedom.

MERHA LAL DUPATTA

1. Scarflike accessory, worn with many South Asian clothes.

THE POLITICS OF HAJJ

1. See Alex Haley and Malcolm X, *The Autobiography of Malcolm X: As Told to*

Alex Haley (New York: Ballantine Books, 1992): 334.

2. Ibid, 332.

3. Ibid, 345.

4. Ibid, 361.

5. See Shawn L. Twing, "Issues in the News: Pilgrims Warned Against Propaganda," *Washington Report on Middle East Affairs* (May/June 1996): 30–34, www.wrmea.com/backissues/0596/9605030.htm.

SARI BLOUSE

1. Glass-nylon is a thin cloth that is extremely hot to wear. It was the first synthetic cloth to be manufactured in British-free India and became a fashion craze for South Asians everywhere.

2. The full body and face covering worn by some women of some Muslim sects.

3. A Shia sect of Islam.

4. A Shia sect that does not view the burkha or *hijab* as a requirement of Islam.

INFINITE AND EVERYWHERE! MY KALEIDOSCOPIC IDENTITY

1. Dipak Gyawali talks about this story in his essay, "Cogito (I'm a South Asian), Ergo Sum!" published in the Spring 2000 edition of the *Harvard Asia Quarterly.*

2. Eid is a Muslim religious holiday celebrated at the end of the holy month of Ramadan. Mohurram is the month of the Islamic calendar when Shi'a Muslims observe a ten-day period of mourning to commemorate the martyrdom of Imam Hussain, grandson of the Prophet Mohammad in the seventh-century Battle of Karbala. Holi and Diwali are both Hindu festivals. Diwali, one of the most popular Hindu festivals, is also called the Festival of Lights. It is dedicated to different gods and goddesses in different parts of India but is generally associated with the triumph of good over evil. Holi, on the other hand, is better known as the Festival of Color, dedicated to Lord Krishna and Kama, the god of pleasure.

3. *Eidi* and *kharchi* are monetary gifts customarily given by elders in the family to the younger generation during the Eid and Diwali celebrations respectively.

4. A *noha* is an elegy recreating events from the Battle of Karbala, where Imam Hussain (a.s.) was martyred.

5. Ganesha is the Hindu elephant god, believed to be master of intellect and wisdom.

6. *Kathak* is one of the major Indian classical dances.

7. While *kafir* is a generic term for "a disbeliever" or "one who rejects the truth" it is mostly used against non-Muslims, often with a derogatory connotation.

8. The term "passing" has also been used to describe people of color who downplay their cultural heritage to emulate a "white" lifestyle.

9. I think it's important to mention here that I've had similar struggles with Hindu culture as well. However, in contemporary Indian society, there is a thriving dialogue to reclaim ideas of sexual liberation for men and women as they are mentioned in several ancient Hindu texts.

10. I would particularly recommend Chughtai's stories, like "The Quilt," "Lingering Fragrance," "The Wedding Shroud," and "Sacred Duty," among others.

11. Irshad Manji's book *The Trouble with Islam Today: A Muslim's Call for Reform in Her Faith* (New York: St. Martin's Press, 2003) is a compelling read—controversial, yet nonetheless thought provoking.

12. For a deeper understanding of liminality and other ways of comprehending multiple and inter-subjectivities, read Shail Mayaram's "Rethinking Meo Identity: Cultural Faultline, Syncretism, Hybridity or Liminality?" published in *Comparative Studies of South Asia, Africa and the Middle East* (vol. XVII No. 2, 1997).

13. For more information, read Judith Butler, "The Question of Social Transformation," *Undoing Gender* (New York: Routledge, 2004).

HOME IN ONE PIECE

1. *Daalpuri*: a breakfast dish of lentils stuffed in bread and deep-fried; *chotpoti*: a snack made with chickpeas, tamarind, onions, and spices; *fuchka*: a crispy outer shell filled with *chotpoti*; *murgi'r thorkari*: chicken curry; *aam bhortha*: mashed mangoes; *kamranga*: star fruit; *laddu*: a type of dessert; *shutki*: dried fish.

2. "my name is chompa, i am bengali."

3. "my name is chompa, i am a bengali muslim _____."
4. An evening meal served to celebrate the end of a day of fasting.
5. Lentil patties, deep fried with onions, commonly served during *iftar*.
6. Verses of the Qur'an.
7. One of the five pillars of Islam, which is to believe that there is no God but Allah, Muhammad is the messenger of Allah.

AFTERWORD

1. See miriam cooke, *Women Claim Islam: Creating Islamic Feminism Through Literature* (New York: Routledge, 2001).
2. See Haideh Moghissi, *Feminism and Islamic Fundamentalism: The Limits of Postmodern Analysis* (London: Zed, 1999).
3. See Fatima Mernissi, *The Veil and the Male Elite: A Feminist Interpretation of Women's Rights in Islam* (Reading, MA: Addison-Wesley, 1991); Amina Wadud, *Qur'an and Woman: Rereading the Sacred Text from a Woman's Perspective* (New York: Oxford University Press, 1999).
4. Several verses from Surat al-Nisa', the fourth chapter of the Qur'an entitled "Women," are devoted to fighting with arms, or *qital*.
5. See Fatima Umar Naseef, *Women in Islam. A Discourse in Rights and Obligations* (Cairo: International Islamic Committee for Woman and Child, 1999): 152.
6. Ibid., 153.
7. Traditions are the sayings and reported actions of the Prophet that, with the Qur'an, are the primary building blocks of the Sharia or Islamic law.

ACKNOWLEDGMENTS

To you I am forever in debt, Amit Rai, for many things, but most of all for editing my writing. This project couldn't have happened without our fights, but also your encouragements and criticism. I cannot thank you enough, Rich Blint, for your consistent support through all the deaths and times. I pray our collective visions continue to strengthen and support each other in more struggles to come. Thank you Mathew Kopka for reading the manuscript from the get-go! Many thanks to all the contributors for believing in this project and being so patient. While I am also very grateful to all the women, and men, who emailed me strong words of encouragement when I publicized the call for submissions, you confirmed that such a project was direly needed. Special thanks to S.N. for all our intense discussions. I want to thank Allah for helping me find this road otherwise I wouldn't have met another better part of myself: sarah abid husain, it's so wonderful to have you in my life! Thanks to Tina Zaman for all those phone conversations and Azza Basarudin for your quick answers to my many questions. Most of all, thank you Hedgebrook for giving me a once-in-a-lifetime opportunity and the privilege of being part of a circle of spirited and powerful women who are *authoring change*. I am blessed to have been part of your community. I've learned that my voice needs more than just words, it needs women spirit, wood, fire, two tea cups, a kettle, and some (hot) water. Also, thanks to All Saints Café, Tallahassee, and my little community there, for providing me a-not-so-comfy chair to do my work in. Thank you, Brooke Warner, for your persistence, patience, and belief in this project.

My love and gratitude to all the organizations and individuals who have supported me and my work throughout many years: South Asians Against Police Brutality and Racism (SAPBR), South Asian Women's Creative Collective (SAWCCi), Desis Rising Up and Moving (DRUM), New York Taxi Workers Alliance, Coney Island Avenue Project, Shaista Husain, Manjula Winjerama, JP Patafio, Jaishri Abichandani, Sougy, Jenniffer, Ahmed, Asif and Arif Ullah, Andrew Blint, Robert Ku, Meena Alexander, Ella Shohat.

Thanks to Social Text, Aljazeera.net, Critical Inquiry, and all the websites who published my call for submission.

A'asia, I don't think I will ever know how to thank you for being so strong through all the changes I've put you in the past year, your two new homes—now your eloquent first words, our too-long separations—your patience. My love, I pray the voices resounding through these pages will also carry you with strength, love, faith, endurance . . . toward change.

CONTRIBUTORS

Ansaro Bah is Fulani (African tribal language) for Aiesha Balde. Born in Manila, Philippines, she immigrated to the San Francisco Bay Area with her parents and siblings at the onset of martial law in her country. She graduated with a BA in English literature from University of California, Berkeley, and holds a degree in nursing as well. A community builder and activist, she cofounded Kifayah Foundation to service the needs of the Muslim population in the East Bay; she also cofounded Timbuktu Educational Foundation, a nonprofit dedicated to preserving the written legacy of early African scholars. She is wife to an imam and has five beautiful children.

Aisha Sattar is a freelance writer/poet. She spent the last year conducting research in Trinidad and is currently working on a series of essays about gender, sexuality, and race in popular Indo-Trinidadian music. Her future plans include attending medical school for a joint degree in medicine and medical anthropology. Through this endeavor she hopes to use her writing for the promotion of peace through health.

Amitis Motevalli was born in Tehran, Iran, and moved to the United States with her family in 1977. She received her BA from San Francisco State University and an MFA from Claremont Graduate University. In her exploration of artwork, she has incorporated a combination of a Near Eastern aesthetic with a Western art education. Motevalli has shown work at Los Angeles Contemporary Exhibitions, Deep River Gallery, and Slanguage Gallery, among other spaces. She has also been involved in art education with youth and collaboration with several community organizations. She is currently living and working in Los Angeles, focusing on a collaboration with students in East Oakland on a multimedia exhibition looking at repressive tactics in local schools.

Anida Yoeu Esguerra seeks an artistic, spiritual, and political exploration of her identity as a nonhyphenated Cambodian Muslim American woman. Esguerra uses an interdisciplinary approach to creating art that mixes the visual, spoken, and written into performed explorations of hybrid identities. She has founded organizations including Mango Tribe, an Asian American women's interdisciplinary performance ensemble; Asian American Artists Collective–Chicago; and the *MONSOON* literary arts journal. She is one of the founding members of the critically acclaimed Pan-Asian spoken word quartet I Was Born With Two Tongues. She is proud to call Chicago home but knows the journey never really ends for the refugee. For more info visit www.atomicshogun.com.

Asma Shikoh is a visual artist who grew up in Pakistan and currently resides in Hoboken, New Jersey. She finished her undergraduate degree at the Indus Valley School of Art and Architecture, Pakistan. Her artwork celebrates and challenges the very vulnerable/sacred ideals of nationalism in Pakistani society. Asma has been showing at group exhibits in New York; most recently, her work was part of the show Fatal Love at the Queens Museum of Art. Presently, her focus is to reach a wider audience, and she intends to develop a language that explores her identity as an immigrant and a mother of an American-born baby.

Azza Basarudin was born and raised in Penang, an old colonial town in Malaysia, and grew up living among a blend of working- and middle-class Muslim, Chinese, Hindu, and Eurasian cultures. She is a doctoral candidate in the Women's Studies Program at the University of California, Los Angeles, where she is working on a comparative study of the cultural meaning of Islam in Muslim women's lives and experiences in Southeast Asia and the Middle East.

Poet, performer, and activist **Bushra Rehman** was born and raised in New York City but has also lived in Pakistan and Saudi Arabia. Bushra is coeditor of *Colonize This! Young Women of Color on Today's Feminism* (Seal Press, 2002) and author of the collection of poetry *Marianna's Beauty Salon*. She has been featured in *NY Newsday* and her work has appeared in *ColorLines* magazine, *Mizna, Curve* magazine, *SAMAR Magazine,* and *Bottomfish*. Her writing is forthcoming in *Writing the Lines of Our Hands: An Anthology of South Asian American Poetry* (Creative Arts Press), and *Stories of Illness and Healing: Women Write Their Bodies* (Kent State University Press).

Chaumtoli Huq is a staff attorney with MFY Legal Services in the Workplace Justice Project. She represents low-income New Yorkers on a wide range of employment matters. Huq is a graduate of Columbia University and Northeastern University School of Law. She has served on civil rights and immigration law committees on the Association of the Bar of the City of New York and is a board member of the New York Civil Liberties Union and member of Community Board 7. She is a part-time lecturer at the Labor Center at Rutgers University, where she teaches Employment Law.

chompa rahman was born in Bangladesh and currently lives in the United States. She is a certified public accountant and has been in the accounting profession for almost ten years. In her spare time she is a pool player, swimmer, and writer.

Engy Abdelkader is an attorney based in the New York/New Jersey area who has worked a number of noteworthy cases, and who served for six months as a civil rights attorney and director of civil rights at the Council of American-Islamic Relations. She has also worked with the American Civil Liberties Union, the Arab-American Justice Project run by the American-Arab Anti-Discrimination Committee in New York, and the Center for Constitutional Rights, where she provided research on the case of Maher Arar. She also has an extensive record of public speaking on civil liberties, and Arab American and Muslim issues.

Farheen Haq is a visual artist working with photo, performance, and video installation. Her work explores ideas of cultural inscriptions of the body, gender, ritual, and gesture. Haq was born and raised near Toronto, Canada, and now resides on the west coast of Canada in Victoria, British Columbia. Haq has exhibited widely across North America, including New York, Los Angeles, Toronto, and Vancouver. She also holds a master's in fine art. For more information and samples of her work, see Haq's website at www.farheenhaq.com.

Fatima Qurayshi is a writer activist living in the United States.

Halimah Abdullah's career as a professional writer began at age nineteen. Since then, she's covered such diverse issues and events as the September 11 attacks and the Justice Department's investigations into Section 8 fraud. Her work has appeared in numerous publications, including *The New York Times,* the *St. Petersburg Times,* and *Newsday,* where she was also a staff writer. She has taught at Brooklyn College, John Jay College, and Gotham Writers' Workshop, all in New York. Halimah holds a BA in journalism from the University of Alabama and an MFA in fiction from Brooklyn College. She lives in Memphis and is a reporter for the Memphis *Commercial Appeal.*

Hend Al-Mansour was born in Hofuf, Saudi Arabia, in 1956. She graduated from medical school in Cairo in 1980 and practiced medicine until 1997. While in the United States, she realized her dream of being an artist. She obtained a master's of fine art from Minneapolis College of Art and Design in 2002. Her work is about her identity as an Arab woman and how that interacts with her Islamic faith.

Jawahara K. Saidullah lives and works in Boston. Originally from Allahabad, India, she has lived in the United States for close to eighteen years. Her first novel, *The Burden of Foreknowledge,* was released by Roli Books in Spring 2006. Her essay "Mirrors" appeared in *Black, White and Various Shades of Brown,* a Penguin (India) anthology. Her short story "A Sound Quest" is included in the upcoming Chowk Press book *Imagine.* Jawahara is a columnist for chowk.com, where she also writes fiction. Her writing can be found in *Siliconindia Magazine* and *Cerebration.* She is currently blogging at jawahara.blogspot.com while juggling a job in technical publishing and writing her second novel.

Khanum Shaikh is a doctoral candidate at the Women's Studies Program at the University of California, Los Angeles. She has been teaching part-time in the Women's Studies Program at California State University, Fullerton. Her research interests include gender, religion, and social movements. Khanum splits her time between Lahore and Los Angeles.

Leila Montour was born and raised in Denver, Colorado. A Muslim since 1996, she holds a BA in English and women's studies and is the mother of two daughters. She is interested in activism, art, and human rights, and her prose and poetry have appeared in independent Muslim magazines in Canada, India, and Australia. Recently, her poetry and essays have appeared in the *Muslim WakeUp!* and Jafaria Association of North America webzines. A member of the

Islamic Writers Alliance, she is currently working on both traditional and free verse poetry, visual digital collages, and photography.

Maddy Mohammed sojourns in the Midwestern metropolis of Chicago. She works on multiple social justice issues and is a researcher and project director at a not-for-profit civic public policy organization, where she works on public policy and race, juvenile justice, education, immigration, housing, and women's and girls' rights.

Maliha Masood is a writer and traveler. Born and raised in Karachi, Pakistan, she has lived in Paris, Rome, Cairo, Damascus, and Beirut while considering Seattle home since 1982. Her upcoming book, *In the Middle of the East: A Muslim Woman's One-Year Odyssey from Cairo to Istanbul,* will be published by Seal Press in the winter of 2007. Maliha is also the coproducer of *Nazrah,* an award-winning documentary film focusing on American Muslim women in the Pacific Northwest. She has a master's degree in international affairs from the Fletcher School of law and diplomacy at Tufts University.

Mansha Parven Mirza is a twenty-six-year-old graduate student at the University of Illinois at Chicago. She was born in Mumbai, India, to a Muslim father and a Hindu mother. She spent most of her childhood and early adulthood in a middle-class Mumbai neighborhood before moving to Chicago in 2002 to pursue graduate studies. An occupational therapist by profession, she has bachelor and master's of science degrees in occupational therapy and is currently pursuing a doctorate in disability studies. Her areas of academic interest include international human rights and public policy, particularly in the area of disability and health.

Maryam Ansari is a twenty-one-year-old junior majoring in English in the San Francisco Bay Area, the most recent place she's decided to call home. She was born in Pakistan and raised in Malaysia. Her passions include thinking, writing, reading, and loving the wonderful people in her life and their Most Wonderful Creator. She plans to teach, write, and travel once she graduates.

Maryum Saifee is a New York–based visual artist. Before moving to New York, she spent two years as a Peace Corps volunteer teaching English at a secondary school for girls in rural Jordan. Prior to working in Jordan, she was an AmeriCorps volunteer and worked at Chaya, a Seattle-based nonprofit, mobilizing South Asian communities around issues of domestic violence and hate crimes. Her most recent job was as a program associate for the Middle East and Asia at Forefront, a New York–based human rights organization. Maryum is currently pursuing a master's degree in International Affairs at Columbia University.

Munerah Ahmed was born in Sana'a, Yemen, to parents from the Yafai region. Her family moved to Flatbush, Brooklyn, when she was a young child. She has worked in social services for the past three years. Munerah has also been a volunteer with the American Red Cross for the last five years. She is currently a graduate student at Columbia University's Mailman School of Public Health.

Nor Faridah Abdul Manaf is a Malaysian Muslim woman living in Kuala Lumpur, the capital city of Malaysia. She is associate professor of English language and literature at the International Islamic University Malaysia. She received her BA (hons) from the University of Waikato in New Zealand, her MA from the University of Liverpool in England, and her PhD from Flinders University in South Australia. She's married and mother to a thirteen-year-old daughter. Nor Faridah was a recipient of the prestigious Utusan Melayu–Public Bank Literary Writing Award (1995 and 1997). Her poems and short stories have appeared in anthologies by Longman, Silverfish Books, and soon by Penguin Books India.

Nuzhat Abbas is a writer presently based in Toronto, Canada. She was born in Zanzibar, educated in Karachi, and immigrated to Toronto in 1981. She works as an educator and consultant on Human Rights and Equity issues. Her work has been published in various magazines in Canada, including *THIS* magazine, *Fuse*, and *Herizons*. She is currently working on a book of essays on Zanzibar and completing a novel.

Saba Razvi received her BA in English and creative writing from Creighton University in Omaha and her MA in the same from the University of Texas in Austin. Some of her works may be found in *Diner, Karamu, Anthology, Crucible*, and *Tahzeeb-e-Deccan*. Born in Chicago to parents who emigrated from India, she has grown up mostly in Houston and is currently in Los Angeles at the University of Southern California, where she is a Middleton Fellow. Her current obsessions include mysticism, dead civilizations, punk and goth subculture, mythology, robots, and fairytale villains.

Salimah Valiani is a researcher in international political economy and economic development, an activist, and a poet. She has lived and worked in Canada, England, and the United States. Her creative writing has appeared in literary journals, alternative newspapers, and in community radio programs. She is presently working in Cape Town, South Africa, with a small think tank and training institute. Her first collection of poems, *Breathing for Breadth,* was released in the autumn of 2005 by TSAR Publications.

Salma Arastu was born in Rajasthan, India. She has been painting for thirty years, since graduating with a master's degree in fine arts from The MS University, Baroda, India, in 1975. Born into the Hindu tradition in her native India, she later embraced Islam through her marriage. Her works are represented in several galleries, including ArtJaz Gallery in Philadelphia; Gmunder in Schwabisch, Germany; Art Heritage in New Delhi; and Bose Pacia Gallery in New York. She has held more than thirty solo shows throughout the world, including in the United States, Germany, Kuwait, Iran, and India. You can find her work online at www.salmaarastu.com.

Samira Abbassy was born in southwestern Iran and emigrated to Britain at age two. During the 1980s and 1990s, Samira established a successful career as a London-based painter before moving to New York in 1998. Her work draws on the visual traditions of both Middle Eastern and Western art. Samira studied painting at Birmingham Polytechnic and Canterbury College in Britain. Her work is included in the British Government Art Collection. She is a recipient of the Royal Academy M&G purchase prize. She has shown with Joan Prats Gallery and Skoto Gallery in New York, and Vernacular Press in London. She is represented by England & Co Gallery.

sarah abid husain is currently a graduate student in the College of Ethnic Studies at San Francisco State University. sarah completed her BA in women and gender studies and cultural anthropology at the University of California, Davis in Spring 2003. In her academic and artistic endeavors, sarah reflects on her mixed cultural and spiritual heritage—Kashmiri, Indian, American, and Muslim—in order to imagine and empower the womyn of color, feminist, transnational, and third-space experience. We will rise up and heal ourselves.

Sarwat Rumi is a bilingual Bengali American Muslim who has been writing since she could read. Sarwat earned a B.A. in South Asian Languages and Civilizations from the University of Chicago and works toward social justice as a vigilante poet, teaching artist, and performance activist. Sarwat has co-written and performed in the Chicago and New York City runs of *Sisters in the Smoke* (2002, 2003); she also co-wrote, co-produced, and acted in *Bombs and Butterflies* (2004). She is the recipient of a Fresh Ink recognition for new music by Serpent Feline, granted by The Chicago Composer's Forum (2005). Sarwat's craft as a solo artist in the touring cast of Mango Tribe and vocalist for Serpent Feline takes her far from Chicago on a regular basis, but her words can always be found in the *Wicked Alice Poetry Journal* and her two chapbooks: *the inverted sun* and *WAR*.

Shadi Eskandani was born in Tehran, Iran, in 1978, a few months before the Islamic Revolution of Iran. She spent her formative years in Tehran until her family emigrated to Vancouver, Canada, in 1987. In Vancouver, she received a B.A. in Socio-Cultural Anthropology and moved to Toronto to complete a M.A. in the same field. In Toronto, she became politically active in anti-racist and anti-war grassroots organizations. As a "secular Muslim" Iranian woman who has experienced the war of bombs and missiles, the war of a fundamentalist regime, the war of patriarchy, and the war of racism, Shadi is committed to pursuing a career that brings together her two passions in life: writing and social justice activism.

Born in Tehran, **Shahrzad Naficy** moved to the United States with her family when she was seven months old, just prior to the Islamic Revolution. She grew up in Los Angeles and attended the University of California at San Diego where she earned a B.A. in Creative Writing and Italian Literature. She recently completed her MFA in Creative Writing from Mills College in Oakland, California. She lives in Los Angeles with her sister and brother.

Sherien Sultan is a freelance writer and activist in New York City who has been exploring the political and social realities of the Arab and Muslim diaspora in the United States. In 2002, she joined the Middle East and Middle Eastern American Center as a research assistant, where she conducted in-depth interviews with Arab and Muslim Americans regarding the effects of 9/11 on their identities. Her work has been featured in *Aramica*, *The Drouth*, and *Alternet*. She graduated with a degree in International Relations from the American University in Cairo and completed her M.A. in Liberal Studies at the City University of New York, Graduate Center.

S.N. is a thirtysomething South Asian poet and writer.

Soniah Naheed Kamal was born in Karachi, Pakistan, and grew up in England and Saudi Arabia. She has been living in the United States since graduating with a B.A. from St. John's College's Great Books program. Her senior thesis won the 1996 Susan Irene Roberts prize and her short stories have been published in Pakistan, Canada, India, and the U.S. Her work has appeared in *A Letter from India* (Penguin, India) and *And the World Changed* (Kali Press, India). Soniah is the senior editor at Monsoonmag.com. She is currently working on a novel and her work can be found at www.soniahkamal.com.

Tina Zaman is a twenty-three-year-old poet and full-time undergraduate at Mills College in Oakland, California, where she is majoring in Critical Studies in Race, Gender, and Philosophy. She is the child of Bengali working-class immigrants who arrived in the United States in 1970, and intends to teach poetry and publish politically empowering poetry as part of her political commitment. Tina represents herself as part of many groups who refuse to identify with one another and she wants to use her privileged voice to make change.

Z. Gaprial Arkles is a white, transsexual, queer Muslim man who grew up in the Philadelphia suburbs and now lives in Brooklyn. He is a law fellow at the Sylvia Rivera Law Project, where he provides free legal services to low-income people and people of color who are transgender, intersex, or gender nonconforming.

Zohra Saed is a Brooklyn-based Afghan American poet and co-editor of an upcoming anthology *Drop by Drop We Make a River: Afghan American Experiences of War Exile and Return* (Rutgers University Press, 2006). She received her MFA in Poetry at Brooklyn College and is currently pursuing a doctoral degree in English at the City University of New York Graduate Center. She is the co-founder of Up-Set Press Inc., an independent publishing house that showcases the works of marginalized voices. She serves as a cultural consultant on scripts focusing on Afghanistan and lectures on the topic of Afghan/Afghan-American film and literature. As a Graduate Teaching Fellow, she also teaches at Hunter College.

ABOUT THE EDITOR

Sarah Husain is a Pakistani American activist, poet, and mother who was born in New York City but grew up in Hong Kong, Sudan, and Pakistan. She has been writing since the age of sixteen and organizing grassroots antiviolence community projects, linking communities of color around issues of police brutality, anti-immigrant policy, detention, and anti-domestic-violence work. In 1997, she cofounded South Asians Against Police Brutality and Racism, a South Asian American grassroots community organization in New York City. Her written and performance poetry deals with identity, memory, nation, violence, bioterrorism, and the female body. She has been published in *Breaking the Silence: Domestic Violence in the South Asian-American Community* and in several journals and websites. Currently she lives in Tallahassee, Florida, with her two-year-old daughter.

CREDITS

"Dikhir," by Nuzhat Abbas, was originally published in 2002 in *Fuse* magazine, v.25(1) pp. 17–21.

"Violence, Revolution, and Terrorism: A Legal and Historical Perspective," by Chaumtoli Huq, was originally published in *New Age,* an English Daily in Bangladesh, on August 11, 2005.

"On Occupation and Resistance: Two Iraqi Women Speak Out: An Interview" by Azza Basarudin and Khanum Shaikh, was originally published in 2004 under the title "Voices of Resistance: Iraqi Women Speak Out" *Middle East Women's Studies Review* (MEWS) v. 18(3/4).

"If This Were My Family: Relearning Important Lessons of Organizing After the Earthquake," by Bushra Rehman was originally published in spring 2006 under the title "My Family" in *ColorLines* v. 9(1) pp. 40–41.

"Farewell," from The Country Without a Post Office, by Agha Shahid Ali. Copyright 1997 by Agha Shahid Ali. Used by permission of W. W. Norton & Company, Inc.

"Poem about My Rights," from Lyrical Campaigns, by June Jordan. Used by permission of Time Warner Book Group.

SELECTED TITLES FROM SEAL PRESS

For more than thirty years, Seal Press has published groundbreaking books. By women. For women. Visit our website at www.sealpress.com.

Nervous Conditions by Tsitsi Dangarembga. Foreword by D. Kwame Anthony Appiah. $15.95. 1-58005-134-0. With irony and skill, Dangarembga explores the devastating human loss involved in the colonization of one culture by another.

Reckless: The Outrageous Lives of Nine Kick-Ass Women by Gloria Mattioni. $14.95. 1-58005-148-0. From Lisa Distefano, who captains a pirate vessel on her quest to protect sea life, to Libby Riddles, the first woman to win the legendary Iditarod, this collection of profiles explores the lives of nine women who took unconventional life paths to achieve extraordinary results.

Stories from Blue Latitudes: Caribbean Women Writers at Home and Abroad edited by Elizabeth Nunez and Jennifer Sparrow. $16.95. 1-58005-139-1. An anthology of stories from new and renowned women writers from the Caribbean such as Michelle Cliff, Merle Collins, Jamaica Kincaid, and Pauline Melville.

Tales from the Expat Harem: Foreign Women in Modern Turkey edited by Anastasia M. Ashman and Jennifer Eaton Gökmen. $15.95. 1-58005-155-3. Female expats from different countries describe how the Turkish landscape, psyche, people, and customs transformed their lives.

Waking Up American: Coming of Age Biculturally edited by Angela Jane Fountas. $15.95. 1-58005-136-7. Twenty-two original essays by first-generation women caught between two worlds. Countries of origin include the Philippines, Germany, India, Mexico, China, Iran, Nicaragua, Japan, Russia, and Panama.